FATHERING BEHAVIORS
The Dynamics of the Man–Child Bond

Perspectives in Developmental Psychology

Series Editor: Michael Lewis
Rutgers Medical School
University of Medicine and Dentistry of New Jersey
New Brunswick, New Jersey

PSYCHOLOGY OF DEVELOPMENT AND HISTORY
Edited by Klaus F. Riegel

FATHERING BEHAVIORS
The Dynamics of the Man–Child Bond
Wade C. Mackey

FATHERING BEHAVIORS
The Dynamics of the Man-Child Bond

Wade C. Mackey

Iowa Wesleyan College
Mount Pleasant, Iowa

Plenum Press • New York and London

Library of Congress Cataloging in Publication Data

Mackey, Wade C.
    Fathering behaviors.

    (Perspectives in developmental psychology)
    Bibliography: p.
    Includes index.
    1. Father and child—Cross-cultural studies. 2. Developmental psychology—Cross-cultural studies. 3. Family—United States. 4. Father and child—United States. I. Title. II. Series.
HQ756.M25   1985   306.8'742   85-6599
ISBN 0-306-41868-1

©1985 Plenum Press, New York
A Division of Plenum Publishing Corporation
233 Spring Street, New York, N.Y. 10013

Printed in the United States of America

To Jennifer Heather, Shannon Rose, Peter Michael,
and Christopher Patrick

Foreword

Like the lines of a secret map made dimly apparent by the chemical potion brushed on a piece of paper from a child's detective kit, the outlines of what may be a substantial behavioral biology of human life seem to be coming clear. From genetic science at its most molecular to demography with its assessment of the vital experience of massive populations, there is a growing understanding of the various ways in which the human species reveals underlying commonalities of experience through the life cycle and over the web of interactions that constitutes the basic matter of social life.

At the same time, research has been successful in two superficially and contradictory directions: first, in showing the enormous variation in human arrangements and consciousness across and within cultures; and second, in showing the similarity between cultures as far as basic processes of physiology, neurophysiology, and even social life are concerned. But the contradiction only exists in the absence of an understanding of the fact that in a species living under as many ecological, historical, and economic niches as *Homo sapiens,* cultural variation is what one would naturally expect.

Romer's Law was developed by Alfred Romer at Harvard and refers to his proposition that animals will undergo minor evolutionary mutations and changes in order that their basic nature be maintained undisturbed. So an animal will change its plumage color to achieve disguise from a fast predator newly arrived in its environment—this is easier in evolutionary terms than, for example, changing from running to flying or developing a large hard shell as protection. We can see human cultural variation as a form of Romer's Law too—cultures change more or less, and this way or that, so that the basic human biosociology or biogrammar can remain undisturbed.

That is to say, far from cultural variation being a demonstration of the irrelevance of human genetic continuities to the contemporary behavior of people, this version of Romer's Law asserts the connection between the human genotype and the array of different human cultures. Once we no longer suffer from what Robin Fox has called "ethnographic dazzle," we can begin to see the relationship between different styles, rhythms, and schemes of human organization.

This requires at once a generous theoretical perspective and an exacting approach to the significance and nature of social information. One of the first great research reports of this quality was Charles Darwin's *The Expression of the Emotions in Animals and Men*, in which Darwin toured the cultures of the world in search for what he felt were reliable data and related such data to common problems animals and people encountered in communicating with each other and in expressing how they felt about what was going on around them. Much later, and in a different style, John Bowlby in his two-volume publication *Attachment and Loss* confronted the central mammalian issue: How does it work between a mother and her children? And what impact does all this have on the wider social structure? In between these publications and since, there has been a resurgence of interest in the phenomenon of pancultural continuity even while there has continued to be a lively criticism of biosocial speculation, often on the grounds that it is something called "reductionist." But of course the work of science is to get to the bottom of things, and far from the addition of biology to the mix of social sciences making things easier and more simpleminded for people, it makes work harder and more complex—even if the mechanisms under investigation may be themselves simplifications revealed by the use of Occam's Razor.

How is one to find variables to study that bear some reliable relationship to biological process? "Living/dead" presents awkward ethnographic problems whereas "male/female" offers sturdy categories, even if the mishaps of nature and the oddities of cultural arrangement will occasionally produce real confusion and uncertainty about the nature of gender. By and large, studying gender seems a reasonable and economic strategy to choose in studying the relationship between genotypically persistent characteristics of *Homo sapiens* and what human groups end up doing. In a paradoxical way, one of the most interesting outcomes of the feminist critique of traditional science has been a renewed attention to the categories "male" and "female" and at the same time, renewed attention to the biology that may underly these. A generation of scholars has emerged who are equally conversant (because it makes their work better) with the arcana of genetic theory, the mass of primate data, the organization chart of the endocrines, the architecture of the brain and how it operates, and the rich record of human cultures. Wade Mackey is one of this group and has in the study that follows these remarks been able to provide genuinely new information about how men act when they are fathers, as well as very useful speculation about how this works and what its significance is for the development of a good human biology. Needless to say, his picture of the behavior of men is firmly different from that cartoon of bloodthirsty, insensitive killers sometimes associated with the biological perspective on human behavior. It turns out that men appear to enjoy having children and being fathers and they spend appreciable amounts of time with them and teach them what they can about how to be grown up. The range of cultures that Mackey and his assistants have examined is impressive, and the impact of what he has found should be benign for a considerable group of researchers working on the study of behavior and also for that by now rather large cadre of commentators who have made a career out of tracking the state of play in gender science. They and their audience should welcome this study, which, with deliberate modesty but equally deliberate imagination, turns our attention to fathers and their acts.

LIONEL TIGER
Rutgers University

Preface

Across the wide swathe of cultures, folklore and myth systems depict and perhaps reflect the regularities of life. If we take several conceptual steps from ourselves and look for common threads within these folk wisdoms, we can see that life forms in general and the human condition itself are viewed as neither random nor chaotic. When broad, fundamental categories are used for scaling purposes, life tends to be patterned and systematic: life is born, life is nurtured to maturity, life reproduces its own kind, life dies. The more we approach with our minds these larger rhythms, the smaller patterns become more and more difficult to perceive and thereby to predict. The moment-to-moment life of a trap-door spider challenges the entomologist. The zoologist can be flummoxed by the path an amoeba may choose to follow. On occasion the botanist can only wonder at the viability of one acorn turning to an oak tree versus the morbidity of the acorn's sibling. When we become enmeshed in our own human patterns, they become difficult to view clearly indeed.

The social scientist, as human as the next person, is faced with the formidable task of dissecting and then reassembling human behavior into a sensible whole. In essence, we have the human central nervous system trying to analyze itself. This self-examination is a problem. The human nervous system has been forged over the epochs more for survival of itself and its kin than for accuracy of self-reflection and introspection. There is no *a priori* reason to believe that veracity in self-knowledge was any more important or useful to our ancestry than was self-deception. Nonetheless, the subject matter is most interesting, and the social scientists seem imbued with high levels of optimism. They do continue unabatedly the formidable task of understanding each other.

So, as seen as part of the biological kingdom and in keeping to wide, coarse categories, people's behavior can be understood to be organized, to be reasonably knowable, and—with huge dollops of qualifications—to be predictable. Common sense and day-to-day intuition can tell us, the sapient ones, just that. Our more finely filtered categories become more problematic in their chances of being perceived, understood, and predicted. Into this void beyond the intuitive step or stumble the social scientists. These brave individuals attempt to complement the visceral folklore of the citizenry with knowledge eked out by the sometimes arcane and often cumbersome character of Western science.

This book is a venture into the specific void of the relationship between a society's men and their children. The intent of the book is to develop a set of norms that can help profile the character and form of the adult male-child bond. Using a method that allows adults and children to exhibit their own priorities, prerogatives, and agendas, their behavior is surveyed and analyzed. It is hoped that the analysis reflects a lifestyle that is unforced, uncontrived, and unhurried by the rigors of a controlled experiment or the constraints of the laboratory. Accordingly, the behavior belongs to the men and women and children, but, for the moment, it is on loan to the regimen of Western science. The core of the book is a data base culled from the behavior of over 49,000 adult–child dyads. Eighteen cultures from five continents were surveyed in the later 1970s and early 1980s.

Two thematic questions were posed by this cross-cultural project: (1) What consistencies, if any, were found in the adult male–child interactions; and (2) what systematic predictable variations, if any, could be expected from the adult male–child relationship as we went from one cultural type to alternate cultural types? By just being themselves, the men and women and children in the sample were most cooperative in the venture. The cooperation, mixed with more than a little good luck in the form of logistical support and first-rate personnel, resulted in a series of candidates for those consistencies and those variations in the man–child bond.

The attempt to view discrete patterns in the continuous stream of behavior is facilitated, for well or for ill, by three interdependent lenses: a biological lens which serves as a foundation for a cultural lens which, in turn, serves as a foundation for a symbolic lens. These three lenses form the springboard of theory such that the behavior can be given a coherence or wholeness.

The effort for coherence or wholeness—that is, this book—is intended for the reader interested in (a) the study of family systems and especially how the father-child relationship melds into its own cultural type; (b) the development of people from the perspective of an evolutionary time scale; and (c) the development of people from the perspective of their birth to their demise. The edges of disciplines have indeed become blurry, but anthropologists, psychologists, and sociologists form the most likely audience of interested readers who would be comfortable with the theoretical orientations and argot of the social sciences.

Special thanks are also extended at this point to individuals without whom this book would not have emerged as it did: M. J. S. Wade, whose tenacious support continuously infused life into the project; anonymous reviewers, who labored well to keep me from straying too far; Lionel Tiger, for illustrating models of ways and means to do science on the sapient ones; and Eliot Werner, editor at Plenum, for his skill in maneuvering this book to completion.

It should be noted, as is the tradition, that all errors by omission and by commission are solely the responsibility of the author.

Acknowledgments

This project was supported by grants from the National Science Foundation and the Harry Frank Guggenheim Foundation. Their generous aid is very gratefully acknowledged. I also thank the fieldworkers whose efforts and enthusiasms were well beyond the call of duty: George Donahue (Virginia, 1974; Karaja, 1977; Brazil—rural, 1980; Brazil—urbanizing, 1980); D. Bruce Carter (Japan, 1977); Roger Griffith (Lima, Peru, 1975; India, 1978; Sri Lanka, 1980); H. James Martin (Taiwan, 1980); Dirk Odland (Hong Kong, 1979); Abigail Sills (Israeli kibbutzim, 1980); Ellen Suthers (Ivory Coast, 1977; Morocco, 1977; Senufo, 1981); Steven Swensen (Ivory Coast, 1977; Morocco, 1977).

Contents

CHAPTER 1

Introduction

In a park in Reykjavik, Iceland, a group of clowns was performing on a stage for a crowd of approximately a thousand people—mostly children. Toward the back of the throng, a father in his thirties had hoisted his daughter of about five years on his shoulders. From her elevated position, the daughter could see the clowns much better and so sat there, enjoying herself rather thoroughly.

She wriggled and bounced at the antics of the clowns, and, when her balance became tenuous, she would grab some part of her father's head and with such a fulcrum she would right herself. For his part, the father made little movement aside from shifting his weight from one foot to another.

For approximately 30 minutes, the clowns cavorted, the daughter enjoyed and bounced, and the father patiently endured. The show ended, and the father lifted the daughter to the ground. They looked at each other only long enough to exchange smiles and a few words. Then she bounded off toward the park's exit with the father following behind at a much slower pace.

In a plaza in Saltillo, Mexico, a barefooted child of three was scurrying after a very mobile phantasm. The child tripped, sprawling in the dust. Whether through loss of dignity or the addition of a bruise, the child stayed prone—only lifting his head to cry and voice a hurt and to scan the immediate area for aid and comfort. A man in his twenties reached down and lifted the child to his feet. The man knelt in the dust and cradled the child with his arms and brushed away some of the dust with his hand. Meanwhile, in lowered, slow tones, the man talked to the child. Within a minute, the child turned to look into the man's face and then quickly resumed the quest of the phantasm. The man stood momentarily, looked at the back of the child, and returned to his seat in the shaded section of a bench.

These scenes are fairly typical ones and, at first reading, seem banal and remarkably uninteresting. A father helps out his child. A father soothes the pain of his child. Any park on any warm Sunday could find repeated examples of these vignettes. Not much of anything extraordinary or noteworthy is in any one of the episodes.

Yet, a second reading poses a more fundamental and intriguing question. Why are the men there with the small children at all? What benefits are there for the man to be with the child? Supporting a 40-pound squirming child on one's shoulders for 30 minutes is fatiguing at the very best. Leaving the shade to kneel in hot dust is not something people ordinarily want to do. Of the many things to do with his time, his final decision is to reject those and to be with a young child. Why would that decision *ever* be achieved? Moreover, why would that decision be reached systematically and predictably in many places at many times? It is the purpose of this book to examine some aspects of the relationships of men toward their children and to offer some speculations on why those relationships exist the way they do.

Within the social sciences, three generalized formats have been used to present data on fathers to those Western readers interested in fathers:[1] (1) a cross-cultural anthropological perspective; (2) a sociopsychological perspective; and (3) a cross-species perspective. Anthropological works have, when referring to the father figure, generally focused on a structural-functional placement of the father within overall dynamics of the different cultures (a notable exception is Rohner, 1975). Cross-cultural compendia or ethnologies tend to seek out common patterns of sociocultural entities; whereas the more idiosyncratic and personal accounts by an ethnographer who has lived in a single community or tribe relate how the father–child relationship fits into the larger mosaic of the culture proper.

When they are depicting the father–child dyads, psychological and sociological conduits have focused, in the main, on variables that impact on the well-being of the developing child as defined by per-

---

[1]The worldview of parents from non-Western states, such as Chad, Laos, or Nepal, is simply unknown by this author. The vast bulk of input from and exposure to data on adult–child interaction is on Western, especially American, subjects as studied by Western, again, especially American, researchers. This parochialism is of course lamentable in that every preclusion of some segment of humanity simultaneously limits the opportunity to understand the full range of texture of that humanity.

sonality constructs of Western culture. The emphasis of these research disciplines is typically on differential effects of differential paternalistic techniques on social, cognitive, and emotional characteristics of the growing child.

The primatologists have made the very reasonable assumption that phylogenetic relatives may well share similar behavioral modes based on a common heritage within a generalized common ecology. Thus, study of the nonhuman primate relationships between adult males and their young would be useful to bracket and to understand some dimensions of the human adult male–child dyad.

CROSS-CULTURAL ANTHROPOLOGICAL PERSPECTIVE

The specifics of actual adult male–child interactions are sparse in the literature. In spite of the lack of specifics, several general points do emerge which bear on this argument. From the multitude of ethnographic accounts, it is clear that societies pay very close attention to marriage rituals and childrearing responsibilities (Broude & Greene, 1976; Fox, 1967; Levinson & Malone, 1980; Schlegel, 1972; Stephens, 1963; Van den Berghe, 1979). If not universal constants, there are certainly universal consistencies that include: (a) the validation of the familial association of each newly born child, that is, his or her lineage or heritage is determined at birth, and (b) the allocation of infant childrearing is not randomly distributed among the community's adults. Near kin, universally female and predominantly the mother, have primary child caretaking responsibilities (Barry & Paxson, 1971; Rohner & Rohner, 1982; Weisner & Gallimore, 1977). Although adult males may be a logical category for the title of primary infant-child caretaker, they are simply not an empirical category for that title (see Brown, 1970, for a concise and cogent assessment of the lack of adult males as primary child caretakers; see also Ember, 1983; Maclachlan, 1983; White, Burton, & Brudner, 1977; and White, Burton, & Dow, 1981).

At birth, the child's consanguine kin is set. The many and otherwise often disparate kinship structures are aligned such that, despite differences in specifics, children consistently have clear and ready access to adult male figures. These male figures may be the mother's husband or, less often, the mother's brother. Nonetheless, an adult male figure is systematically proximate to the developing child (Mackey, 1983; Schlegel, 1972).

Although males are not given the primary child-caretaking responsibilities, they are reported, when compared to mother figures, to have considerable levels of interaction with the child and to show substantial amounts of concern and affection toward children (Mackey, 1983; Rohner & Rohner, 1982). Once a child leaves infancy, and the exclusive primary caretaking of the females, the males often begin to enter progressively more intrusively in that child's life (Barry & Paxson, 1971; Barry, Lauer, & Marshall, 1977). This increased participation, although highly variable across cultures, is more salient with young boys than with young girls.

Although it is extraordinarily difficult to validate degrees and variants of emotional cathexes across very divergent cultural bases, there does seem to be a consensual, thematic pattern suggesting that men consistently and importantly do not like adulterous wives. To be more precise, *their* wives' adultery is disliked; the adultery of the wives of other men is quite a different matter (Broude, 1980; Gaulin & Schlegel, 1980; Rosenblatt & Hillebrant, 1972; Stephens, 1963; Han der Berghe, 1979). Because adulterous wives make the overlap between "social" fathers and "biological" fathers more problematic or equivocal, the omnipresent onus against or of philandering wives bears directly on the father–child relationship.

Inherent in the status-role complex of the father figure are the two prerogatives of provisioning and protecting. Although it is certainly the case that the ecological character and sustenance techniques of the world's community of cultures vary widely, there is an invariant in that foodstuffs are systematically and consistently funneled toward children—either directly to them or mediated through the mother figure. The proportions, amounts, and quality of the shared provisions do fluctuate across subsistence type as well as across time within a culture. Nevertheless, the consistency across the societies is that when men do produce or extract foodstuff from the environment, they are socially sanctioned to redistribute the food to children. This cultural charge or sanction is followed with remarkable amiability by the world's community of men (Levinson & Malone, 1980, HRAF numbers 22–26).

With equal predictability of inferred congeniality, adult males serve as active defenders of hearth and kin when hostilities occur either within their own community or when males from a competing community threaten their community (Divale & Harris, 1976; Ember & Ember, 1971; Whyte, 1978).

SOCIOPSYCHOLOGICAL PERSPECTIVE

Until the late 1960s, the American and Western European versions of the father figure were presented in the social science literature as being either neutral or irrelevant in their impact on the psychosocial development of young children. In terms of the emotional and intellectual growth of the developing child, the mother–child bond was the preeminent focus in the professional and the popular literature (Bowlby, 1969, 1973; Parsons & Bales, 1955; see discussions by LeMasters, 1974; Nash, 1965; and Rapoport, Rapoport, Strelitz, & Kew, 1977). For one example, in the Foss series Determinants in Infant Behavior, there are over 600 references cited (Foss, 1961–1969). Of those 600 references, 91 refer directly to "mother/maternal," whereas only one citation refers directly to "father/paternal" and this is Itani's (1963) work with the macaque monkey.

With the advent of the early 1970s, a shift slowly occurred in the paradigmatic view by the authors who reported on the American father figure. From being viewed as an unimportant parent, the paternal figure was being recast as a potentially important and significant parent; yet he was not adequately fulfilling that potential (Appleton, 1981; Colman & Colman, 1981; Levine, 1976; Yablonsky, 1982). The template being used—invariably tacitly—to make a determination of paternal adequacy was the mother–role, and thereby any alleged decrement of the fathering behavior was adjudged by the standard of the mother figure. The barometer of evaluating the appropriateness of father behaviors became the template of the status-role complex of the mother (for review works see Hamilton, 1977; Lamb, 1981; Lynn, 1974; Maccoby & Jacklin, 1974; McKee & O'Brien, 1982; Price-Bonham, 1976).

Any unique aspects of the father qua father which benefitted the child would be difficult to emerge in the scientists' research designs. In addition, the level of adequacy of the American father figure would only be available to be known if knowledge of father–child dyads from non-American cultures was similarly available.

The parenting (i.e., maternal) model which is used to bracket the paternalistic behaviors is itself of interest. Research on parenting tends to cluster around the well-being of the human condition. For rather understandable reasons, research efforts have focused on the different effects that different parenting strategies and techniques may have upon the well-being of developing children.

Special emphases have been targeted on the well-being, social competence, emotional profiles, cognitive abilities, and gender-role assumption (e.g., Cooper-Holman & Braithwaite, 1983; Hofferth, 1983; White, 1983). The (again usually tacit) value underpinning the rationale for constructing and executing such research was that there were some personality constellations which were preferred over other constellations. Research designs were thereby constructed to isolate and profile variables that would magnify those elements in the preferred constellations. The thrust of any typical project would be to select a trait and then establish an environmental situation that would theoretically optimize that trait. For example, high IQ, or good adjustment or proper and acceptable emotional and social maturation are generally viewed as desirable traits. Nearly any child development text or reference work is replete with examples of such studies (e.g., Biehler, 1981; Gardner, 1982; Hurlock, 1983; Lawton, 1982).

From just about every civilian's point of view, the finding of optimal societal formulas for brighter, more creative, and secure children would be an unqualified good thing. Certainly any individual in favor of dumber, duller and anxiety-ridden children would be a peculiar individual in the Western world and would undoubtedly be aberrant within the human condition.

Any cult advocating good attributes for children would undoubtedly receive more public support than a competing cult promulgating an inferior brand of children. (Within this context, let me, as a civilian, very quickly align myself on the side of the angels and join with all those forces for "good" and against "bad" by endorsing happy, clever, and socially competent children—the more, the better.)

However, it is incumbent that social scientists be able to separate out what would be nice to enjoy as a member of society from what people are in fact doing as directed by their own priorities and their own agendas.

Seen from a different angle, the Western research regimens are filtered by the tendency to study behaviors and phenomena which society would tend to want optimized, for instance, children in the United States are encouraged to be achievement oriented, obedient and popular, creative, organized, spontaneous, self-sufficient, caring and warm, loving human beings (cf. Barry, Bacon, & Child, 1957; Barry, Child, & Bacon, 1959). It is also not unreasonable to suspect that preferences expressed rather than logical categories which are available help to choose which variables are included into research designs and which variables are excluded from research designs.

Funding agencies which support social research are, of course, part of the overall society, and they tend to be consonant with societal vectors. The social dynamics and forces which generate optimal, if not maximal levels of particularistic cognitions and emotions are actively sought by those foundations. The research efforts which more clearly promise to expose facets of these valued traits are those same research efforts which tend to be funded (see the Grants Register, 1983, for current examples of preferred targets of research).

Unhappily, there are only a very few social scientists who are independently wealthy. Therefore, to be able to do that which they do best, the social scientists must parallel their research interests with the interests of the funding agencies (both public and private). These agencies provide the largesse which, in turn, provides the necessary base from which the investigations can begin. Funding agencies tend to want to be part of those forces upgrading the human condition and developing happier, more responsible, self-actualizing and productive citizens. Which set of variables to affect in order to slant individual's behavior toward such fine ideals becomes the epicenter of attention of the social scientists, the funding agencies, the media, and the public. A variable is isolated. A variable is profiled. A variable is discussed. A variable is acted on. A variable is chosen as a consequence of a preferred personality type.

There emerges a small structural problem both in terms of a correspondence between scientific research and the public's behavior. Optimal states for different conditions do not necessarily run parallel with each other. The creation of the brightest, most achievement-oriented child may not involve the same milieu which creates the most empathetic, most compassionate child. Both of which, in turn, may not be the same wellspring which creates the most effective leadership in children. None of these factors may have much influence upon the child's physical health.

Rearing children does not lend itself to the punctual orderliness of a laboratory environment or the politeness of a structured interview. In terms of maneuvering in subtle nuances, young children are simply terrible negotiators. Their lack of manipulative acumen, however, is well balanced by high energy levels and by a persistence, not to be confused with patience, of the force of gravity. To parents, this passage is superfluous. To nonparents, I simply have to ask for either a leap of faith or a suspended judgment. For those individuals with a skepticism and a bent for the empirical, let me suggest spending a Saturday morning in any large American food market. Placing oneself in either the breakfast cereal section or near the cashier should suffice rather nicely.[2]

Current breakfast cereals and their advertisements usually feature ecstatic, winsome children who are laughing and giggling while eating a particular brand of grain and sugar. A parent on top of his or her game would, all other things being equal, opt to buy nutritious breakfast food, of which these cereals are not good examples. If nothing else, healthy children require less attention from parents than do ill children. However, the young child is influenced more by colors, premiums, prizes, and images of joyous peers than by "minimum daily requirements." The result of the two noncongruent preferences is a compromise—a maintenance formula between the two preferences—but not an optimum for either. The compromise could be reached in the relatively safe and private domain of the home, but is often reached in the store's aisle after both sides have expressed their preferences in the modalities of their own developmental statuses.

Exhibiting unparalleled marketing verve, food store managers place chewing gum and candy just before the cash register is reached. The parent must often wait in line at the cash register to pay for his or her wares. At this juncture the parent–child dyad is immobilized while being surrounded by enormous temptations in the form of sugar, chocolate, and artificial fruit flavors.

The child is at this point aided in the quest for the creature

---

[2]Perhaps the only category of the human condition to which I feel morally superior would be that category that imagined and then actually did put marshmallows in children's cereals.

comforts of taste by the immobility of the parent, the presence of other adults, and the ease of being placated. The adult's optimum strategy of avoiding a poor diet for the child and the child's optimal strategy of enjoying "sweets" on demand clash (see Trivers, 1972, 1974, for a much more technical analysis of parent–child asymmetrical strategies). The compromise is again a maintenance formula rather than an optimum formula. Balances are struck. Enter to center stage the invention of "sugarless" chewing gum which is without the disadvantages of "sugared" chewing gum yet is flavorful and chewy enough for children to enjoy. The inventor of sugarless chewing gum is someone whom I would heartily support for the Nobel Peace Prize.

Although these two examples of compromise are innocuous enough and trivial in the context of geopolitical spheres of influence, the basic notion is of fundamental importance in the study of family networks. The implementation of scenarios or strategies to develop *optimal* levels of several behaviors or emotional conditions is a very expensive procedure. In current parlance, the "costs" of marginal units toward the optimum are high, whereas the "benefits" may be ambiguous.

Parents, as well as children, play multiple roles which have conflicting demands. It is unlikely that there would be more than a few traits that could receive highly concentrated, undiluted time, energies, and resources. What is more likely to occur is a shifting amalgam of parental behaviors and priorities that reflect an attempt to reach a *maintenance* of acceptable levels of cognitive, social, and emotional traits in their children.

I use the plural "children" in the preceding sentence advisedly. It requires no exotic mathematical skills to divine that a society which averages less than two children per woman ("family" if monogamy is taken seriously by the natives) is a maladaptive society. Unless repopulation by immigration is allowed (i.e., exploiting the fertility of other women in other societies), a society which chronically and systematically reduces fecundity to less than two children per female must depopulate itself. The depopulation may be rapid (zero children per female) or slow (1.9 children per female). In either event, the social structure is maladaptive and would be replaced by an alternate social organization that generated in excess of two children per female.

Now, if—as *is* the case—child psychologists make a concentrated effort of studying family networks of father, mother, and one child triads, then the child psychologists are studying a maladaptive system. One child per female cannot a society make. An advantage to the study of a triadic family, especially if the one child is an immobile infant, is that there is a relatively simple network of only four relationships available for analysis: mother–father; father–infant; mother–infant, mother–father–infant. A more successfully adaptive family network of four (mother–father–older child–younger child) has eleven relationships (mother–older child; mother–younger child; father–older child; father–younger child; mother–father; younger child–older child; mother–younger child–older child; father–older child–younger child; father–mother–older child; father–mother–younger child; father–mother–older child–younger child). A family system averaging three children (probably societally viable if infant–child mortality is low) has 46 relationships (30 dyads + 10 triads + 5 quartets + 1 quintet = 46) available for analysis.

As mentioned earlier, cross-cultural data indicate that women are exclusive primary caretakers of infants, but that men are given increasing access or responsibility/opportunity to tend to slightly older children. Accordingly, the family configuration of at least two children and a father figure and a mother figure may more funnel the older child toward the father figure and the younger child toward the mother figure. A study of singletons can never reveal that type of dynamic. Certainly it is a reasonable hypothesis that unique fathering behaviors are more triggered in the toddler stage and above rather than by the infant gestalt, which is arguably more efficiently directed at and eliciting to the mother figure. Once again the structural problems of focusing on the socially maladaptive triadic family system to gain knowledge of paternalistic behavior become clearly profiled: it is impossible to study maternalistic and paternalistic behavior differentials toward two children if there is but one child available.

Forty-six relationships along (only) three dimensions—cognition, emotions, social effectiveness—is a very disorderly research design if optimal levels of functioning are the quest or terminus of the research project. The logistics of such a project would seem to be awesome enough to create a myopia blurring the imperatives of the project into a hazy oblivion. The paradox is quite clear. A ratio of two adults (mother figure; father figure) per child may well maximize the opportunity for optimum growth and development of a *single* child. Howsoever, the average of one child per family, even as bright, content, and able as he or she may be, is maladaptive at the societal level.

A maintenance formula, allowing for two or more children, is much more viable from the perspective of society. With a goodly measure of optimism, I will posit that families opt for maintenance: the reaching of socially acceptable levels of behavior on many dimensions for all of their children. Compromise is the order of the day, the decade, the generation. With less optimism and perhaps more realism, I can posit that there are probably nonzero families in which survival is not achieved. Child abuse and infanticide are both logical as well as empirically filled categories (Inglis, 1978; Kempe & Kempe, 1978; Lenington, 1981; Starr, 1979).

The research strategies seeking optimal values on selected variables are, of course, self-evidently valuable for a restricted range of questions with qualified interpretations. Complementing these research tactics is the additional option of trying to reflect the mosaic of balanced, compromised behavioral patterns that parents do develop in response to, and for, and perhaps in defense against, their children.

Letting the men and the women set their times, their agendas, and their priorities as they prefer and *then* trying to read that tapestry of interactions become prime foci of this book. In addition, with very few exceptions (and this book will not be one), the psychosocial research on fathering is uni-directional. The impact of the father on the child is almost exclusively studied. The impact of the child on the father (especially at different developmental stages of the father) has received minimal research effort (exceptions include Clarke-Stewart, 1977; Lewis & Rosenblum, 1973). The impact by the developing child on the developing adult male may be trivial or it may be substantial and important. An interesting thought is that children domesticate and otherwise tame and settle down the proximate adult males as those males leave the final phases of puberty. However, social fathers and childless males may be quite similar on many if not most psychosocial scales. To bring that friendly chestnut to the fore: only further studies will address these questions.

A few words ought to be offered on the generalized view of the human condition as seen through the telescopes and microscopes of the social sciences. Overall, the view is rather benign and favorable.

From the literature one infers that the unwritten substratum of the imagery, myth system, and symbolism of most writers is that humans, by and large, are a fairly decent lot; we would like to be good, to do good things, and treat and be treated with decency; and that, given a chance to perform a nice act versus a tawdry act, the benefit of any doubt is given to us by us: we would be nice, not tawdry. Whether this view is crisp and clear description or a flagrant obfuscation via self-vested, self-inflicted cultural illusion is an interesting notion in its own right. In any event, a Rousseauian or Wordsworthian image of Western humanity seems more in line with the givens and covert culture of the bulk of social scientists than a Hobbesian view in which we would be a nasty, scruffy collection of folk barely kept from mutual carnage by that "thin veneer of civilization."[3]

The seemingly ever present continuous mayhem and sufferings humans inflict upon each other is conceptualized by the social sciences as a series of unfortunate personal histories, economics, disparities or political inequities. If better childhoods, fairer economic distribution systems, and political egalitarianism were to be achieved, then people would, in the main, be without reason to be injurious to each other and, without such reasons, would not thereby be injurious.

A brief digression is in order concerning a broader facet of the philosophy of Western social sciences in particular and of the tone of popular literature in general. In discussions of a wide array of social problems, a set of solutions is conjectured whose basis is essentially that a "better quality of people" is needed to solve this or that or some other social blight. The route to procuring better people is often "more education"—more education would result in better people— or the route is not mentioned, just the destination.

Spouse abuse, drug addiction, unemployable adults, crime, illiteracy, juvenile delinquency, obesity, child abuse, and so on and on and on are bracketed within the rubrics of "if only a better quality of people were about," then these social problems would be unnecessary and thereby dissolve away.

Included in such sentiments is the rather charming and op-

---

[3]Acknowledgment and appreciation are extended to Edgar Rice Burroughs and Lord Greystoke for the phrase, if not the content.

timistic premise that "better people" are in fact on their way and will emerge perhaps as the plurality or even the majority, or even beyond the majority to the totality of the human condition.

A measured response to such a scenario would include the notion that "better" families, however defined, would systematically have to provide increasingly more children to society than "non-better" families. People do not arise from the void, in whole cloth. People have histories—one to a person. The collective histories of many people, one at a time, would have to be affected to nudge the entire unit of the huddled masses toward the quasi-idyllic notion of being "better" people. Whether by genetics or by socialization traditions or some combination of the two, the primary conduit through which all or nearly all children pass is some version of the family as a massively influential socialization device. For the arrival of the millennium to occur, a mechanism would have to be in place which would limit "non-better families" the access to unfettered fecundity while allowing or encouraging or mandating increased fecundity on the part of "better families." It seems infinitely unlikely in the highly individualistic Western world that any population policy which could be enforced would be allowed by the citizenry to operate effectively. Current democracies are just not structured along those lines of coercion in the twentieth century—free-lance birthing is alive and well. Any realistic notion of social problems dissolving with the oncoming of better people is questionable. This argument of better people having fewer problems can obviously be applied to many human adventures. It certainly may be argued that there may be social problems or social anomalies which result, in part or in whole, from bad fathering, however "bad" is chosen to be defined. Consequently, the arrival of better fathers would simultaneously occur with the departure of any particular social anomaly or problem. Such new, improved fathering, of course, must come from a generation in which the old, subpar fathering was extant and prevalent. In nearly allegorical terms, the two competing socialization matrices—the newly emerging and the previously established—would vie for societal prepotence. The winner, by definition, would be the matrix producing the most (not the best, but the most) father–child dyads over many generations. Disregarding the herculean tasks of definitions and implementing tests for "good," "better," and "best," there is not, nor will there be in the near or distant future, any way to enforce a policy dictating the number of offspring per male or per female or per family. Over time, any societal lurching in the direction of improved fathering must result from mothers selecting improved husbands, and these improved husbands/fathers must provide more of the next generation than alternate versions of husbands/fathers.

My banner indicating that I too am an appropriate citizen is still unfurled. I too am in favor of better people with proper childhoods, a just and thriving economic system, plus the virtues of a democratic political system. However, my other banner, that of a social scientist allows me the luxury of not evaluating behavior in terms of "the right, the moral, and the really quite proper" or of "the wrong, the immoral, and the something one ought not think, much less do." I have the additional luxury of asking: What do we do and why do we do it? More specifically, I can ask the question: How are men as father figures and women as mother figures maintaining in the bewilderingly complex ecological system known as culture?

Level of Analysis

There is a temptation to call such analysis of behavior patterns without reiterating strong societal preferences of personality type, a "Mackeyvellian" analysis. However, this label seems somehow inelegant and the more conventional appellation of Darwinian more aptly fits the concepts in effect.

A Darwinian analysis shifts the focal point from the well-being of individuals to that which those individuals *do* to survive, and if lucky, to flourish. In other words, there is no overriding reason to suppose that happiness is a driving force either in a successful family system or, painting with a larger brush, a society (see Szasz, 1967, 1970, for an extended discussion on this topic). Whether seen as a derivative of cultural evolution or as a derivative of coevolution of cultural-and-biological evolution (Barkow, 1980; Durham, 1979), the "natural selection" of extant families in extant communities depends directly upon the referent population being able to have and rear viable, socially competent children. Those groups consistently having more children will obviously, over many generations, have the opportunity to supplant those with less children. The relative "happy" or "content" quotients may be only very indirectly related, if related at all, to the success or survivability of a family or a community. It is at least arguable that a pervasive societal value system of self-sacrifice, humility, hard work, and the veneration of the polyparous mother figure could be systematically advantageous over time in competition with a value system of self-indulgence and antinatalism—regardless of what the other chips in that cultural mosaic may be.

The current scientific research paradigm on childhood development illustrates a most benign and optimistic view of the human condition. The fundamental thrust of the paradigm is the attempt to elevate the well-being of the society's citizenry. This attempt may not be consonant with the core culture of those natives whose habits, mores, folkways, and symbolic and myth systems have been forged most certainly from an ancestral matrix generating survivability and maintenance. If personal happiness, contentment, and autonomy, in other words, well-being, happen to be included within the cultural traditions, so much the better; yet such well-being is neither necessary nor sufficient for the survivability of a society. It is probably a moot question whether the benefits and costs accrued from a "self-actualized," "happy" citizenry can be competitive with a society chronically indifferent to personal satisfaction.

My intuition is that a happy citizenry is an expensive, ecological luxury, ill-suited for cultural competition against alternate cultural forms. This intuition may be partially influenced by the social fact that I grew up when children's television fare included "Howdy-Doody" rather than either "Sesame Street" or "Mister Rogers," and I am, at this juncture, potentially prone to the vice of temporocentrism. A cross-cousin of ethnocentrism, temporocentrism may be more pernicious in that everyone is exposed to it at the same time and it is thereby that much more difficult to counter. Whereas a person can travel from culture to culture and experience first-hand different lifestyles, travel back and forth in time is available only in the imagination, and the imagination may not be a particularly accurate barometer for analyzing human social behavior second and third hand.

To return a moment to an earlier topic, it is also arguable that the members of a man–woman dyad could maximize their own personal well-being without the addition of even one child. From the perspective of the two relevant individuals, that well-being is a fine and proper sequel of a lifestyle (Huber, 1980; Lorber, 1980). From a societal point of view, such a condition is suicidal: no children, no future adults, no society. A triad of mother-father-(one) child may result in a satisfying or even optimum life for the trio. Howsoever, from a societal perspective, such a trio represents a maladaptive system. One child fails to achieve replacement level for the population.

A quartet—one father, one mother, two children—is adaptive if and only if child mortality asymptotes at zero. Although perhaps adaptive, such a society is, over generations, probably not competitive with an alternate system based on three or more children per woman. If all other factors were held consistent, if not constant, a single child may receive more resources, parental (or adult) affection, supervision, and guidance, than a set of three or more children—that is, the optimal well-being of children is vulnerable with the addition of competing siblings. However, the maintenance of family, community, and society are clearly vulnerable with the onset of a system of optimizing well-being of singletons.

Accordingly, the thrust of a major sector of research on child development is operating on a separate plane from that which families or societies operate. Despite a high laudability quotient which may be derived from a formula for optimal socialization among one or two (albeit important) dimensions of personality, that formula is also to be weighted within the context of the larger familial or community networks or systems whose background was filtered for maintenance and survival.

Using this context as a background, a supplementary research strategy to one which would isolate key variables in the emergence of different amounts or types of personality characteristic is the alternate strategy of developing behavioral maps of what people do, how they behave when they get to follow their own prerogatives, their own agendas, and their own priorities. The rationale here is that behavior is not a chaotic assemblage of random, Brownian movements, but that behavior is structured, organized, and reasonably purposeful. Behavior is also that property of the organism which interacts directly with the environment. Although the cognitive images and symbols of an individual lend meaning and understanding to the environment, it is that individual's behavior which, with varying success, meets the demands and opportunities of the environmental vagaries. From the kalaidoscope of diverse, reinforcing, and mutually exclusive images and symbols within each individual, a discrete behavior pattern or habit eventuates. The cognitive dynamics and decision making may be complex or simple for any given behavior. Nonetheless, a behavior either does or does not occur. Emotions and ideations may tend to be continuous; behaviors tend to be discrete.

The theme or focus of this book is on the behaviors of father figures. Holding in abeyance for the moment an analysis of the nuances and subtleties of any articulated reasons concerning the image of fathering expectations and the evaluation of the father status-role complex, we may say that the primary interests to this book are (1) how do fathers actually behave and (2) why in a broad sense do they behave as fathers at all and then (3) why do fathers behave in some particularistic ways rather than in others.

CROSS-SPECIES COMPARISONS

Humans, with the capacity and flexibility of the metaphor, can classify themselves in what amounts to an infinite number of ways as they exercise their humanity. Within the Linnaean world of taxonomy, "we" are transfigured into genus *Homo*, species *sapiens*—a species of the order Primate (Eimerl & DeVore, 1965; Nelson & Jurmain, 1982; Simons, 1972). The level of description which Primate entails involves a diverse assemblage of fellow primates including: pottos, lemurs, tarsiers, aye-ayes, baboons, lorises, gorillas, gibbons, and orangutans. As will be discussed later, this level may in fact be more broad than is needed for the most useful scrutiny. Nonetheless, Primate has the most current coinage, and for the moment, will be used here.

A small, yet influential and increasing, number of studies on nonhuman primates has been used to bracket and profile the human father–child relationship. The rationale for the advisability and utility of these "within order" and "cross-species" comparisons has an intuitive appeal.

The rationale is hinged upon the premise that, as ontogeny unfolds, behavioral tendencies, like morphological and physiological tendencies, are canalized or funneled along some particular routes rather than others (Breland & Breland, 1965; Hinde & Stevenson-Hinde, 1973; Immelman, Barlow, Petronovich, & Main, 1981; Piaget, 1978; Roe & Simpson, 1958; Seligman & Hager, 1972; Waddington, 1975; Wilson, 1978). The correspondence for humans between morphological or physiological genetic programming and behavioral programming is met, as would be expected, with a wide spectrum of acceptances and rejections. In spite of the legitimate queries and criticisms, the premises or assumptions, in theory form, do become available for generating hypotheses about human instincts and for synthesizing otherwise divergent bits of data.

Given the possibility that genetic information from the phylogenetic heritage of an organism *can* bias or direct, however generally, then it is reasonable to surmise that the closer two organisms are phylogenetically, the more that they may share inherent behavioral tendencies. Increased phylogenetic relationships ought to be associated with increased behavioral homologues. Primates such as chimpanzees, baboons, and macaques, when compared to nonprimates like whales, birds, and horses, are close cousins indeed to *Homo* (cf. Yunis & Prakash, 1982). Consequently, analysis of shared and unique paternalistic behavior strategies for nonhuman primates in diverse ecologies can be reasonably entertained to shed light and insight into *Homo*'s paternalistic strategies.

Such preliminary analyses have been made and the trends of the results are interesting. Two modes of behavior from adult male nonhuman primates to their young have been found across different taxa of primates. Although there are individual differences within groups and population differences across species and species differences across larger taxa, in general, adult males have been surveyed offering protection toward females and young, and these males have been recorded as exhibiting tolerance toward their young along a template or model which could be called "nurturing-parenting" (Kleiman & Malcolm, 1981; Mitchell, 1979; Redican & Taub, 1981).

A Preliminary Test of American Father Figures

In an attempt to generate initial behavioral analogues to the then current and prevailing sociopsychological model of assumed minimal input of the father figure on the child, a pilot study was conducted in the state of Virginia in 1972. The resultant data were surprising in that they were not consonant with the model of the neutral or irrelevant father figure. Parks, pools, shopping malls, sporting events, and restaurants found men and children, both boys and girls, in substantial numbers and in substantial proportions (compared to women and children). Not only were men found with children, the men seemed to be holding and watching these children and monitoring their behaviors in a manner comparable to that of the women's responses to the children. The imagery of a detached father figure would not have predicted the high level of men's parenting behavior which was actually observed. This older model of unimportant, indifferent, aloof father figures was not sustained. In addition, as shall be seen, the newly emergent model of the potentially important, yet underachieving father figure was also not supported.

A more complete survey in Virginia and subsequent research in additional cultures sustained the discrepancy between the image of the detached father figure in the United States and the empirical data on the man–child dyad. The stereotype or imagery suggested irrelevance or aloofness, while the data indicated substantial associations between men and children and relatively high levels of interaction from men toward children. This ill-fitting match between expectation and data necessitated what Kuhn (1962) called a paradigmic adjustment. The lack of correspondence between emic/subjective reality of the image of the uninvolved father and the etic/behavioral reality of substantial man–child interaction allowed two domains of questions to present themselves:

1. What behavioral patterns are extant between men and children (boys and girls analyzed separately and then combined to be analyzed within the single taxon: children)?
2. What are the expectations or images held by a society in terms of the relative importance of the father as co-primary child caretaker?

It should be noted that any answers to these two questions may result in a great deal of overlap—essentially the perceptions of reality may turn out to be equivalent to that reality—or the data from an inquiry into the two questions may tap different domains. Whether the overlap is sparse or is substantial, the two questions should be treated as diagnostically separate and as tapping into two different kinds of inquiry: one primarily symbolic and one primarily empirical.

As the project evolved, the importance of an empirical data base was emphasized, and fieldwork concentrated on observing and recording behavior patterns between men and children across cultures. The resultant patterned behaviors were kept conceptually separate from the symbolic domain to ascertain what degree of correspondence in fact existed between the behavior of the subjects versus their perception of their own behavior.

With a final flourish of my good citizen banner, let me agree that healthy, good parenting, however defined, would, of course, be viewed with approval and enthusiastic encouragement. Certainly I would say as much in a public arena, whether I believed it or not. When in Rome, one wears the symbols of Rome. As my banner is furled and put away, it should be made very clear that this project has no special expertise or familial recipes to offer on successful fathering or on the emergence of successful childhoods as a function of stylized parental milieus. Thresholds or criteria that separate hygienic parenting from unhygienic parenting, for both mothers and fathers, are currently unavailable. No illusions are entertained here that this project can demarcate the character or form of whatever parameters "good fathers" may manifest and "bad fathers" do not, especially when the measuring instruments are aimed at children-turned-adults in two or three decades. This book is targeted to survey how men and children interact and what myth structures surround the man–child bond in America. The book is arranged in a sequence that parallels both the order of events as they occurred and the generalized scientific method: (1) a question was posed; (2) a method was designed to answer the question; (3) data were gathered that it is hoped addressed the question at hand; (4) the data were discussed within the constraints and structures of theories upon which a loose consensus of germane specialists has agreed were profitable (Chapter 2).

Three tiers of theory allowed diagnostically separable analyses: (1) the influence on social behavior by genotypic information, that is, a phylogenetic analysis; (2) the influence on social behaviors by economic and ecological variables; and (3) that segment of a society's symbolic and myth structures which surround the man–child relationship (Chapter 3).

Human paternalistic behavior is then interpreted through the prism of evolutionary history or, to use current nomenclature, through the lens of the newly emerging discipline of sociobiology (Chapter 4).

As a complement to the evolutionary perspective, the influence that a traditional division of labor by gender has on the man–child bond is investigated. It is suggested while the basic template that generates man–child interaction is more affected by the age of the child than the gender of the child, the relative dependence of a culture on the male's greater brute strength to achieve important societal tasks is a very sensitive marker to the gender of children as their association with adults are allocated (Chapter 5).

Following the presentation of the dynamics of the 18 culture sample, the American man–child dyad is described in relation to the other 17 surveyed cultures. The form and frequency of interaction from the American father figure toward his children are compared to similarly constructed indices from the total cultural sample. The resultant comparisons are viewed within the perspective of the generalized image of American fathers as portrayed by both the professional and popular authors (Chapters 6 and 7).

The place of parenting within a high technology egalitarian society is then discussed as a candidate to exemplify G. Hardin's (1968) "Tragedy of the Commons." That is, when seen within the context of individual freedom and societal viability—two highly approved yet often contradictory values—what are the dynamics of parenting in America as the twenty-first century begins to loom on the horizon? Finally, a synopsis is given on what the project had accomplished and what of value might have stemmed from its completion.

The Adult Male–Child Bond

An examination of any human behavior pattern faces five immediate problems of some magnitude:

1. Whom are you going to study—that is, who are your subjects?
2. Where are you going to study your subjects?
3. Is your method of research influencing the character of the data that are being gathered on your subjects, in this instance man–child dyads? Framed in a different way, are you viewing behavior reflecting your subjects' own priorities, agendas, and decisions or are you viewing behavior which is reacting to your scientific intrusion?
4. What behaviors are to be coded, and at what level of coarseness or refinement?
5. From what perspective or vantage point will the collected data be organized and interpreted?

With an infinite number of options available for choice, the following decisions were made early in the project's inception. Each selection that was made simultaneously eliminated the benefits and unique facets to be gained from the rejected options. However, no study has an infinite number of variables with an infinite number of subjects; so decisions that reject and make information unavailable are not merely convenient, they are necessary.

SUBJECT SELECTION?

The people to be surveyed would include men, as well as women, who were interacting with at least one child. The question can be quickly asked: Why study the woman–child relationship if the man–child bond is the real focus of interest? The response to this question is in two parts.

1. There was, and still is, every good reason to believe that child rearing and child caretaking are vital and irreplaceable components of the social structure of a viable society. Living, socially competent children are a sine qua non of a culture, be that culture a tribe, a village, or a nation-state.

The form, mode, rhythm, and character of child rearing seem to be sensitive to a large array of variables impacting on the overall functioning of any society (Levinson & Malone, 1980, pp. 185–228). Accordingly, there could be a mosaic of culturally unique prescriptions and proscriptions, the do's and don'ts , orchestrating the behavior of men (and women) toward their society's children. In other words, the man–child bond of any society is operating within the context of the cultural traditions and prerogatives of that society (Rohner, 1975; Whiting & Whiting, 1975). This context becomes an integral component in the analysis of the man–child bond. Different cultures may have different starting places or givens in the realm of interpersonal behavior. For example, touching, holding, or hugging may be more appropriate within one culture than within another. The minimum amount of interpersonal distance felt to be comfortable may be quite small in one society while large in an alternate society. Any list of the covert, tacit behavioral rules in a cultural infrastructure can be extensive indeed. Touching, eye contact, facial expression, speaking voice, terms of address, posture, and so on are subtly and effectively regulated by culture (Hall, 1959, 1966).

The problem faced with this project, as in any cross-cultural project, was to find a baseline against which the man–child dyad could be compared within each surveyed culture and then compared with some sense of legitimacy across cultural boundaries (Moore, 1961; Naroll, 1973; Rohner, Naroll, Barry, Divale, Erickson, Schaefer, & Sipes, 1978). Fortunately, the sexual phenomenon and its derivative linguistic analogue "gender" are available as diagnostic instruments in the analysis of societal dynamics. Every society recognizes gender differentials and uses those differences to stratify its social structure (Levinson & Malone, 1980, pp. 267–278; Murdock, 1937; Murdock & Provost, 1973; Stewart, 1977). Women thereby became the baseline with which to evaluate man–child interaction. Within each society the level of activity between men and children would be compared with levels of activity between women and children. On this point, let me accede that men and women within any culture do not experience that culture identically or even equivalently. In the sense that cultures can expect distinct responses from the two genders, men and women do not experience congruent cultures. On the other hand, the culture that the men experience is the same culture viewed by the women, and the culture experienced by the women is the same culture viewed by the men. In the sense that one gender is the actor and the other gender is the potential spectator, the two genders are from the same culture. There is symmetry in the two asymmetries. It is this sense of similarity of shared overview that serves as a pylon underpinning this section of the project.

Once an ordinal relationship (more than, less than, or equal to) that would index fathering behaviors compared to mothering behaviors was established within a culture, the ordinal relationships could be compared directly with each other across cultures. Using this technique, the problems inherent in cultural relatively, the judging of a society on its own terms, and of highly variegated cultural bases were lessened, if not completely countered.

2. The second part of the decision to survey women in a man–child project is as follows. Family life and familial dynamics tend to be integrated, interactive sets of activities. Men and women and children triangulate their behaviors off of feedback mechanisms and the expectations that they offer to one another. Not only would the macro-aspects of a culture, for example, the subsistence technique, kinship systems, and political structures affect the man–child relationship, but the simple micro-aspect of having a woman present or not may affect how a man responds to a child. As the pilot study strongly indicated, it did indeed matter if a woman was present or absent from a man–child dyad. Patterns of the man–child relationships were different when there was a woman present with them versus when there was no woman present.

To encapsulate the rationale of studying women in a project about men and children: to avoid tapping purely idiosyncratic socialization traditions (of Western Europe/United States), cross-cultural data are essential. To minimize the inherent problems of different cultural bases, comparable units of analysis were constructed within each society of the man–child relationship as compared to the woman–child relationship. The ordinal relationship developed within a society can then be compared across societies. Because of potential interpersonal dynamics operating within a man, woman, and child triad, the recording of woman–child interaction was mandated to make available for analysis any influence that the presence of a woman had upon a man–child dyad.

WHERE TO STUDY SUBJECTS?

The options for places to investigate the man–child bond include three prototypes: the laboratory, the home, and the public.

The advantages of the laboratory are profound. The control of variables (the environment) is most available in the scientist's laboratory. Because the isolation of important variables versus trivial variables is the very goal that the scientist is seeking, a laboratory environment, with its control of extraneous variables, becomes a valuable research tool. The laboratory setting is well tailored for finding the capacity or limits of subjects' sensorimotor skills or for divining the relative prepotence or penetration of variables which were selected prior to the study. In addition, and not inconsequentially, the "lab" is the scientist's home turf with the attendant emotional security and confidence of the familiar. The subjects enter into a strange, often peculiar and intimidating place, and follow instructions that often include "act natural, and just be yourself."

The disadvantages of a laboratory regimen are primarily that the subjects *are* in an alien place, knowing they are under scrutiny, and thereby may be acting unnaturally (Rosnow, 1974; Rubin, 1974). The laboratory setting is not well met to profile the subjects' priorities and agendas as they choose to execute them.

The home of the subjects, as a place for investigation of the subjects' behavior patterns, gives the home turf or home team advantage to the subjects with a probable increase in allowing their typical habits to unfold and become available to be recorded. However, it is problematic whether or not their knowledge of the presence of an observer or recording device is massively affecting the normal range and central tendencies of their behavior patterns. It is certainly possible that in this instance the means of gathering data can fundamentally affect the character of the data themselves.

The other option, that of observing behaviors in public places, is somewhat the mirror image of the laboratory milieu: whereas the laboratory setting minimizes spontaneous, "feral" behavior of individuals who are interacting ad lib, and maximizes control of variables or immediate input which the subjects receive, an alternate study based upon merely observing behavior in a public place maximizes the naturalness or spontaneity of the subjects' behavior and minimizes any control that the experimenter may wish to exercise.

The aims of this project were to seek what father figures actually do. Consequently, the lure of the laboratory was rejected for the great outdoors—where humidity, rain, dust, mud, lack-of-shade, and a very formidable Doberman pinscher avail themselves. All observations were to be during daylight hours, in public places which had equal access by gender. The project might retain the prerogative of selecting which public places with equal access for male and for females would be the observation sites, but after that decision was made, the subjects selected themselves. They came when they wanted. They left when they wanted. They behaved as they so chose at the speed, amplitude, and direction that they chose.

Once the type of observation locus was decided, the next problem was where to distribute those loci. A cross-cultural study, by its name, should include a number of different cultures, but which ones? Several immediate filters limited the potential pool of cultures as exemplified by the World Ethnographic Sample or the Ethnographic Atlas or the Human Relations Area File. Not unlike the stars, cultures too seem to have a life cycle. They are born. They flourish. They die. Large numbers of cultures from antiquity such as the Aztecs, the Incas, the Mayas, Pharoah's Egypt, Socrates's Greece, Caesar's Rome, the Vikings, and Babylonia, are no more. In addition, large numbers of preliterate societies, for example, Tasmanians, the Kiowa, the Cheyenne, the Caribs, the Yahgan, and the Ona are simply gone. Analyses of their citizens' behaviors are likewise permanently unavailable.

Political considerations and health considerations further winnowed down the field. Not every government is unabashedly enthusiastic to have (especially Western) anthropologists scrambling among its peasantry and doing any number of things, from censuses of menstrual cycles to consciousness raising. In addition, a number of areas of the globe are clearly dangerous to life and limb—and thereby are good places in which to lose a fieldworker, even if he or she could gain access. A single example will suffice. One cultural niche scheduled to be surveyed were the Pushtun of Afghanistan, and, just in case something would go awry, the backup culture was in Iran. One invasion and one revolt later, the cultural niche actually surveyed was rural Taiwan, a relative paragon of stability.

Geographically, the five major continents were to be represented: North America, South America, Europe, Africa, Asia. In addition, urban-rural sites were to be represented plus places with ethnically homogeneous populations as well as ethnically heterogeneous populations. Within the further limitations of funding personnel, there was an attempt to maximize cultural diversity.

Fieldwork proceeded in two stages. Four cultures were surveyed to develop a baseline: Virginia, and Coahuila, Mexico (North America); Spain (Europe), and Lima, Peru (South America). Then 14 additional cultures were surveyed to test more fine-grained hypotheses: Reykjavik, Iceland, Ireland (Europe); Israeli kibbutzim, India, rural Taiwan, rural Sri Lanka, Japan, and Hong Kong (Asia); Morocco, Ivory Coast, the Senufo of the Ivory Coast (Africa); and the Karaja of Brazil, Brazil—rural, and Brazil—urbanizing (South America). To date a total of 18 cultures have been surveyed.

It should be made clear that these cultures are not meant to be exhaustive ethnographic accounts of the referent cultures. That is, the data from India are not intended in any way, shape, or form to profile the huge kaleidoscope of India's great diversity of peoples, customs, and lifestyles. The data should be viewed as data from India. Similarly, the data from the Israeli kibbutzim were not developed to reflect all of the various subcultures in Israel. These data are most diagnostically useful when interpreted as data from the Israeli kibbutzim.

If it can be agreed that India is distinct from Ireland which is distinct from Israel which is distinct from Virginia, and so on, then data sets drawn from within these distinct cultures can be conceptualized as representing different cultural bases. The various amounts of similarity and dissimilarity of behavior found among these (agreed upon) different cultures can then be analyzed further.

METHOD OF STUDYING?

All observations were to be conducted as anonymously as feasible, if not possible. The influence of the observer upon the responses of the observed was ideally to be restricted to only the influence of the observer's sedentary, physical presence within the vicinity. In larger areas—playgrounds or parks in large urban areas—anonymity was fairly easy to adopt. Sunglasses, tourist guidebooks, and newspapers hid eye direction and recording notebooks effectively. For small villages or towns effective anonymity of the fieldworkers was more of a challenge and the fieldworkers exercised their skills in creativity and interpersonal relations in appearing benign, nonthreatening, and unobtrusive. The infusion of cash into the very local economy for bread and board of course helped, but engaging personalities probably aided the most. In any event, anonymity of the fieldworker and his or her observing duties were key elements to the study and were, I do believe, maintained effectively. The gathered data reflect men and women and children allocating their preferences and their priorities and their choices, as they decided. It became the requirements of this study to reflect accurately what were the behavioral results of those decisions made by the subjects, that is, by the men and the women and the children.

There would be no questionnaires, no interviews, no intrusion on the private space and time of the observed subjects. With such a decision, much information of great value becomes unavailable. However, the importance of anonymity generated benefits which were judged to be at least equivalent to the heavy costs incurred.

Behavior to Be Coded?

A cross-cultural project such as this one required comparable units of analysis. That is, whatever behaviors were coded in one culture had to be comparable or equivalent to the kinds of behavior coded in alternate cultures. To achieve comparability, the level of behavor coded had to be generalized enough or abstract enough to be available to all or nearly all of the cultures surveyed. Vocabulary, for example, would be far too specific across societies for any kind of useful comparison. The heart pumping blood or the direction of peristalsis would be equivalent across societies but too obvious to be interesting.

After a good deal of trial and error—mostly error—four basic behaviors were selected from the pilot studies to be coded across cultural boundaries. The four dimensions (from Hall, 1961) were essentially:

1. A person could be present with or absent from the presence of another person.
2. A person could be touching or not touching someone else.
3. A person could be near or far from someone else.
4. A person could be looking at or not looking at someone else.

A more detailed and technical description of the coding categories is presented below in the Procedure section.

It may be useful to note that verbalization (Talk—Not Talk) was a major disappointment as a candidate for inclusion in the study. The logistics of determining whether someone has spoken or not were invincible. Smell and taste were only logical categories of even then but short duration. Problems of validation overwhelmed. However, many of the names for the proposed scales were innovative.

THEORETICAL PERSPECTIVE

In what amounts to a totally arbitrary decision, the emergence or development of human social behavior is seen as a triune phenomenon—three major forces acting simultaneously on the actual emitted response. It is certainly possible that another theoretician might be more comfortable with two forces; still others may find solace in four, five, or seven. For this project, however, three is a manageable, useful number and true to the notion of an epigenetic unfolding of the human condition. The three forces or tiers of analysis include:

1. The symbolic tier
2. The cultural or socialization tradition tier
3. The biological or phylogenetic tier

What is being suggested here is that behavioral development and variance can be conceptualized as emerging from two "main effect" variables (genotypic information and cultural information) plus the multitudes of interaction effects (from Jensen, 1972). Because of the interdependency and short term and long term feedback loops that exist amongst these three tiers, any dissection of ongoing human social behavior will always have elements of the artificial and the arbitrary. With final interpretations tempered by this caveat, the threefold analysis can then be accepted as being diagnostically useful.

The Symbolic Tier

The universal proclivity by humans to symbolize and to form metaphor and simile has been richly documented by ethnographers for decades (e.g., Geertz, 1974). It is self-evident that analyses by symbolic anthropologists have been and will continue to constitute a broadly useful and informative discipline. However, a systematic relationship between symbols as a class of events and the referent behaviors is very difficult to ascertain (Harris, 1974a). Symbols can reinforce and parallel behavior tendencies, but they can also camouflage or obfuscate the accurate perception of empirical behavioral patterns. The symbol, in the form of an image or a rule or a spoken phrase which attempts to profile "the-way-things-are," may be actualized more in the breach than in the observance. In addition, contrasting symbols or images can reflect the same trait, for example, "fools rush in where angels fear to tread," "strike while the iron is hot," "haste makes waste," "time and tide wait for no man." The symbols of Western folklore give no real aid on how to manage one's time.

Because of the equivocal consonance between symbols, including verbal reports from informants, and the referent behaviors, this study will concentrate upon the cultural and biological tiers. This concentration can in no way be construed to suggest that work within the symbolic or verbal domain is not important. Emic analyses are of course necessary for a more complete understanding to the problem of what it means to be human. Nevertheless, the current lack of a paradigm which would allow the matching of empirically normative behaviors across cultures with parallel imagery or symbols across cultures simultaneously severely limits and constrains the utility of a symbolic analysis toward the *validation* of causal agents generating the emergence of human social behavior.

Socialization Tradition Tier

In a rare display of consensus amongst social scientists, the notion has been accepted that socialization or enculturation of traditions that surround and immerse each citizen of a society most definitely influences the form and intensity of the individual's behavior. There is virtually no theorist who discounts the impact on a culture's populace of their assimilation of that culture. The importance of norms, expectations, and worldviews of each culture on its citizenry is agreed to be broad, deep, and pervasive.

To accede to the strength of cultural prerogatives on the ontogenetic development of human behavior, however, by no means disavows or argues against an additional (causal) influence on behavior by biological processes. Moreover, an acceptance of the power of social processes to affect behavior does not also necessitate a further acceptance of idiosyncracy or total arbitrariness of each culture. Regardless of any proposed genotypic penetrance into behavior, the notion that cultural elements often follow regular, predictable relationships with each other has been well documented (White, Burton, & Brudner, 1977; White, Burton, & Dow, 1981; Whiting, 1964).

For this study, it is also accepted that culture and phylogeny "track" each other (i.e., coevolution), and that feedback loops align the biological substrate of *Homo* with the cultural manifestations which are found with that substrate (Barkow, 1980; Durham, 1979). The genotype held in common by *Homo* would generate thematic modes of behavior whereas the cultural circumstances would generate variants of that theme.

Personality type and subsistence technique are good examples of a systematic linkage between theme and variation: (1) the acquisition of a personality is panhuman: (2) the various facets of the personality are differentially emphasized or de-emphasized as a function of a culture's mode of procuring food from the environment (Barry, Bacon, & Child, 1957; Barry, Child, & Bacon, 1959). The ability to generate grammar (theme) and the myriad of languages and dialects (variations) is an example of a linkage which, at present, points to no scaled relationship.

The Phylogenetic Tier

This study accepts the proposition that the development of human behavior, in addition to human morphology and physiology, can be biased and canalized by genotypic information which is mediated by the neural system and endocrine system, that is, the motivation system. The central nervous system in particular is viewed here as not only processing information originating from the external and internal environments, but as autogenetically creating motivation states (Lorenz 1958, 1965; Tinbergen, 1951). These motivational states are then available for selection, both phylogenetically and ontogenetically, from a wide range of other potential motivations to be actualized into overt behaviors and finally to be directed and molded by the culturally idiosyncratic milieu in which the individuals happen to reside.

This study also accepts the feasibility that the man–child bond is a partial function of genotypic information which in turn has eventuated from the phylogeny or evolutionary history of the human taxon. The genotypic information, conceptualized within a "blueprint" metaphor, constructs the central nervous system and the endocrine system which, in concert, allow some behaviors to be learned more easily, more efficiently, and with more completeness than other behaviors (Hamburg, 1963; Hinde & Stevenson-Hinde, 1973; Immelmann *et al.*, 1981; Seligman & Hager, 1972). Operating within a normative environment consonant with the environment in which hominids developed the human biogram, the neurohormonal system will "forge" the man–child bond with particular characterisitics. These characteristics should be recognizable as such and thereby become available to be recorded across cultural boundaries.

Because all humans are included within the taxon *Homo sapiens,* a core commonality or constellation of genetic material is, by definition, shared amongst all humans. This shared genetic material can be hypothesized to generate thematic behavior patterns common to humans. The task then becomes the ferreting out and delineating these thematic behavior patterns, that is, the validation of species-characteristic traits in humans. Given the likelihood that the central nervous system was positively selected for flexibility and plasticity in its adaptation to the environment, as well as selected for appropriateness in the sensory detection of stimuli and the accuracy of motor responses, the thematic patterns will be nested within the concept of a reactive range of behaviors (Freedman, 1974, 1979). The notion of a reactive range takes the blueprint metaphor one step further in that it would be apparent that various readings of an architect's blueprint or that a lack of components required by the blueprint, for example, bricks, timbers, cement, or tiles, would result in variations of the same type of house. Similarly, any genotype finds itself in a complex biological world with potentials of vitamin shortages, ph excesses, mechanical traumas, and viral invasions. It would be expected, therefore, that variations of phenotypes would occur from the same generalized genotypic instructions. The variations, however, would be limited in range. Much higher or much lower variants would be lethal to the organism, either directly through gestation or indirectly in its inability to be socially competitive enough to have viable progeny. Plasticity is intrinsic to the genetic blueprint, but the plasticity is not infinite. Moreover, as stated earlier, some behavioral themes may be found only at very abstract levels. At these polar levels, for example, the knee reflex or the breath cycle, the genetic penetrance may be quite true but also remarkably uninteresting.

A few added points might be useful here and these involved two illustrative traits that can be assumed to be shared by most humans: people have emotions, and people dream.

One of the fundamental premises in this brief would be that the affective segment or content of an emotion cannot be taught by one person to another. Although the label or the name of the emotion can be learned by one individual from the examples and teachings of other individuals, how that emotion *feels* is immune from pedagogy and is restricted to one individual at a time. The appellations "hungry," "angry," "sad," "happy," and "lonely" can be transmitted from one generation to another. Nevertheless, how hunger, anger, sadness, happiness, loneliness actually feel cannot be so transferred. In addition, although it is true that the behavioral, hence social, manifestation of emotions can be controlled or modulated by cultural rules, this manipulation is based on the prior existence of the emotion. The manipulation can magnify, diminish, or orient; it cannot create.

For example, one society may deem crying to be an acceptable release for pain or for grief. Another society might view such behavior as crying to be a totally unacceptable mode of response to pain or to grief. What such cultural options cannot generate is the actual components of the subjective experience itself. On this matter, the epistemology of the solipsists seems well founded indeed: "one may know one's own emotional self, but one cannot know another person's subjective reality." At base, emotions are solidly individualistic and private domains. Yet, yet, and yet again (sliding from solipsism to induction), the existence and ubiquity of human emotions are rarely challenged. They are tacitly accepted as being in existence. But given that emotions do exist, and their subjective content cannot be socially transmitted, then the question arises: From whence do they come? Presuming that all events have causes and that human phenomena do not emerge out of nothingness, then there must be a causal agent or set of agents causing human feelings to exist—at all. Socialization traditions simply cannot be that agent. Socialization traditions can label or can direct emotions, but they cannot generate or create emotions. The only other available candidate operating within the currently knowable time–space continua is the genetic material blueprinting the construction and functioning of the human motivational system. The ability to have feelings or emotions is the derivative of having a motivation system (a central nervous system plus an endocrine/hormonal system) which in turn is constructed from information blueprinted within the genetic material.

The inherent capacity to possess emotions can be actualized, and then, at this juncture, the emotion can be integrated into social structures and social expectations that would amplify and direct appropriate behaviors for the outward expression of those feelings. Conversely, some emotions and their behavioral derivatives known by the "natives" to exist can be inhibited or ameliorated by social censure and ostracism, for example, anger followed by retaliation.

It should be made obvious that this discussion is emphasizing that it is the emotion's genetic template, or rephrased as a template for a motivational state, that is inherited. The behaviors, of course, cannot be inherited. However, the tendency—read emotions, read motivation—to behave in some ways rather than in others and at some times or developmental stages rather than at others can be inherited.

Some motivating states, such as hunger, thirst, and cold can energize behavior quickly, and, according to one culture circumstance, the procurement of manioc and water and an adjustment of fiber blankets will occur. Following another cultural circumstance, eggs Benedict, a sauterne, and a readjustment of the thermostat could result to defuse the motivations and return the individual to homeostasis. A third response may involve a hungry, thirsty, cold ascetic.

It is clear that the overt (voluntary) muscular patterns and sequences need not be closely aligned with the motivations, hence with the genetic material. The muscular patterns could be tightly aligned, that is, as reflexes, but the point being made here is that they need not be. The extreme plasticity of human behavior is not paralleled with an equally plastic motivational system. In more than an analogous manner, the motivation system can be conceived of as "fossilized behavior."

Another human trait of interest is the ability to dream. Dreams, in addition to being able to have emotional overtones, are certainly cognitive events: scenes, strategies, scenarios, plots, jokes, and grammar are all available for dream content. Current documentation suggests that dreaming exists as a panhuman event (Hunter & Whitten, 1976, p. 134). Although the vocabulary in the dream, the grammar, and the format or story line of the dream would certainly reflect cultural variations, the capacity, ability, and tendency to dream at all seem to be a consequence of having a central nervous system biased to dream. The central nervous system on its own can generate this complex cognitive phenomenon.

As in the example of emotions, the logic involved here is through the process of elimination: dreams exist. They must be caused. The capacity and dynamics of the dream phenomenon seem to be well beyond the skills and techniques of socialization agents; yet dreams still occur. What other source could serve as a causal system? The choice here for that causal system is information coded in the genotype.

The argument is presented that, at a minimum, the motivational system (central nervous system plus the endocrine/hormonal system) can create emotions and can create intricate cognitive sequences (dreams). The construction of our motivational system is a consequence of the genetic blueprint. Although we can know the minimum of what our motivation system can do, a crucial question whose answer is a long procedural way away, becomes what is the maximum subtlety and intrusion that the genetic material can exercise into human social behavior. The minimum influence is impressive; the maximum may be even more admirable.

Part of the job description of social scientists is the charge to separate which sets of information forging the various sectors of human social behavior is heavily biased by the genetic material and which sets of information are lightly touched by genetic material, but very sensitive to environmental histories and changes. Framed differently, the hoary nature and nurture controversy is still alive and annoying. It will not do to announce that this problem is specious or unanswerable or to declare as an explanation that there is interaction between gene and environment. These are nonanswers to a real question. Both the variation (heritability) and the central tendency of human social behavior could be trivially or massively caused by genetic material operating through the motivation system.[1] Whether this influence will be found to be small or to be large will depend on the craft and enthusiasm of the social scientists meeting their charge.

It is useful to point out that the validation of predictions concerning behavior must be achieved through behavior. Perfect knowledge of the structure and physiology of the neurohormonal system would not allow predictability of integrated social behavior of a human who has a past, a present, and a future, and who is behaving ad lib in a cathected social environment. Only behavior can validate hypotheses about behavior (Hinde, 1982).

It should be further noted that, although behavioral differences between populations can be argued to reflect genetic differences between populations, the demonstration of such an argument, though theoretically possible, is logistically and methodologically an awesome and most difficult task. A more feasible approach in a preliminary construction of a behavioral biogram of *Homo* is to seek behavioral consistencies across cultural boundaries, that is, to hold the genotype constant (*Homo sapiens* as the referent population) and to vary the cultural configurations. Ekman's work on facial expressions is, to date, the classic example of this method (Ekman, 1973, 1980). Freedman's (1974) work with infants, a quasi-deprivation study, is a good example of a useful type of controlled study. The more similar that the recorded behaviors are found to occur across increasingly different cultural matrices, the more reasonable becomes the hypothesis of species-characteristic behavior.

In other words, the more concordant the surveyed behaviors are with each other across widely disparate cultures, the less likely it is

---

[1]For a series of the state-of-the art presentations on the influence of genetic influences on differences between and among individuals, see *Child Development, 54,* 1983.

that the cultural variables explain the concordance. If the varied socialization traditions are viewed as an unlikely source of the consistent behaviors, then the only other source of influence available with which to affect human behavior is genotypic information inherent in the human condition. Said in another way: a constant, when compared to a variable, has a better opportunity to explain the existence and form of another constant.

Assuming that the above model is reasonably accurate, the researcher's task is to select likely behavioral candidates and then to survey the candidates' levels and forms of occurrence in distinct cultures, that is, to seek the validation of their existence as species-characterisitc traits.

Four necessary, and it may be argued sufficient, conditions must be met to legitimize the claim that the behavioral candidates are in fact part of the human biogram.

1. The thematic trait is catholic in scope. That is, the behavior is found in diverse cultures with distinct social structures and ecologies.
2. The behavior is potentially arbitrary in that the behavior is one of many available response sets which could achieve the same results. To avoid an antinomous condition of competing hypotheses that cannot be logistically disentangled, the behavior should not represent a technologically highly functional adaptation. The use of fire, weaving, the making of pottery, and the use of agriculture are examples of widespread traits; yet the universality of these highly utilitarian traits is undoubtedly a consequence of their technological efficiency rather than reflecting any relevant genotypic information. The widespread occurrence of these tratis would thereby more represent cultural diffusion rather than genetic displacement.

    It should be noted that, among the six major dyads within a social structure, the man–child dyad operating within the diagnostic time intervals of this study appears least mandated by the political, social, or economic imperatives of a society. The other five dyads (man–man, woman–woman, man–woman, woman–child, child–child) can be better argued to reflect a functional utility which emerged from social formulae operating over the eons (Fox, 1978, p. 126; Harris, 1979).[2] High levels of man–child associations during the diagnostic observation intervals would not be predicted by current psychological or sociological theories.

3. To complement cross-cultural variability, a large number of observations in which the germane trait could occur is required to allow the emergence of the trait's prevalence in a culture.

4. The incidence of the trait must occur at a substantive level which is judged to be greater than the error variance. The number of observed occurrences of the trait should not reflect either serendipity or examples of extreme deviance. With the occurrence of a sizable number of extant behaviors, the likelihood is increased for finding homologues rather than collecting coincidental analogues.

Once these four conditions are achieved, acceptance of a candidate as a species-characteristic behavior is enhanced by the demonstrated (inductive) predictability of the type and the level of the trait in subsequently surveyed cultures.

PROCEDURE

The generalized hypothesis that organized and catalyzed the empirical direction of the project is from Money and Ehrhardt (1972, p. 258), who postulated that parenting behaviors were not gender dimorphic, but that the threshold for activating and maintaining parenting behaviors was lower for women than for men.

As mentioned earlier, the definitions and coding system were tested and modified from a pilot study conducted in Virginia in 1973.

---

[2]Other authors have concisely dealt with the five dyads from alternate perspectives. For example, the man–man dyad has been viewed as an economic and sociopolitical adaptation (Divale & Harris, 1976; Tiger, 1969). The woman–child dyad has been analyzed as a socialization derivative of lactation (Ainsworth, Bell, & Stayton, 1978; Bowlby, 1958; Count, 1973; Rajecki, Lamb, & Obmascher, 1978). The importance of peer groups for children was argued by Harlow (1971). The woman–woman relationship was reviewed by Tiger and Fowler (1978), and the man–woman relationship has been dissected voluminously by a legion of authors.

The basic parameters of the data-gathering techniques are reiterated below.

This project used naturalistic observation as the means to gather data. All observations were conducted during daylight hours at sites that were places of public access with equal access for both males and females. There was strict anonymity concerning the project. Observers were not to interact with the people being observed in any manner over and beyond whatever impact the observer's physical presence had upon the people within the surrounding vicinity. The potential of the method of observation to influence the results of observation was very real; therefore, the anonymity of the observer and the project was essential to minimize such influence.

Of utmost importance were the time intervals which were used for observation. Observations were coded in one of two categories: observations occurred in time intervals in which adult males may normally be expected to be precluded from association with children because of cultural norms, for example, tilling fields, tending herds, being at work, and attending special ritual events. The code for this time interval was Males Precluded (MP).

Observations also occurred in time intervals in which adult males would be expected to be available to children, for example, sabbaths, festival days, after-work hours, weekends, and holidays. The code for this time interval was Males Not Precluded (MNP). The MNP times tended to be "free" time for men when they had numerous alternatives for their time and presence. These men *could have been* with their children, but they were not forced or coerced to be with them. That is, a "not precluded interval" was not the same as either a men-are-present interval or a men-must-be-present interval. The individual times for the MP and MNP intervals could vary considerably within the same culture at different communities as well as between cultures. The boundaries separating MP from MNP intervals were developed by the judgment of each field researcher at each site.

For any given culture, if the total percentage of adult male–child association was significantly different between the MP intervals and the MNP intervals, thereby indicating two populations, then the *diagnostic intervals for subsequent analysis would be only the MNP intervals.* (The MP figures generated the expected frequencies.) If the percentage of adult male–child association was *not* significantly different between the MNP intervals and the MP intervals, thus indicating one population, then the diagnostic intervals for subsequent analysis would be the totals (MP plus MNP intervals). A lack of difference in adult male–child association between MP and MNP intervals did not occur for any of the cultures.

Definitions

A social *bond*, from Tiger and Fox's (1971) usage, is defined as a social relationship in which predictable social patterns of behavior occur as major regularities of a species. Available bonds for humans would include the man–man bond, the man–woman bond, the woman–woman bond, the man–child bond, the woman–child bond, and the child–child bond.

Proxemic behavior, from Hall's (1959, 1963, 1966) work, is defined as the structured use of microspace as an elaboration of culture. The proxemics utilized in this study included a society's allocation of associations between categories of people (e.g., by age and gender—both of which are universal attributes that divide and subdivide a social structure) and their use of interpersonal space when the individuals are proximate to each other. This study was to investigate who associates with whom, the level of touching from adults to children, how close adults stay to children, and how much adults tend to keep children within visual sighting.

The meanings of the terms *child* and *adult* vary enormously across cultures and often vary between genders within the same culture. To facilitate comparability, this project arbitrarily defined anyone of either gender as a *child* if that individual was not well into or finished biological puberty as determined by physically observable secondary sex characteristics. A child was defined as a prepubescent. An *adult* was arbitrarily defined as anyone of either gender who was either well into puberty or had finished puberty. Adults were defined as pubescents and postpubescents. Given that an adult was defined as a pubescent or a postpubescent and a child was defined as a prepubescent, a logical category existed of an association between a person who has just become a pubescent (15 years), and a person who was late in childhood and was still a prepubescent (e.g., 13 years). This association is nominally one of peers, not one of a caretaking dimension. To avoid the distortion of counting peer groups as caretaking, the judgments of the fieldworkers were the best barometers. A perceived gap of at least eight years between the postpubescent and the pubescent was available to demarcate an adult–child dyad from a child–child dyad or an adult–adult dyad. However, the judgment of the fieldworker at the site was relied upon to make the distinction between a play/peer group and a caretaking group.

Prepubescence (childhood) was further divided into three arbitrary age brackets: birth to 4 years, 5 to 7 years, and 8 years to onset of puberty (14 years of age for census purposes). See below for the symbols used in coding the gender of adult, the gender of child, and the age brackets of the child.

Coding System

The coding system developed to define operationally adult–child interaction was a modified version of Hall's "A System for the Notation of Proxemic Behavior" (Hall, 1963).

Symbols were used for recording the adults and children during all observation intervals.

Adult male ♂; Adult female ♀; Infant—gender undetermined ⊖.

To code a child in the category of the birth–4 year bracket, a dot was placed *below* the appropriate figure, for example: ♀ ♂.

To code a child in the category of the 5–7 year bracket, no additional markings were included: ♀ ♂.

To code a child in the 8 year to onset of puberty bracket, a dot was placed *above* the figure, for example: ♀ ♂.

There were five categories of measurements; two for association and three for interaction. The two association indices were (1) adult proximity to child, and (2) group size and composition. The three interaction indices were (3) tactile contact—adult to child; (4) personal distance—adult to child; and (5) visual orientation—adult to child.

Adult Proximity to the Child

The occurrence of adult–child association was recorded noting the gender of the adult and the child. An adult was judged to be in association with a child when there was a general orientation of one to the other, for example, they both arrive or leave the vicinity together, one periodically visits the other, one carries the other, they exchange items, or one grooms the other.

To aid in achieving independence of observations, any given group of adults and children was recorded only once per day per observation site. For sites with extremely few groups to record (e.g., in a playground during a thunderstorm), all groups that were visible to the observer were recorded. For sites with large numbers of groups streaming by the observer, a systematic randomization of selecting groups was used. For example, the third-group-to-appear-after-the-last-recorded-entry was the criterion used in Madrid's Puerto del Sol.

There were three categories of adult groups with which a child could associate: a men-only group, a women-only group, and a men and women group. As evidenced by the pilot study, some proxemics of the adult male–child dyad (with no women present) were distinct from proxemics of the adult–child dyad (with women also present). Hence, the dyads of men and children (with no women present) were recorded and analyzed separately from those dyads of men and children (with women also present). The association of record was between the category of adult group, regardless of the number of adults in the group, and each child. For example, a group of three adult females and one girl would have been recorded as one girl associating with one women-only group.

It is important both to note and to emphasize that the method used here could not allow an analysis of genealogical relationships among the men, women, and children recorded. Consequently, an investigation of the dynamics between kinship structures and the proxemic indices is not available. Furthermore, the use of parenting behavior, which replaces the more accurate but more arcane *epimeletic* behavior, refers only to caretaking behaviors and does not necessitate any geneological relationship between any given adult and any given child. Paternity is a very delicate matter to bring up even in the best of settings. A stranger in a strange land who is challenging, with a question, the virility of other men is not in the best of settings. Uncles, aunts, grandparents, older siblings who are acting in the child caretaking role will reflect culturally expected modes of behavior toward children. These modes may or may not be the same as those presented to and by the biological or social parents. The basic question addressed here is whether the cultures develop fundamentally similar or fundamentally different modes of caretaking behavior for children by men versus women. Kinship analysis is one turn more fine-grained than these data, by themselves, can address.

Because of different cultural bases, the comparison of indices of adult male–child interaction across-cultural boundaries required minimizing as far as feasible the effects of different cultural matrices (Moore, 1961). To help reach this goal, the ordinal relationships between the adult male–child dyad and the adult female–child were developed within each culture and then the ordinal relationships were compared across cultures. Of course, within each culture, the adult male–child dyads (with no women present) were compared exclusively with the adult female–child dyads (with no men present), and the adult male–child dyads (with women also present) were compared exclusively with the adult female–child dyads (with men also present). The value of constructing comparable units for cross-cultural work is also relevant here. Across cultures, man–child dyads are compared only with other man–child dyads (and not to woman–child dyads). Men in man, woman, and child triads are compared only with other men in man-woman-child triads.

Group Size and Group Composition

The joint association of two or more people with at least one adult and at least one child was defined as a *group*. As well as recording the age bracket of each child, the composition of each group was recorded by the number of individuals, by gender, and by adult/child status. The statistical instruments for within-culture comparisons were chi square and *t* test.

Tactile Contact—Adult to Child

As soon as the group composition was determined, a 30-second observation interval was begun. Within the 30 seconds, the most active physical contiguity from the adult's hands to the child was recorded. See the Appendix for the coding system: tactile contact—adult to child.

For the tactile contact scale as well as for the following two scales, adult males in men-only groups were compared exclusively with adult females in women-only groups. Adult males in men and women groups were compared exclusively with adult females who were also in men and women groups. For the three interaction indices, the interaction as defined by the germane operations was recorded for each adult with each child per group. For example, a group of one adult male, two adult females, one boy and one girl had six ($3 \times 2 = 6$) interactions recorded. However, when large groups (with more than one adult and more than three children) occurred, only the interactions toward the three children most proximate to each adult were recorded. Proximity was determined by the personal distance scale.

Personal Distance—Adult to Child

With the adult's head and trunk as the locus, the closest in terms of (spatial) distance that the adult came to the child, within the 30-sec observation limit, was recorded. See Appendix for the coding system of personal distance—adult to child.

Visual Orientation—Adult to Child

The immediate visual field was considered to be directly in front of any individual's eyes plus segments to the left and right of center. The coding interval for visual orientation was the last 5 sec of the 30-sec observation interval. If, during the full 5 sec, the child was never in the visual scan of the adult, the child was recorded as being out of the adult's visual field (coded NONSEE). If, during any portion of the 5 sec, the child was within the visual scan of the adult, then the child was recorded as being in the adult's visual field (coded SEE). See Appendix for the coding system of visual orientation—adult to child.

Reliability of the Coding System

Each fieldworker was trained and pretested prior to his or her field-work. Gender, child/adult status, and the age brackets were reliably coded (both for intra- and for inter-rater reliability). For the pretest, 35-mm color slides were used. For all indices discussed below a 90% agreement was the minimum standard for passing the pretest. For gender and adult/child status, no one scored below 95% ($r = .99$). Identifying gender of adult in the field is virtually error proof when the temperatures do not necessitate heavy overcoats. Hence, the project's fieldwork was geared to the warmer months. Similarly, the gender of child after infancy was quite reliably coded (during infancy the child was coded as infant—gender undetermined).

The placing of a child in the birth to 4-year old bracket had very little overlap with the 8 to onset of puberty bracket. There was nearly 99% agreement.

As would be intuitively expected given the normal distribution of size and maturational development of children, the placing of individuals at the border of the birth to 4, and 5 to 7-year brackets and the 5 to 7 and 8 to onset of puberty brackets (i.e., 4–5 and 7–8 year olds) was somewhat more difficult and was approximately 70%.[3] The individual raters were internally consistent which is especially important, and the inter-rater errors that did occur were not systematically biased in either direction (younger/older). For interaction scales, reliability for both inter- and intra-rater agreement was good (90% minimum).

Levels of Significance

For a statistical test run within a single culture, the level of significance was set at .05—two-tailed where appropriate. For a statistical test run across or between cultures which was testing for commonalities or trends, the criterion mandated that at least one-half ($18 \div 2 = 9$) of the cultures meet the within-culture criterion with no more than four cultures reaching criterion in a competing direction. In other words, at least nine cultures must reach the within-culture criterion in the predicted direction. In the event that the within-

---

[3]The arrangements for fieldwork in Taiwan had to be conducted via airmail. As a result of the time lag and unnecessarily ambiguous instructions, the data from the 5 to 7 year-old category, as an age bracket, were also potentially ambiguous. The most conservative approach dictated the deletion of the 5 to 7 year category when age was an independent variable. The data from Taiwan for the birth to 4 year age bracket and the 8 year to puberty bracket, which presented no such ambiguities, were thereby the analyzed units for age and developmental status.

culture criterion was reached in a competing direction, the numbers of cultures reaching the within-culture criterion in the predicted direction must significantly exceed the numbers of cultures reaching the within-culture criterion in a competing direction (sign test, $p <$ .05). For example, nine cultures reaching the within-culture criterion in the predicted direction versus one culture reaching the within-culture criterion in a competing direction would satisfy the between-culture criterion (sign test, $p <$ .05). Similarly 15 cultures reaching the within-culture criterion in the predicted direction versus three cultures reaching the within-culture criterion in a competing direction would also satisfy the between-culture criterion (sign test, $p <$ .05). Allowing three cultures to reach the criterion in a competing direction in regards to the hypothesized direction reduces the potential of a Type II error: falsely rejecting a true relationship.

Tests across cultures that were seeking linear relationships (Kendall's tau, Pearson's product moment correlation) used a standard two-tailed level of significance at .05.

Selection of Communities within each Culture

The selection of communities within each culture depended in part on logistical accessibility, geographical dispersion, and the type of culture being researched. For example, rural Taiwan dictated communities that were agrarian based and were within ready traveling distance of each other. Urbanized Iceland was restricted to Reykjavik. See Table 1.

Selection of Observation Sites per Community

A minimum of four observation sites per community were used. One site was to be where children were playing. A second site was to be at a place of commerce. Subsequent sites were developed by the fieldworkers as circumstances dictated.

Length of Fieldwork

Fieldwork varied in time from two weeks (Lima, Peru) to approximately 24 weeks (the Karaja of Brazil). Urban sites generated a large

TABLE 1
Communities within the Cultures that Were the Sites of Adult–Child Association

Culture/total number of children	Communities
Mexico (2,212)	Saltillo, Sabinas, Piedras Negras, Allende, Morelos (all in Coahuila state)
Spain (1,738)	Madrid, Guadalajara, Lerida, Zeura
United States (14,499)	132 sites throughout the state of Virginia
Ireland (3,213)	Dublin, Tralee, Cashel, Athlone, Sligo
Karaja, Brazil (840)	(The villages of) Sao Felix, Fontoura, Tapirape, Macauba
Ivory Coast (2,658)	Korhogo, Bouake, Dimbokro, Ferkessedougou, Abidjan
Morocco (2,265)	Marrakech, Ouirgane, Casablanca, Azrou, Fes
Lima, Peru (573)	Greater Lima area
Japan (2,578)	Okayama, Ogi-Megi, Seto, Takamatsu, Nagoya
India (1,336)	New Delhi, Madras, Khajuraho, Allahabad, Bombay
Israel (3,018)	Givat Brenner, K'far Monash, K'far Blum, Givat Hay'yin, Sde Nitzan, Moshen Tsofet
Reykjavik, Iceland (2,587)	Greater Reykjavik area
Sri Lanka (2,538)	Colombo, Kandy, Nagambo, Rathapura, Hatton, Polanurawa, Chilow
Hong Kong (164)	Hong Kong island
Taiwan (4,336)	Lu Kang, Ma Kung, Da Yuan, Lung Tan, Chu Nan, Tung Hsiao, Ching Shui
Brazil—rural (722)	Bom Jardim, Silvania, Vianopolis
Brazil—urbanizing (562)	Monte Mor
Senufo, Ivory Coast (3,320)	Ferkessedougou, Dabakala, Gbon, Boundial, Siempurgo, Dikogougou, Niakaramandougou

number of dyads quickly. An appropriate number of dyads was slower to develop at rural sites. Consequently, seven weeks for observations was the modal duration in rural cultures, while four weeks of observation was the modal duration in urban cultures.

RESULTS

The following nine patterns of adult-child proxemic behavior are offered as candidates for species-characteristic behavior in *Homo* and thereby are suggested to reflect genotypic information ''blueprinting'' behavioral tendencies. Using a similar method under similar conditions as described above, these thematic patterns would be suggested to exist and be recognized as such panculturally.

Components of the Man–Child Bond that are Candidates for Species-Characteristic Traits

Association Data—Association Patterns between Adults and Children

Candidate 1. When cultural norms do not preclude men from associating with children, men associate with children in significant proportions—both with women also being present and with no women present.

TABLE 2

Percentage of Associations between Adult Groups by Gender Composition and Children in 18 Cultures (Diagnostic Time Intervals Only)

Culture	Percentage of children associating with adult groups consisting of			Number of children
	Women only	Men only	Men and women	
Israel	53.5	31.9	14.6	2,139
Reykjavik	39.6	29.0	31.4	1,694
Morocco	56.8	28.5	14.7	1,398
India	43.0	28.5	28.5	1,104
Brazil—urbanizing	46.4	24.4	29.2	562
Taiwan	56.8	23.8	19.4	2,790
Ireland	36.5	22.9	40.6	1,852
Japan	38.3	22.9	38.8	1,336
Brazil—rural	54.3	22.8	22.9	549
Senufo (Ivory Coast)	41.5	21.0	37.5	1,132
Hong Kong	32.3	20.7	47.0	164
Sri Lanka	64.7	20.5	14.8	1,973
United States	43.5	17.5	39.0	8,953
Ivory Coast	67.4	17.4	15.2	1,642
Lima (Peru)	52.2	17.4	30.4	490
Spain	31.5	16.8	51.7	1,058
Mexico	50.2	14.2	35.6	1,355
Karaja (Brazil)	40.8	8.3	50.9	399
Mean	47.2	21.6	31.2	1,699
sd	10.4	5.9	12.4	

The mean percentage of children associating with men-only groups (no women present) was 21.6% of all adult–child dyads. See Table 2. The mean percentage of children associating with groups of men and women was 31.2% of all adult–child dyads. Both the 21.6% and the 31.2% are suggested to be greater than error variance.

Of very special note is the projected "teeter-totter" relationship between the percentage of man–child dyads and the percentage of children with men and women. For the current sample ($N = 18$), there is a negative correlation between the two indices ($r = .547; p < .05$; two-tailed). See Figure 1 and Table 3. The negative correlation indicates that there may be a finite threshold of adult male–child association below which neither the men nor the cultures tend to go. Supporting the notion that the "teeter-totter" effect is a real event in the mosaic of the man–child bond is the relationship between the proportion of adult–child dyads that were man–child dyads versus the proportion of adult–child dyads that were woman–child dyads. The correlation between these two sets of dyads was virtually zero ($r = .089; p > .05; N = 18$). In other words, if the children, for whatever

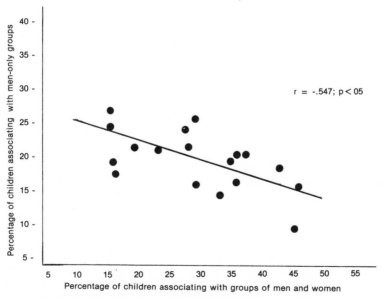

FIGURE 1. Percentage of children (associating with adults) who are associating with men-only groups and who are associating with groups of men and women: 18 cultures.

TABLE 3

Correlations between Percentages of Adult-Child Dyads that Were in Man–Child Groups and in Man-Woman-Child Groups, Correlations between Percentages of Adult–Child Dyads which Were in Woman–Child Groups and in Man–Woman-Child Groups, and Diagnostic Time Intervals Only: 18 Cultures[a]

| | Men and women category of children | | | | |
| | | | | | |
Adult group	All children	Boys and girls (no infants)	Boys only	Girls only	Infants
Men only	−.547*	−.542*	−.617**	−.051	+.450
Women only[b]	−.833***	−.627**	−.637**	−.443	+.151

*$p < .05$; **$p < .01$; ***$p < .001$; two-tailed.

[a]The linear relationship between these variables is considered an *a priori* hypothesis. The data do not suggest an *a posteriori* consideration of a better fit for any other curvilinear regression (from Wollan, 1982).

[b]Note that the woman–child dyad follows a pattern somewhat parallel to that of the man–child dyad. Although there is a similarity in behavioral outcomes between the patterns of the men-only group and the woman-only group, there is no imperative to assume similarity in the forms of the causal mechanisms. An argument of functional adaptation to explain the same teeter-totter effect between the men-only groups and the women-only groups could take the form: women lactate (men do not), and women universally are primary caretakers of infants/children; hence, societies have independently developed a social formula of norms and socialization traditions which funnel women and children together quite removed from genetic predispositions.

reason, reduce their association with men (no women present), they do not systematically increase their association with women. The children *do* systematically increase their association men and women. The children were thereby insured regular proximity to men (with women present or not) and hence to whatever of value that might be accrued to them from their associations with the men.

Candidate 2. The mean number of men per groups of men and children (no women present) is significantly lower than the mean number of women per groups of women and children (no men present). (For within-culture analysis: t test $p < .05$; two-tailed). See Table 4 for data from the current sample. For the entire sample, the average number of men per men-only group was 1.125 ($SD = 0.107$). The average number of women per women-only group was 1.305 ($SD = 0.116$). It is apparent that men are more reluctant to join a man–child dyad than are women to join a woman–child dyad.

Across the 18 culture sample, the mean number of children, for the three adult groups, followed an interesting pattern. As Table 5 illustrates, larger numbers of children tended to occur with men and women groups ($m = 1.738$; $sd = 0.274$, range = 1.451–2.519; $n = 18$) compared either to men-only groups ($m = 1.404$, $sd = 0.150$; range

TABLE 4

Mean Number of Men per Groups of Men and Children Compared to the Mean Number of Women per Groups of Women and Children:[a] 18 Cultures

Cultures in which		
Mean number of men is greater than the mean number of women	Mean number of women is greater than the mean number of men	No differences in the mean number of men or women exist
0	16*	2

*p < .01; sign test.
[a]For the men-only groups: $m = 1.125$, $sd = 0.107$; range 1.00–1.181; $n = 18$. For the women-only groups: $m = 1.305$; $sd = 0.116$; range 1.124–1.541; $n = 18$. If the initial man and the initial woman in the men and women groups are counted as one individual, then the mean for the men and women groups was 1.385; $sd = 0.308$, range 1.085–2.241; $n = 18$.

1.150–1.696; $n = 18$) or to women-only groups ($m = 1.536$; $sd = 0.162$; range $= 1.330–1.895$; $n = 18$). In 24 comparisons men and women groups had more children per group than the single gender adult groups. In no culture did men-only or women-only groups average more children than groups of men and women. For the remaining cultures (12 cases), single gender adult groups averaged the same number of children as did the men and women groups.

TABLE 5

Comparisons of the Mean Number of Children among the Three Adult Groups,[a] 18 Cultures

Compared adult groups	Cultures in which the mean number of children				
	Is the same for both groups	Is greater in men-only groups	Is greater in women-only groups	Is greater in men and women groups	Total
Men only vs. women only	10	0	8	—	18
Men only vs. men and women	5	0	—	13*	18
Women only vs. men and women	7	—	0	11*	18

*p < .001; sign test.
[a]For the men-only groups: $m = 1.404$, $sd = 0.150$; range 1.150–1.696; $n = 18$. For the women-only groups: $m = 1.536$; $sd = 0.162$; range = 1.330–1.895; $n = 18$. For the men and women groups: $m = 1.738$; $sd = 0.274$; range = 1.451–2.519; $n = 18$.

Compared to women-only groups, the men-only groups averaged either fewer children (8 cases) or the same number of children (10 cases). In no culture did men-only groups average more children per group than did the women-only groups. The data indicate that men tend to avoid being with other men when associating with their children, but, with the exception of being with infants (as we shall see in a moment), men associate with as many children as do women.

Candidate 3. Compared to census data,[4] associations between men and older children (8–14 years of age) are underrepresented. This underrepresentation is found both in men-only groups and in men and women groups as well as in women-only groups. Rephrased more concisely, adults are with younger children more than they are with older children. This pattern is true for men as well as for women. See Table 6 for data from the current sample.

Candidate 4. As a refinement of Candidate 3 (levels of association between men and children are inversely related to the age/developmental level/status of dependency of the child), men, with no women present, associate with infants at a lower percentage of their total number of associations with children than do men who are also with women ($t = 3.755$, $p < .01$; two-tailed, $df = 17$). See Table 7. In other words, for men-only groups, there is a curvilinear relationship between age of children and the level of association. Men-only groups are highly underrepresented in their associations with infants. After infancy, man–child associations increase in the toddler stages and then decrease again.

The level of association between men and women groups with infants is fairly high and then the levels decrease linearly by age of child. Hence, appreciable proportions of man–infant associations oc-

---

[4]The expected frequencies were generated from census data from the relevant area. The expected frquencies for Hong Kong, Taiwan, Sri Lanka, Iceland, Isreal, the Ivory Coast (including the Senufo), Morocco, Spain, India, Japan, Peru, and Ireland were developed from the *United Nations Demographic Yearbook* (United Nations 1974, 1975, 1976). The figures used were primarily nationwide census data. Hence, the expected frequencies used can only be thought of as rough approximations. However, the magnitude and direction of the results, despite the crudeness of the measuring device, still strongly support the interpretations. The state of Virginia data were compared to a detailed United States census compilation (Department of Commerce, 1972). The Mexican data were compared to figures from the state of Coahuila (Brito, 1969; Ruddle & Barrows, 1974). The Karaja and Brazil (rural and urbanizing) were compared to George Donahue's field notes taken during his fieldwork in Brazil.

TABLE 6

*The Relationship between the Age (Developmental Status/Dependency) of Child
and the Child's Tendency to Associate with Adults: 17 Cultures;[a] Expected
Frequencies Were Generated from Census Data from the Relevant Area*

	Cultures in which					
	Older children (8–14 years) are underrepresented			Age of child and associations with adults are independent		
Adult group	Girls	Boys	Total	Girls	Boys	Totals
Men only	15*	15	30*	1	1	2
Men and women	17*	17*	34*	0	0	0
Women only	17*	16*	33*	0	1	1

*p < .001; sign test.
[a]The Hong Kong sample was too small for analysis. The men-only sample for the Karaja was too small for analysis.

curred only when the woman was also present. Because the man–child dyad is heavily represented in the literature in the form of the man–infant dyad, the relatively low level of man–infant association contiguous with relatively high levels of man–toddler association is of some importance. See Pedersen (1980) for an excellent review of the literature on the man–infant bond.

It is of further interest that the proportion of the associations

TABLE 7

*Comparisons among the Three Adult Groups of the Percentage of Children
Associating with Them Who Are Infants (18 Cultures)*

	Cultures in which the percentage of infants is				
Compared adult groups	Greater in men-only groups	Greater in women-only groups	Greater in men and women groups	The same in both groups	Total
Men only vs. women only	0	12*	—	6	18
Women only vs. men and women	—	3	4	11	18
Men only vs. men and women	0	—	14*	4	18

*p < .001; sign test.

between men and children that was man–infant dyads was less than a comparable figure for woman–infant dyads ($t = 3.621$; $p < .01$; two-tailed, $df = 17$). The proportion of associations between women and children which was woman–infant dyads was not different from the proportion of man, woman, and infant triads in the total number of children associating with men and women groups ($t = 0.239$, n.s.).

The key to be gleaned from these data is that men, unaccompanied by women, are very rarely proximate to their infants (when in public places which have equal access by gender during daylight).

Candidate 5. Compared to other adult–child groups, the man-older boy dyad is uniquely overrepresented. That is, compared to the other five combinations of adult group-older child, the man-older boy dyad is overrepresented. See Table 8 for data from the current sample.

Candidate 6. When men and women are associating together with children, boys and girls are equally represented in these adult–child groups, that is, with census data generating the expected frequencies, neither boys nor girls are overrepresented in the association with men and women. See Table 9 for data from the current sample.

TABLE 8

Comparison among Adult Groups of Associations with the Higher Percentage of Older Children (8 Years to Puberty); Boys and Girls are Analyzed Separately: 17 Cultures[a]

	Compared adult groups		
	Women only vs. men only	Women only vs. men and women	Men only vs. men and women
Number of cultures with the higher % of girls in the older age bracket	9 vs. 7	12[b] vs. 4[b]	10 vs. 4
Number of cultures with the higher % of boys in the older age bracket	0 vs. 16*	7 vs. 10	15 vs. 1*

*$p < .001$; sign test.
[a]Hong Kong's sample was not large enough for inclusion. The Karaja sample had an insufficient number of cases in the men-only group for analysis. The Brazil—rural and the Brazil—urbanizing samples had insufficient numbers for analysis of girls in the men only versus men and women comparison.
[b]Tie in Ireland.

TABLE 9

Differential Association by Men and Women Groups with Children by Gender of Child: 18 Cultures; Expected Frequencies are Generated by Census Data

Cultures in which			
Boys are overrepresented	Girls are overrepresented	Neither boys nor girls are overrepresented	Total
4	0	14*	18

*$p < .05$; sign test.

Interaction Data—Interaction from Adults to Children

Candidate 7. Using the proxemic indexes (touching, seeing, personal distance) as measuring instruments, men interact toward children at the same level that women interact toward children. This congruence occurs both when men, without women present, are compared to women when no men are present and when men and women are compared with members of the opposite sex also being present. See Tables 10 and 11 for data from the current sample.

Candidate 8. The gender of the child is independent of the level of interaction received from the adult male (also the adult female). This independence is found when adults (men and women) are compared to each other and when men (or women) are analyzed separately in their interaction with children (boys, girls). See Tables 11 and 12 for data from the current sample.

Note that from Table 10, 70.4% of the 108 comparisons indicate no differential in intensity of interaction from adult (by gender) to children. However, for the 32 cases in which a differential *did* occur, an interesting pattern emerged. In the single gender comparisons (i.e., men-only vs. women-only) men showed more active interaction than did women: 10 to 4. In the plural gender comparisons, that is, men (with women present) versus women (with men present), women showed the greater activity in interaction: 16 to 2. The relationship between gender composition of adult group and gender of adult manifesting greater interaction was significant ($\chi^2 = 12.226$; $p < .001$; $df = 1$). From Table 11, there were 213 comparisons of levels of interaction from men and women to children: boys and girls analyzed separately. Of these 213, 80.3% (171 cases) indicated similar levels of interaction

TABLE 10

Comparison between Men and Women in Relation to the Level of Interaction toward All Children
(Boys + Girls + Infants): 18 Cultures

Adult group	Gender of adult responding more actively	Interaction category			
		Tactile contact	Personal distance	Visual orientation	Total
Men only versus women only	Men more active	4	2	4	10
	Women more active	1	3	0	4
	Neither more active	13*	13*	14*	40**
	Total	18	18	18	54
Men (with women present) vs. women (with men present)	Men more active	1	0	1	2
	Women more active	6	5	5	16
	Neither more active	11	13*	12	36**
	Total	18	18	18	54

$*p < .05; **p < .001$; sign test.

TABLE 11

Comparison between Men and Women in Relation to the Level of Interaction toward Children (Boys and Girls Separately): 18 Cultures[a]

Adult group	Gender of adult responding more actively	Tactile contact		Personal distance		Visual orientation		Total
		Boy	Girl	Boy	Girl	Boy	Girl	
Men only vs. women only	Men more active	1	4	2	5	1	4	17
	Women more active	2	0	0	0	1	0	3
	Neither more active	14**	14*	15*	13*	15**	14*	85***
	Total	17	18	17	18	17	18	105
Men (with women present) vs. women (with men present)	Men more active	3	0	2	0	1	1	7
	Women more active	0	2	0	5	3	5	15
	Neither more active	15**	16**	16**	13*	14*	12	86***
	Total	18	18	18	18	18	18	108

*p < .05, **p < .01, ***p .001; sign test.
[a]The Karaja had insufficient number of boys in the men-only groups for analysis.

TABLE 12

Comparison of Level of Interaction from Adult (Man or Woman) to Child by Gender of Child and Composition of Adult Group: 18 Cultures[a]

Gender of adult and adult group composition	Gender of child receiving more active interaction	Interaction category			
		Tactile contact	Personal distance	Visual orientation	Total
Men only	Girl	4	2	0	6
	Boy	0	0	0	0
	Neither	13*	15**	17***	45***
	Total	17	17	17	54
Women only	Girl	0	0	0	0
	Boy	0	3	2	5
	Neither	18***	15**	16**	49***
	Total	18	18	18	54
Men (with women present)	Girl	0	0	1	1
	Boy	2	4	1	7
	Neither	16**	14*	16**	46***
	Total	18	18	18	54
Women (with men present)	Girl	1	3	0	4
	Boy	0	0	0	0
	Neither	17***	15**	18***	50***
	Total	18	18	18	54

*$p < .05$, **$p < .01$, ***$p < .001$; sign test.
[a]The Karaja had an insufficient number of boys in the men-only groups to allow analysis.

from men and women toward children. There were, however, 43 instances of differential interaction by gender of adult. In single gender adult group comparisons men illustrated greater interaction: 17 to 3. In plural gender adult group comparisons, women showed greater interaction: 15 to 7. The relationship between gender of adult manifesting greater interaction toward children and the composition of the adult group was significant ($\chi^2 = 12.099$, $p < .001$; $df = 1$). See Table 13. These patterns are supportive of the basic hypothesis entertained here that parenting or epimeletic behaviors are inherent in both men and women, but that the threshold is lower for women than for men.

Candidate 9. For all adult groups, interaction levels decreased as a function of the age of the child for the categories of tactile contact and personal distance. For the category of visual orientation, the patterns of decreased interaction aligned with increasing age held only for the single gender adult groups. In sum, older children, when

TABLE 13
Relationship between Gender of Adult Responding more Actively with Children (Boys and Girls Analyzed Separately and Boys + Girls + Infants Combined)

More active gender[a]	Adult group composition interacting with children (boys and girls analyzed separately)			More active gender[b]	Adult group composition interacting with children (boys + girls + infants combined)		
	Single	Plural	Total		Single	Plural	Total
Women	3	15	18	Women	4	16	20
Men	17	7	24	Men	10	2	12
Total	20	22	42	Total	14	18	32

Note. Only the interactions from dyads that have reached the within-group criterion are analyzed.
[a]$\chi^2 = 12.099$; $p < .001$.
[b]$\chi^2 = 12.226$; $p < .001$.

compared to younger children, were touched less by adults, were more distant from adults, and were watched less by adults. See Table 14 for data from the current sample.

Components of the Man–Child Bond that Systematically and Predictably Respond to Cultural Processes

A controversial and important debate is currently being pursued as to whether or not selective pressures developed gender dimorphic behaviors which maximize the efficiency of executing any exclusively male tasks, for example spatial skills (math) for hunting. See Benbow and Stanley (1980) for a similar debate. Although there is room for active debate upon the role of genetics in the traditional division of labor by gender, there is virtually no disagreement that cultural institutions have amplified and reinforced such divisions.

So far, it has been shown that consistencies do appear in the man–child dyad across cultures. Do systematic variations also occur? The answer here is *yes*. A mosaic of predictable variations did coalesce. The chips in this mosaic include: (1) man–boy dyads, (2) man, woman, and child triads, (3) man, man, and child triads, and (4) woman, woman, and child triads. An additional chip, the woman–

TABLE 14

The Relationship between Age of Child and the Level of Interaction from Adult to Child; by Men and Women Separately in Single and Plural Gender Adult Groups: 17 Cultures[a]

	Number of measurements in which there is												Total
	An inverse[b] relationship between age and level of interaction				No relationship between age and interaction				A relationship (noninverse) between age and level of interaction				
	Single		Plural		Single		Plural		Single		Plural		
Interaction	Men	Women	Men	Women	Men	Women	Men	Women	Men	Women	Men	Women	
Tactile contact	16**	16**	16**	14**	0	1	1	3	—	—	—	—	67
Personal distance	13**	13**	10**	13**	3	3	7	4	—	1	—	—	67
Visual orientation	10*	11*	5	5	5	3	12	9	1	3	—	3	67
Total	39***	40***	31***	32***	8	7	20	16	1	4	—	3	201

*p < .05, **p < .01, ***p < .001; sign test.
[a]The Hong Kong sample and the men-only groups in the Karaja had too few cases for analysis.
[b]An inverse relationship occurred when within-group criterion was achieved and the youngest age bracket (birth–4 years) was overrepresented in the more active levels of interaction from adult to child.

TABLE 15
Rankings of the 18 Cultures by Five Proxemic Indexes (from MNP Time Intervals Only)

Culture	Boys associating with men-only groups		Girls associating with women-only groups		Children associating with groups of men and women		Women's Plural Group Score (WPGS)		Men's Plural Group Score (MPGS)	
	Rank	Percentage	Rank	Percentage	Rank	Percentage	Rank	Percentage	Rank	Percentage
Israel	12	60.0	7	56.2	18	14.6	12	65.2	15	84.0
Ivory Coast	1	77.4	2	61.0	15	15.2	18	47.7	16	83.7
Sri Lanka	5	70.0	16	51.9	16	14.8	16	52.6	14	85.6
India	11	60.6	11	53.8	12	28.5	8	73.6	11	87.7
Morocco	4	71.8	12	53.7	17	14.7	17	49.8	18	81.1
Mexico	6	69.7	5	59.4	8	35.6	10.5	67.8	8.5	92.6
Brazil—rural	3	73.1	4	59.6	13	22.9	14	56.8	12	87.5
Taiwan	10	61.5	17	49.6	14	19.2	13	62.2	6	94.5
Senufo	7	66.7	8.5	54.8	7	37.5	9	70.2	17	81.8
Lima (Peru)	9	62.7	6	56.3	10	30.4	15	54.8	3	98.0
Brazil—urbanizing	2	77.3	10	54.5	11	29.2	10.5	67.8	13	86.3
United States	14	58.9	8.5	54.8	5	39.0	5	76.3	8.5	92.6
Spain	16	50.6	15	52.4	1	51.7	2	83.3	10	92.1
Ireland	15	56.8	3	60.6	4	40.6	3	82.3	4	95.6
Hong Kong	17	45.2	13	53.5	3	47.0	6	74.6	1	100.0
Reykjavik	8	65.1	14	52.7	9	31.4	4	80.9	7	93.4
Japan	13	59.6	18	46.7	6	38.8	1	88.8	5	95.2
Karaja	18	32.1	1	73.0	2	50.9	7	74.5	2	98.8

TABLE 16

Correlations (Pearson's Product Moment Correlation) among the Five Proxemic Indexes: 18 Cultures (MNP Time Intervals Only)

Index	Percentage of children who are			Women's Plural Group Score (WPGS)	Men's Plural Group Score (MPGS)
	Girls associating with women-only groups	Associating with groups of men and women			
Percentage of boys associating with men-only groups	−.334	−.722***		−.562*	−.690**
Percentage of girls associating with women-only groups	—	+.224		−.135	+.141
Percentage of children associating with groups of men and women	—	—		+.774***	+.665**
Women's Plural Group Score	—	—		—	+.518*

*p < .05; **p < .01; ***p < .001; two-tailed.

girl dyad, marched to its own tune, and tended to distribute itself randomly when compared to the other groups. See Tables 15 and 16.

There are two generalized interrelationships among these which are relevant to this discussion:

1. The relationship of the preference of men to associate with boys (rather than with girls) and the other indices
2. The relationship between the adult–child dyad's tendency to associate with the same-gender adult (man, man, and child or woman, woman and child triad) or with cross-gender adults (man, woman, and child triad) and the other indexes.

To address this second interrelationship, ratios were constructed in the following manner. The number of occasions in which a man–child dyad associated with a woman (to form a man, woman, and child triad) was added to the number of occasions in which a man–child dyad associated with another man (to form a man, man, and child triad). This number was divided into the number of man, woman, and child triads. Accordingly, if there were an increasing number of man, woman, and child triads compared to a decreasing number of man, man, and child triads, the ratio would approach one (unity). However, if there were diminishing numbers of man, woman, and child triads, but increasing numbers of man, man, and child triads, the ratio would approach zero. This ratio is labled the Men's Plural Group Score (MPGS). An analogous score is computed for women: the Women's Plural Group Score (WPGS). The only difference in the computations is that the number of woman, woman, and child triads replace the number of man, man, and child triads. See below for examples from the Ivory Coast sample.

Computation of the Men's Plural Group Score:

$$\frac{\text{Number of man, women, and child triads}}{\substack{\text{Number of man, woman,} \\ \text{and child triads}} + \substack{\text{Number of man, man,} \\ \text{and child triads}}} = \frac{164}{164 + 32} = .837 \text{ MPGS}$$

Computation of the Women's Plural Group Score:

$$\frac{\text{Number of man, woman, and child triads}}{\substack{\text{Number of man, woman,} \\ \text{and child triads}} + \substack{\text{Number of woman, woman,} \\ \text{and child triads}}} = \frac{164}{164 + 180} = .477 \text{ WPGS}$$

What advantage lies in composing such a cumbersome index? What would it tell us? Primarily, the ratios lend insight into the soci-

etal milieu surrounding the adult–child bond. Is the adult–child relationship stripped of a social context and isolated or does society incorporate it into a larger context? If there is a context, what kind is it, and
is it systematic? Secondarily, the ratios help construct a benchmark
which calibrates the reliance a society may entertain on the nuclear
family: a father figure, a mother figure and one or more children.

Results

The results are presented in Tables 15 and 16. In Table 15, the
societies are ranked from 1–18 on each of the five proxemic indices. In
Table 16, the correlations among the five variables are shown.

Looking at the man–boy dyad first, the following relationships
occurred: as the preference for the men to associate with boys, rather
than girls, increased:

1. The percentage of children (associating with adults) who were
   with men and women decreased ($r = .722$; $p < .001$).
2. The more woman–child dyads associated with other women
   rather than with men ($r = .562$; $p < .05$).
3. The more man–child dyads associated with other men, rather
   than with women ($r = .690$; $p < .001$).

As the percentage of children (associating with adults) who were with
men and women increased:

1. The more woman–child dyads associated with men rather
   than with women ($r = +.774$; $p < .001$),
2. The more man–child dyads associated with women rather
   than with other men ($r = +.665$; $p < .01$).

As would be expected, an increase in woman, woman, and child
triads (in proportion to man, woman, and child triads) was paralleled
by a proportional increase in man-man-child triads ($r = +.518$; $p
< .05$).

It bears repeating that women's preferential association with
girls, rather than with boys, did not correlate significantly with any of
the other proxemic indices.

To summarize the key patterns found here, the data indicate

that—across-cultures—when the percentage of children (who were with adults) were associating with men and women decreased: (1) men's preferential association with boys increased and (2) adult–child dyads, pulled from association with a cross-gender adult, increased their association with same-gender adults. The patterns in the woman–girl dyad did not correlate significantly with changes in any of the other proximate indices.

CHAPTER 3

Parameters of the Man–Child Bond

Two sets of data have presented themselves to be analyzed. One set suggests a behavioral commonality which in turn suggests a similar factor or cluster of factors causing the commonality. The second set reveals systematic change in how the variables predictably relate to each other.

The next step in analysis is to avoid the seduction of promiscuous empiricism in which hordes of data are collected and then left to speak mutely for themselves. This avoidance mandates that some fairly reasonable theory be presented that would lend coherence and a sense of order to the otherwise inchoate and potentially chaotic data base.

Let us deal first with the consistencies found across the disparate sample of cultures. It was stated in the last chapter that human social behavior can be conceptualized as triune or as a trinity—three forces acting simultaneously. These forces were the (1) symbolic or myth structure of a society which pervades much, if not all, that a human does; (2) the cultural imperatives underpinning those myths, symbols, and images, whether they support or camouflage those imperatives, and (3) the phylogeny or biological heritage of *Homo sapiens* as blueprinted in the genetic code.

This chapter and the next one will examine the consistencies found in this study from the biological or phylogenetic perspective. In Chapter 5, the systematic variations will be discussed from a cultural perspective.

When humans—*Homo sapiens*—are discussed in the literature as a zoological taxon, they are often classified as Primates. Although this classification is accurate enough, the order Primates does cover a wide beach indeed, and includes prosimians, New World monkeys, the Old World monkeys, plus apes and humans (from Simons, 1972; Nelson & Jurmain, 1982). To investigate how our phylogeny, or evolutionary history, may be influencing paternalistic behaviors, a frame of reference is going to be needed to see our own behavior in a wider context. The order Primate with the prosimians, such as the lemurs, lorises, and aye-ayes, is a little unwieldy. The super family Hominoidea, which includes just apes and humans, is too narrow. The infraorder Catarrhini, which includes Old World Monkeys, apes and humans, seems a reasonable platform or level of abstraction for further analysis.[1] Given that the Catarrhini becomes the frame of reference. The line of reasoning becomes thus:

1. Several candidates for species-characteristic behavior have been proffered for men's paternalistic responses.
2. Because we share a relatively recent (in geologic time) ancestry, hence a gene pool, with other Catarrhini, it is reasonable to expect generalized patterns of paternalistic behavior from other Catarrhini males to their young to be similar to the man–child patterns recorded in the 18 culture sample.

There are two central types of data to be sought among the other Catarrhini, and these are (1) finding substantial numbers of adult males and young proximate to each other with no adult female present and (2) finding levels of interaction between adult males and young consonant with the levels of interaction between adult females and young.

The literature on catarrhine paternalistic behavior, virtually the null set before 1960, has increased many fold within the last two decades. This recent literature suggests that our catarrhine cousins exhibit, compared to other zoological taxa, a complex interrelation-

---

[1]A focus upon Catarrhines leaves out the marmosets of which there are many examples of extremely active and intense interactions from adult males to their young. These marmosets are monogamous, small in size, arboreal, normally give birth to twins, and live in small social units. The paternal ecological niche seems to resemble more that of monogamous birds (Jolly, 1972; Mitchell, 1979; Redican & Taub, 1981) than the niche of the humans whose ecology is one of a large sized, terrestial, highly social creature with a variegated sexual life with singleton births.

ship between adult males and their young (Bales, 1980; Kleiman & Malcolm, 1981; Mitchell, 1979; Redican & Taub, 1981). The form and extent of the behaviors from adult males toward their young varied enormously. The higher levels of interaction usually involved an active defense of the social group including the young and a fairly benign tolerance of the young colliding into and scurrying over and around the elder statesmen. The arboreal and monogamous[2] male gibbon represents comparatively high levels of contact and nurturing with his young in the presence of the adult female (Chivers, 1972, 1975), and the male hamadryas baboon (Kummer, 1968), the barbary ape (MacRoberts, 1970), and the chacma baboon (Busse & Hamilton, 1981), will occasionally have intense interactions with one of the tribe's young. The interpretations of these latter interactions as unambiguous nurturing behaviors are confounded with mating strategies or "buffering" behaviors between two adult males.

However, no report was found which described adult males and young systematically associating with each other outside the perimeter of the troop or band without the additional presence of an adult female. When adult males and young were proximate to each other, so was an adult female. In addition, while the degree of reported paternalistic interaction was quite variable, the data consistently showed far lower levels of interaction from adult males toward their young compared to that of the adult females toward those young (Brown, 1975, p. 265; Hrdy, 1976; Goodall, 1979; Goss-Custard, Dunbar, & Aldrich-Blake, 1972; Mackinnon, 1974; Lawick-Goodall, 1971). In terms of paternalistic behavior, men are deviant Catarrhini. A pre-

---

[2]Monogamy and polygyny used in the social sciences refer to a cultural device describing a marriage system. Marriage systems and sexual systems may well contain a good deal of overlap in terms of partners, but these two systems can be diagnostically separated. When the zoological literature refers to *monogamy* and to *polygyny*, the reference is to breeding strategies. Because humans have elaborate cultural symbols and images, and nonhumans (to our knowledge) do not, monogamy in infrahumans cannot be a segment of their cultural superstructure. A modicum of intellectual mischief has occurred by the equating of a restrictive mating format with an expansive sociocultural pattern. Sexuality and marriage are not identities for humans, nor are nonhuman sexual patterns easily paralleled by the diffuse and textured symbolic and behavioral patterns of the human marriage institution. In addition, a marital state of polygyny for a man indicates a marital state of monogamy for a woman; all of which allows for a situation wherein a family can be polygynous and monogamous at the same time. In sum, sex and marriage are two distinct concepts, and marriage systems are best analyzed with reference to one gender at a time.

diction about man–child bonding based upon monkey and ape field data would widely underestimate the men's involvement.[3]

Men are typically associating with children and responding to them as no other Catarrhine does.[4] Knowledge of our phylogeny on this one point would misrepresent our extant behavior.

If the investigation were stopped at this cul-de-sac, then Huxley's definition of a true tragedy would unfold: a beautiful theory killed by an ugly fact. The theory was that our catarrhine genotype blueprinted an active central nervous system and endocrine system that, across cultures, eventuated in high levels of man–child interaction. The fact was that other catarrhine males were not that interested in their young.

So: either the theory is extremely damp, if not all wet, or the human genotype, *after* separating from the gorilla and (especially) the chimpanzee, was under intense selective pressure to favor increasingly high levels of paternalistic behavior and to punish, that is, let die, those individuals with low levels of paternalism.

It is argued here that the theory is basically sound and that, indeed, as the genus *Homo* emerged, adult males were stringently selected to be fond of their children. The stimulus which favored fathering was the increasing dependence of hunting and scavenging by our ancestors for food—read for survival. This stimulus (a consensus of theorists seems to suggest) asserted itself after the split occurred between humans and the great apes (Andrews, 1982; Johanson & White, 1980; Leakey & Walker, 1980; Pilbeam, 1982; Yunis & Prakash, 1982).

---

[3]Harlow (1971) and Adams (1960) in fact did go through this scenario. From predominately rhesus macaque data (whose adult males exhibit low levels of nurturing behaviors to their young), they argued that the human males do not possess an independent bond with their children. Their argument is that the relationships among men and children are a derivative effect which results from the man–woman bond and the woman–child bond. That is, men are with children because men like women and women like children.

[4]Other adult male platyrrhines (New World monkeys) and prosimians, compared to the respective adult females, have low levels of paternalistic involvement (with the important exceptions of the marmosets). Furthermore, the field reports (including the marmosets) do not describe adult male–young association (in the absence of adult females) at some distance from the perimeter of their "home" territory. Hence, the lack of correspondence between human paternalism and the platyrrhine, prosimians, and other Catarrhines can now be truncated to a lack of correspondence between human paternalistic behavior and the paternalistic behavior of nonhuman Primates.

A generally accepted reconstruction of the prehistory of emerging *Homo* depicts an increasing reliance upon hunting/scavenging as an important subsistence technique (Bunn, 1981; Chagnon & Irons, 1979; Fox, 1980; Isaac, 1978; King, 1975; Lee & DeVore, 1968; Lovejoy, 1981; Potts & Shipman, 1981). Hunting is viewed as a male prerogative either from the inception of systematic hunting or as being progressively assumed by males at the gradual exclusion of females. Whereas hunting has been reported for other (adult male) Catarrhini (Lawick-Goodall, 1971; Sturm, 1975; Teleki, 1973, 1975), the hunts tend to be close to the perimeter of the social unit, often precipitated by a serendipitous chancing upon a prey, unsystematic over time, and highly variable across bands. The reconstruction of the *Homo* hunt is usually presented as wide ranging beyond visual or vocal contact of the tribe, systematic and structured or preplanned, and consistent over time within a tribe and consistent across tribes. The envisioned lifestyle of early male *Homo* was not merely a magnification of catarrhini tendencies. Male *Homo* would have had to take hunting seriously and include it as a major facet of his life-style and life cycle.

Once the schism between male hunting and female nonhunting occurred, the two genders embarked upon two evolutionary tracks. Selective pressures were introduced and made possible to favor successful hunters and to disfavor the unsuccessful ones. The relevant intrusion and power of those selective pressures and two distinct tracks is a matter of much conjecture and discussion (e.g., Ardrey, 1961, 1976; Laughlin, 1968; Montagu, 1973; Tiger, 1969; Zihlman & Tanner, 1978).

It does seem reasonable to argue that one important component of this division of labor by gender would be a positive selection for a motivation system that would allow or encourage the men to bring the procured food and to share that very valuable commodity with women and children. Any alleles that would have increased the motivation (mediated by the central nervous system and the endocrine system) to share with women and children have proven inordinately successful. A strong universal across cultures is the active sharing of food from men to women and to children. That is, men transport food from a locus outside the perimeter of the domicile to that domicile. There the food is distributed and then consumed. See Human Relations Area File code numbers 22–26 for examples. Although this is a human trait, it is not a catarrhine trait.[5]

Competing alleles have been displaced by alleles that can blueprint a neurohormonal system that is biased to learn, integrate, and emit sharing behaviors toward women and children (see Dawkins, 1976, and Alexander, 1979, for an overview of allelic displacement within genetic theory).

It is argued here that the sharing was and is facilitated if an affection bond is extant between men and children. That is, if men are fond of their children, they will more willingly, and with greater generosity, share food with those individuals. Framed differently, the all male hunting groups would increase their likelihood of survival across generations if the men returned to camp and shared food with the next generation (Isaac, 1978; Lancaster & Lancaster, 1982; Lovejoy, 1981; Mackey, 1976, 1979a).

Let us go back and reexamine Money and Ehrhardt's original hypothesis: that parenting behavior was not gender dimorphic but that the threshold was lower for women than for men. The catarrhine data on the mother–young relationship seems fairly similar across species: mother chimpanzees, mother gorillas, mother gibbons, mother baboons, and mother macaques, as well as mother humans, all tend to spend a lot of caretaking time with their young. The difference between humans and the infrahumans lies in the men. Human men, as a class, are far more solicitious than their simian cousins. The argument here has a bit of the ironic in it. The all-male, symbolically masculinized endeavor of hunting resulted in increasing nurturance and caregiving in men. A parenting template increasingly emerged and solidified itself in the motivation (emotional) substrate of men as a derivative of this masculine prerogative.

What then is the nature or gestalt of this putative parenting template in men, and how would this relate to the data base from the 18 cultures? A segment of such a gestalt, Money and Ehrhardt's position

---

[5]A number of reports (e.g., Starin, 1978; Teleki, 1973) report food sharing amongst Primates. The character of the sharing is invariably the eating from the same source or successful food begging. To my knowledge the systematic return from a point outside the group's perimeter by an adult male to the female–young dyad with the active relinquishing of the food for consumption by female and young has not been reported.

would predict, is that men would be expected to associate with children less often than women, but once the men were proximate to their children, they would behave in a manner which would be thematically similar to that of women responding to children. That is, the threshold for activating or for triggering caregiving to children would be lower in women than in men, but once the threshold is reached in men, they would respond to children in a manner rather similar to the way women would respond to children. It is simply harder to stimulate men to respond in a care-giving way to children, but once stimulated they parent as do women. See Figure 2.

A synopsis of Table 2 shows that in all 18 cultures, women do predominate in adult–child dyads, even during MNP intervals. However, men-only groups were well represented (21.6% of adult–child dyads, sd = 5.9%) and the men and women groups contained nearly a third of all the surveyed children (31.2%, sd = 12.4%). See Table 17.

For the three interaction indexes, there were a total of 321 comparisons between men and women in their level of responding to children. There were 108 comparisons involving all children (boys +

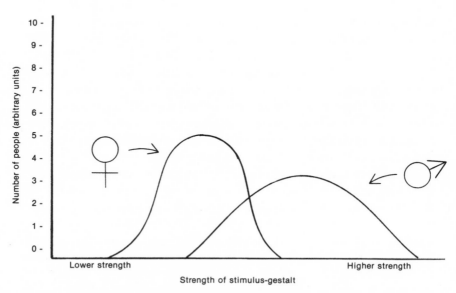

FIGURE 2. Schematic depiction of distribution of relative strength of stimulus-gestalt needed to initiate or to maintain adult–child interaction in a population of adult males and in a population of adult females.

TABLE 17

Percentage of Associations between Adult Groups by Gender Composition and Children in 18 Cultures (Diagnostic Time Intervals Only)

	Percentage of children associating with adult groups consisting of			Number of children
Sites from	Women only	Men only	Men and women	
Israel (kibbutzim)	53.5	31.9	14.6	2,139
Reykjavik, Iceland	39.6	29.0	31.4	1,694
Morocco	56.8	28.5	14.7	1,398
India	43.0	28.5	28.5	1,104
Brazil—urbanizing	46.4	24.4	29.2	562
Taiwan	56.8	23.8	19.4	2,790
Ireland	36.5	22.9	40.6	1,852
Japan	38.3	22.9	38.8	1,336
Brazil—rural	54.3	22.8	22.9	549
Senufo (Ivory Coast)	41.5	21.0	37.5	1,132
Hong Kong	32.3	20.7	47.0	164
Sri Lanka	64.7	20.5	14.8	1,973
United States	43.5	17.5	39.0	8,953
Ivory Coast	67.4	17.4	15.2	1,642
Lima, Peru	52.2	17.4	30.4	490
Spain	31.5	16.8	51.7	1,058
Mexico	50.2	14.2	35.6	1,355
Karaja (Brazil)	40.8	8.3	50.9	399
Mean	47.2	21.6	31.2	1,699
sd	10.4	5.9	12.4	

girls + infants) and 213 involving boys and girls analyzed separately (Table 18). Of the 321 (108 + 213) comparisons, men and women had similar levels of interacting with children in 247 of the cases (76.9%). Women were more active 38 times (11.8%) and men had a higher level of response 36 times (11.2%). In sum, the men were treating the children in much the same way that the women were—the men just were not proximate to the children as often.

A second aspect of the gestalt would be that the variance or distribution of parenting behavior would be greater in men than in women. Said another way, it would be more difficult to activate simultaneously the care-giving motivational triggers in two or more men than in two or more women. Women would be more homogeneous in having their mothering elicited than men would be in having their fathering elicited. See Figure 2. As Table 19 (from Table 4)

TABLE 18
Comparisons between Men and Women in Relation to the Level of Interaction toward All Children (Boy and Girls and Infants Combined) and toward Boys and Girls Analyzed Separately: 18 Cultures[a]

Category of children analyzed	Gender of adult responding more actively toward the child	Number of occasions higher level of response occurs	
		Number	Percentage
All children	Men more active	12	11.1
(boys + girls +	Women more active	20	18.5
infants)	Neither more active	76	70.4
	Total	108	100.0
Boys and girls	Men more active	24	11.3
separately	Women more active	18	8.4
	Neither more active	171	80.3
	Total	213	100.0

[a]Abstracted from Tables 10 and 11, Chapter 2.

illustrates, it was difficult to find two or more men associating with children; whereas two or more women associating was a relatively frequent occurrence. In 16 cultures, the mean number of women in women-only groups exceeded the mean number of men in men-only groups. In two cultures, there were no differences in the mean number of men and women per group. It is simply harder to trigger simultaneously the parenting threshold in two men than it is in two women. If a man–child dyad were going to associate with another

TABLE 19
Mean Number of Men per Groups of Men and Children Compared to the Mean Number of Women per Groups of Women and Children: 18 Cultures[a]

Cultures in which		
Mean number of men is greater than the mean number of women	Mean number of women is greater than the mean number of men	No differences in the mean number of men or women exist
0	16*	2

*Sign test; $p < .01$.
[a]For men-only groups: $m = 1.125$, $sd = 0.107$; range 1.000–1.181; $n = 18$. For women-only groups: $m = 1.305$; $sd = 0.116$; range 1.124–1.541; $n = 18$. (Repeated from Table 4, Chapter 2.)

adult, that adult was invariably a woman—not another man. Over the entire 18 culture sample, there were nearly 9 man, woman, and child triads for each 1 man, man, and child triads (from Table 15). The woman–child dyad, however, was much more prone to replace a man with another women. The ratio of woman, man, and child triads to woman, woman, and child triads was approximately 2 to 1.

A third segment of the template's gestalt would be that it would be sensitized to react more to the age, or dependency of the child, and less to the gender of the child. Men, just as women, will react to the level of dependence of the child more so than to whether the child is a boy or a girl. Younger children, who are more dependent receive more attention than do older children, who are more independent. From Table 20 (which revises Table 6 and Table 14), both the men and the women were not only more proximate to younger children than to older children in 97 of 100 indices (97%), but it is clear that the men and the women tended to respond more actively to younger children compared to older children. For the 102 interaction indexes analyzing women's level of responding to children by the age or developmental status of the child, 70.6% (72 cases) of the indexes show that younger children (compared to their older siblings) received more active response sets from the women. The analogous figure for men was

TABLE 20

The Level of Association between Adults and Children and the Level of Interaction from Adults to Children by the Age of the Child[a]

| Adult groups | Number and percentage of cases in which younger children received a higher level of interaction | | | Number and percentage of cases in which older children (8–14 years of age) are underrepresented in associations with adults | |
	Number	Percentage of total cases	Percentage of cases reaching significance	Number	Percentage
Men-only groups	39	81.3	97.5	30	93.8
Women-only groups	40	78.4	90.9	33	97.1
Men and women groups					
Men	31	60.8	100.0	34	100.0
Women	32	62.7	91.4		

Note. The three interaction indices are combined.
[a] Abstracted from Tables 6 and 14, Chapter 2.

70.7% (70 of 99 cases). Thus, men and women were discerning age differences in their children and reacting selectively to those differences.

Even as the age of the child was affecting the adult's behavior, the gender of the child was less intrusive. See Table 21. Of 105 cases in which men's behavior toward girls was compared to men's behavior toward boys, 91 (86.6%) comparisons indicated no gender differences or preferences. For women, the analogous figure was 91.7% (99 of 108 cases).

There are important nuances, if not exceptions, to the notion that men (and women) are more attentive to the age of the children than to the child's gender. The first is that men in men-only groups will be with infants rather rarely. See Table 7. This lack of association with infants can probably be traced down to the biological reality that men cannot nurse infants, whereas women can. Accordingly, the lack of association between men-only groups and infants can be quickly conceived as being a reflection of economy and efficiency of meshing adult schedules and infant appetites.

The second and more interesting wrinkle represents a fourth segment of the gestalt which entails an interaction between the age of a child and the gender of a child. This segment is the tendency for males to create and maintain all-male groups. Part of the selective

TABLE 21

Comparison of Level of Interaction from Adult (Man or Woman) to Child by Gender of Child (Single and Plural Gender Adult Groups are Combined and the Three Interaction Categories are Combined[a])

Gender of adult	Gender of child receiving more active responses	Number of occasions higher level of interaction is received	
		Number	Percentage
Men	Girl	7	6.7
	Boy	7	6.7
	Neither	91	86.6
	Total	105	100.0
Women	Girl	4	3.7
	Boy	5	4.6
	Neither	99	91.7
	Total	108	100.0

[a]Abstracted from Table 2.12, Chapter 2.

pressures from a hunting lifestyle included the need to recruit older boys into all male hunting groups (Mackey, 1981; Tiger, 1969). Table 22 clearly shows the distinction between the man–older boy dyad and the other five adult group–older child dyads. Accordingly, older boys and men would isolate themselves from females, and do things together. Although very little actual hunting or scavenging occurs in the latter part of the twentieth century, the neurohormonal system forged and successful for millions of years is oblivious to the silicon chip and shopping malls, but replays the themes which survived over those millenia. In a special manner, men like to be with their older boys.

In summary, a closing of the parenting gap between men and women is suggested which does not reflect a catarrhine heritage in particular or the heritage of Primates in general. The ecological imperative that, over generations, nudged men into the nursery was foodsharing from the successful hunt or scavenge. The human males had shaded over from a selfish gatherer of seeds, nuts, and fruits to incorporate the life-style of an altruistic social carnivore.

Whereas the field data from monkeys and apes generally revealed spare individual attention from adult males to their young, the field data on other social carnivores/omnivores (the canids), wolves, coyotes, jackals, and hunting dogs, was a different matter. Adult

TABLE 22

Comparison among Adult Groups of Higher Percentage of Older Children (8 Years to Puberty) Boys and Girls are Analyzed Separately: 17 Cultures[a]

	Compared adult groups		
	Women only vs. men only	Women only vs. men and women	Men only vs. men and women
Number of cultures with the higher percentage of girls in the older age bracket	9 vs. 7	12[b] vs. 4[b]	10 vs. 4
Number of cultures with the higher percentage of boys in the older age bracket	0 vs. 16*	7 vs. 10	15* vs. 1

*$p < .001$; sign test.
[a]Hong Kong's sample was not large enough for inclusion. The Karaja sample had an insufficient number of cases in the men-only group for analysis. The Brazil—rural and the Brazil—urbanizing samples had insufficient numbers for analysis of girls in the men only versus men and women comparison.
[b]Tie in Ireland.

male wolves (Allen, 1979; Mech, 1966, 1970; Mowat, 1963; Murie, 1944), adult male coyotes (Dobie, 1949; McMahan, 1976; Ryden, 1974; Young & Jackson, 1951), adult male jackals (Lawick & Lawick-Goodall, 1971; Moehlman, 1980), and adult male hunting dogs (Kühme, 1965; and Lawick & Lawick-Goodal, 1971) are solicitous toward their young and interact with them at high levels. They play with their young. In addition, and of some importance to this argument, the adult males of this group return to their pups and share food by regurgitating the food for their pups to eat. Here again, high levels of response from adult males to the young are found associated with the sharing of food from those males to their young. The problems of their life-style as social hunters led to behavioral solutions that, compared to other genera, involved very high levels of adult male–young individualized interaction (Crook, Ellis, & GossCustard, 1976; King, 1980; Kleiman, 1977; Rabb, Woolpy, & Ginsberg, 1967; Schaller, 1972b; Schaller & Lowther, 1969). In an ecological niche in which food is gained and then relinquished, it is probably much easier to give food away if the benefactor happens to like the recipient. Men who liked their children would feed them—either directly or mediated through the mother. These men were more likely to have more great-grandchildren than were those men who simply, or complexly, considered their own children, in addition to their nephews and nieces, plus any strangers' children, to be merely additional competitors for resources.

It should be noted that although spotted hyenas and lions are also social carnivores, the adult males have not been reported either to return to their young in order to share food actively with them or to play with their young (Guggisberg, 1963; Kruuk, 1972; Lawick & Lawick-Goodall, 1971; Rudnai, 1973; Schaller, 1972a). Hence, for the analysis presented here, the lion and the spotted hyena are not appropriate analogues for the proposed hominid model.

What presents itself is a model of convergent evolution in which different taxa or groups independently solve similar problems in similar ways. Within the confines of the adult male–young dyad, men moved away from the catarrhine heritage and toward an analogous ecological heritage of the social carnivore that shares food with its young and has a strong division of labor by gender. In the meantime, they also converged toward the parenting role which had long been the females domain within the primate, if not mammalian, heritage.

A Test for the Hypothesized Adult Male–Child Bond

The previous chapters suggest that the form and texture of a human social bond are consistently and meaningfully influenced by genotypic information which blueprints an active motivational system (the central nervous system and the endocrine system). The evidence adduced for this position was consistent behavioral patterns found in different cultures.

In addition to evidence to support a theory, another fundamental construct in Western science is the prerequisite of predictability. If a theory can predict, rather than merely explain ad hoc, a phenomenon, then the theory is bolstered and becomes one notch more credible. Another important concept in our version of science is falsifiability; can a prediction be refuted or shown to be incorrect? Generally a statement which can be falsified is given more attention than a similar statement which offers little or no opportunity to be shown to be wrong.

A theory is usually quite broad and abstract and thereby fairly immune from direct testing. Radiating from a theory would be derived hypotheses which can be very particularistic and specific and thereby testable. The results from such tests either can sustain or confirm the hypothesis that would indirectly lend credibility to the theory, or the test results can be inconclusive, ambiguous, equivocal, or much more embarassingly they can support unequivocally a competing theory. A lack of supportive predictability limits the half-life of the theory in question as it vies for acceptance in the marketplace of ideas.

This chapter will take the generalized theory that there is a man–

child bond forged, in part, from information coded in the human genotype and test the theory against empirical reality. To flesh out better how and why the test can be constructed, a brief summary of Darwinian evolution and the definitions of five concepts should be presented first.

DARWINIAN THEORY IN A NUTSHELL

Below are five steps in Darwinian evolution (from Barash, 1977). For more detailed and technical discussion on the topic see Darwin (1859) and Dawkins (1976).

1. Living organisms have the capacity to overreproduce. Salmon, rabbits, wolves, beetles, and humans all produce many sperm and eggs, which, if they all survived to maturity, would soon have the universe awash with salmon, rabbits, wolves, beetles, and humans.
2. Given the capacity to overreproduce, populations tend to remain reasonably stable. The universe is not awash in any one species.
3. There are individual differences among individuals within a population. A portion of these differences is under genetic control and can thereby be inherited as tendencies.
4. If differences between individuals can be affected by inherited differentials and if fairly stable populations exist in the context of a tremendous capacity to overreproduce which is *not* utilized, then there exists a strong potential for differential reproductive success. Some individuals will have a disproportionately large number of progeny, whereas alternate individuals will have a disproportionately small number of progeny.
5. The process by which the traits of some individuals are better suited to survive and propagate (i.e., better adapted) than alternate traits in other individuals is usually called "natural selection." *Natural selection* is the evolutionary history of differential reproductive success whereby the increase/decrease in the proportion of different genes or alternate gene forms—alleles—manifest themselves in the form of differences in anatomy, in physiology, and, this brief argues, in behavior.

A concise example may be useful here. Let us say that a small tribe on an isolated island has only five women: These women are Ms. Able, Ms. Beatrice, Ms. Cassandra, Ms. Dravidian, and Ms. Pinnip. These five women share a great many traits in common; nonetheless, there are differences:

- Ms. Able has red hair, green eyes, excellent teeth, and has great difficulty in digesting lactose.
- Ms. Beatrice has blonde hair, grey eyes, good teeth and has great difficulty in digesting lactose.
- Ms. Cassandra has blond hair, blue eyes, moderate teeth, and also has great difficulty in digesting lactose.
- Ms. Dravidian has brown hair, black eyes, fair teeth, and, she too has a great difficulty digesting lactose.
- Ms. Pinnip has brown eyes, black hair, her teeth are soft, ineffective, crooked, or missing since puberty. Ms. Pinnip has awful teeth. However, Ms. Pinnip can digest lactose efficiently and is very fond of its taste.

Let us agree that hair color, eye color, teeth construction and the ability to digest lactose are under at least some genetic influence.

At their own generation (which shall be labeled G_0), each of the five women represent 20% of the village's adult female population. At the next generation (G_1) Ms. Able died in childbirth. Her child died also. Ms. Beatrice had one daughter. Ms. Cassandra had two daughters. Ms. Dravidian had three daughters, and Ms. Pinnip had four daughters. Because females are the limiting resource which can determine the rate of population change, the family trees of the daughters will be followed. For nine additional generations each daughter had the same number of daughters as did her own mother. The results of these ten generation family trees are presented in Table 23.

After ten generations, the percentage of females who descended from each of the original five founders differs markedly from the original 20% that each of the five founders represented. The tendencies for red, blond, and brown hair, for good teeth and for the inability to digest lactose efficiently were all much reduced in the village life. Ms. Pinnip's awful teeth, brown eyes, and skills in digesting lactose predominated. Her fertility over time dictated the form and character of the village's gene pool. At base, this process of evolution,

TABLE 23
Illustration of the Evolutionary Process in a Human Community

Generation	Women and number of daughters				
0	Ms. Able	Ms. Beatrice	Ms. Cassandra	Ms. Dravidian	Ms. Pinnip
1	Deceased	1	2	3	4
2		1	4	9	16
3		1	8	27	64
4		1	16	81	256
5		1	32	243	1,024
6		1	64	729	4,096
7		1	128	2,187	16,384
8		1	256	6,561	65,536
9		1	512	19,683	262,144
10		1	1024	59,049	1,048,576
Percentage of the population at G_{10}	0.0%	0.001%	0.09%	5.3%	94.6%

the changing of the proportions of alleles over time, is elegantly simple. The actual matching of traits with reproductive success/failure and the matching of alleles with traits (behavior) are elegantly elusive. The crucial concepts in the theory of natural selection are rather straight forward. The validation of the integration of a phenotype with its referent (putative) genotype is a very difficult task.[1]

The application of the principles of Darwinian evolution to human behavior has, in its relatively brief history, encountered a

[1]Part of the problem in testing for genotypic influences in human behavior is the ethical constraints placed upon the scientific community by the larger society. The overall American society is not the least bit willing to let scientists rear children, even orphans, in isolation or under scientific conditions. As part of my introductory classes near the beginning of the semester, I annually ask the classes whether they would support the purchase of Vietnamese, or El Salvadorean, or Kampuchean war orphans (infants). These purchased infants would be reared under controlled conditions and important questions could be addressed, perhaps answered, on the development of human behavior. It is suggested further that, although some of the orphans would suffer irreversible damage, generation after generation of humans would be able to benefit from the knowledge gained at the expense of the few. Over the years, there have been a few individuals who have responded enthusiastically to the idea; yet the thundering majority of the people and classes have thought such an approach a terrible idea.

series of ebbs and flows in the arena of public acceptance. Human instincts and racial differences were popular ideas in the 19th century and in the early part of the twentieth century. These ideas were fairly useful in a justification of extant social structures. Darwin's theses were usurped to give a modern or contemporary explanation to social and ethnic differentials that had existed certainly since agriculture encouraged social stratification and it is arguable that the notion of ethnocentrism has separated contrasting groups for the millenia (Beach, 1955; Freeman, 1983; Harris, 1968).

Social circumstances changed by the first quarter of the twentieth century. Instinct was deleted from the human repertoire and was generally replaced with the reinstated "blank tablet." The vehicle to write on this slate was learning or experience by psychologists and culture by anthropologists. In turn the learning or experience or culture was viewed to be mediated by a largely passive brain that operated not unlike a telephone system: output from the system was highly congruent with the input into the system without prepro- grammed influence or biased processing within and by the system itself. The idea of inherited behavioral potentials in humans was not seriously entertained by the mainstream social scientists nor was funding available to research such an idea. An ebb time for human instincts. This view of the genesis of human behavior was also, not unexpectedly, borrowed by the larger society in general (at least in the Western world) to justify social programs and social engineering. The logic was not difficult: if the clay is infinitely malleable, then the sculpture can take any form. The better the artist/sculptor, the better the finished product.

The second half of the twentieth century began and the nature- nurture pendulum, reaching the end of one sweep, began another. Epitomized by two very public books *On Aggression* By Konrad Lorenz (1963) and *African Genesis* by Robert Ardrey (1961), both the public and the scientific community began to reexamine the notion that humans were a part of the natural world rather than apart from it. The winning of the 1973 Nobel prize in medicine by Konrad Lorenz, Karl von Frisch, and Nicholaas Tinbergen for the inheritance of behavior tendencies in infrahumans (birds, bees, and fish, respec- tively) lent a dollop of credibility to the asking of such questions as the inheritance of behavioral tendencies in humans. Further work by, for example, Tiger (1969), Tiger and Fox (1971), Morris (1967, 1969), and Ashley Montagu (1973), plus additional offerings by Ardrey (1966, 1971, and 1976) kindled the continuing dialogue. In 1975 a watershed work, *Sociobiology: The New Synthesis* by Wilson (1975), was published. Of incidental interest is the fact that Wilson's book has 546 pages of text, of which 29 pages or 5% is devoted specifically to humans. In terms of attracting notice, few five percents have been so effective.

As noted earlier, the nature–nurture debate concerning humans is probably worthwhile; although a nature–nurture solution is equal-ly probably a happenstance well beyond the immediate temporal horizon. Unequivocal scientific facts are excruciatingly difficult to ob-tain and to find consensus on when the subject is the development of human behavior. Even the existence of such facts, as facts, are of problematic influence unless prevailing social and political forces are served by their existence.

The latter quarter of the twentieth century is a segment of the seeming oscillation between both public and scientific polar visions of *Homo*, the zoological entity, and of Humanity, which is composed of rational beings with free will, who transcend a biological heritage. In this segment a middle if somewhat muddled ground has been, mo-mentarily, achieved (Freedman, 1979; Freeman, 1983; Fox, 1980; Hinde & Stevenson-Hinde, 1973; Tiger, 1979; Van Den Berghe, 1979).

A solid intellectual success that became available to subtend and promulgate the recent paradigmic shift involved the notion that the gene, rather than the individuals or the groups of individuals, was the unit or engine driving evolution (Dawkins, 1976; Fisher, 1930; Haldane, 1932; Hamilton, 1964; Maynard Smith, 1964). It was the gene/allele which increased or decreased its proportion of the gene pool. If their phenotypic expression increased the referent alleles' relative reproductive potential, then those alleles would more domi-nate the population. If the phenotypic expression of the referent al-leles decreased their relative reproductive potential, then the alleles would dwindle in their representation until extinction would occur.

Keeping the gene/allele as the focus, the following concepts and their definitions become useful (from Barash, 1977; Trivers, 1974; and Wilson, 1975).

1. Genetic fitness: the contribution to subsequent generations within a population of genes/alleles relative to the contribu-tions of alternate genes/alleles. By definition, the more preva-

lent forms are the most fit and the least prevalent forms are the less fit.

2. Inclusive fitness: the sum of an individual's own genetic fitness plus all of its influence on the genetic fitness in its relatives other than direct descendants (kin selection).

3. Kin selection: the selection of genes because of their effect on favoring or disfavoring the reproductive success of relatives other than offspring, for example, nephews and nieces.

4. Personal fitness: the genetic fitness of an individual as measured by the individual's own children.

5. Parental investment: behavior of a parent toward his or her offspring that increases the chances of that offspring's reproductive success at the cost of the parent's investment in other offspring.

From these five concepts, an argument can be constructed that can lead to an empirically investigated hypothesis.

It is assumed that in past epochs, men who helped women nurture children had more descendants than did men who allowed their children to be reared by women only and who did not participate in their direct nurturance. In other words, it is suggested that paternal nurturance aided the woman–child dyad in sustaining and expanding the population level of a tribe or band or village. A very fit strategy for a man to execute would be to inseminate his own wife and then help her in rearing his own children—plus inseminating as many wives of other men and then having those surrogate fathers aid in the rearing of his children to the point of their social competence and independence.[2] Such a genetic strategy and motivational and behavioral derivatives would surely and eventually supplant and displace an alternate strategy of a man dispassionate and indifferent to the genitor of his social children whom his wife has borne and whom he will nurture with his time and resources to maturity (see Dewsbury, 1982, for a complementary discussion).

An complementary strategy for the woman would involve hiding

---

[2]As is customary, the use of the word *strategy* does not imply or preclude a consciousness or awareness of the organism's capability of developing and testing methods which would achieve desired goals. *Strategy* is used here as a shorthand term to note that particular patterns of responses have been selected which tend to result in predictable ranges of consequences (see Barash, 1977; Dawkins, 1976; van den Berghe, 1980, p. 158, for similar usages).

when she ovulates both from herself and from her consort, but to become continuously sexually receptive, if not proceptive. She then develops the options of keeping one male interested in her for extended periods of time, or of keeping several men interested in her at different times. This very unusual human trait of continuous receptivity runs counter to other species, in which chemical and visual cues are utilized to advertise the adult female's fertility, and whereby frequencies of copulation become clustered around those times of fertility. The obvious disadvantage to this trait of hiding ovulation is that a large amount of sexual activity, with attendant time and calories expended, can occur without procreation, and thus seems to be counterintuitive if an efficient relationship is sought between costs of copulation and benefits of progeny. An advantage to this trait is that a large amount of sexual activity can occur. See Spuhler (1979), Hrdy (1981), and Daniels (1983), for expanded discussions on female sexuality.

A sequela to hidden ovulation and continuous rather than discrete receptivity, is that rape for the male becomes a potentially useful genetic strategy. Because rape, either actual or threatened, is deeply entertained in symbolic systems as well as in criminal ledgers, it is suggested that, in the emergence of *Homo*, the motivation system generating the behavioral trait of forced copulation was a successful adaptation to the new microecology of hidden ovulation and continuous receptivity (see Alexander & Noonan, 1979, for additional discussion). It seems reasonable that a counterstrategy to rape potentials would include (1) the usefulness and intensification of the invention and assimilation of the emotion jealousy into the man, woman, and child triad. Men fight over women—a lot (as described by such diverse theorists from Mead, 1935, to Chagnon, 1977), and (2) the two successful cultural innovations of the cuckholded husband as a figure of negative stereotypy (whether the imagery takes the form of a fool, a figure of ridicule, or emasculation), and the cultural rules prohibiting and punishing adultery and rape, plus more rarely, rules prescribing the virgin bride (Broude, 1980; Levinson & Malone, 1980; Schlegel, 1972; Stephens, 1963; van den Berghe, 1979).

To summarize the preceding: it would be expected that men would marry according to the immediate cultural rules of their society, sire children, raise and nurture their own children, and avoid expending resources on other men's children.

It is important to emphasize that these men of course would not recognize genes. They would recognize individual features and personalities. As the saying goes "it *is* a wise child who knows his own father." Whereas even the dimmest of females can figure out who the mother of her children is, men never know—but only assume—paternity. To the child such information is irrelevant. From the child's point of view, the only relevant rule is to stay alive. To survive, the child's arsenal of weapons includes looking cute, acting cute, and being cuddly. If cute and cuddly are not enough, the child possesses an insistent determination to intrude noisely into the immediate social environment. The child needs food, lodging, and protection. Our altricial children depend on adults for the necessities of survival. If the child's behaviors can tug and pull and pluck on the emotional strings of one or any proximate man to feed, shelter, and protect the child, then that child would be infinitely indifferent to the karyotype of the man. For his part, the man would be more vulnerable to becoming fond of proximate children, assumed to be his children via his high-fidelity wife, through the children's survival strategies of being lovable. Conversely, the man would be less vulnerable to distal children—who, in turn, have neither the time nor the opportunity to meld and emotionally entangle their personalities with those of the men. The unity of his status of father and the survival package of the child serve to bond the man to the child. The cognitive category of genetic fitness, if understood at all, would not work nearly as well.

As a happy side effect of these processes, the adoption of genetically distant babies by nonrelatives can be very effective for both adults and children. A cute child and a susceptible-to-cuteness adult can work wonders. The men, as well as the women, react to the phenotype of the baby that scans the environment searching for adults with whom to attach and to mold and to manipulate. It is a very old game and a very widespread game. It is also a game with very few losers.

With this prolegomenon as background, the next task is to find a way to test out the theory. The divorce rates in the United States offer such a way.

It is important to point out that the data underpinning the argument which follows is, of course, unique to the culture of the United States. The people involved are United States citizens, immersed in the culture of that social, political entity. Although thematic predictions and confirmations are argued here to be available across cultures, blanket highly particularistic analogies from the United States cannot be made. The closer a divorce system of another culture parallels that of the United States, the more generalizable are the specifics of the United States patterns to that culture. However, the more divergent the divorce systems are, the less generalization of subtleties is warranted. The United States culture, with its emphasis upon the nuclear family, monogamy, neolocality, bilateral inheritance, and with equal numbers of men and women, cannot be immediately compared with, for example, a social structure that emphasizes the extended family, polyandry, matrilocality, matrilineal inheritance, and with an unbalanced sex ratio.

Operating within the confines of data from the United States social system, this section investigates the adequacy of parenting strategies executed by United States men. In a rather antiseptic manner, an *adequate strategy* is defined here as the production of *at least* replacement value in the form of offspring, that is, fathering two or more children who are viable and are sexually and socially competitive. To coincide with the U.S. Census procedures, children will be defined as individuals under 18 years of age.

Within the United States social structure, the adult male who has the predominant social power over children is the father. In other societies, it may be the mother's brother, for example, among the Truk (Schlegel, 1972). In the forthcoming analysis, the United States men's effective influence upon consanguineal kin—"blood" relatives—of the next generation is usually restricted to their own offspring.

DIVORCE AND DARWIN'S THEORY—A PROBLEM?

The phenomenon of divorce, as practiced in the United States, is, at face value, troublesome for Darwinian and genetic theory. Divorce represents a behavior pattern not immediately reconcilable to the basic genetic or (to use current vernacular) sociobiological tenets of genetic fitness, inclusive fitness, kin selection, personal fitness, and parental investment.

Divorce in the United States separates spouses and, simultaneously, sexual partners; for although sexual activity and marriage are undoubtedly not coterminous in the United States, there is probably a great deal of overlap. Even greater overlap would exist between procreation and marriage. Accordingly, the dissolution of a marriage between two people is assumed to be congruent with the dissolution of shared procreation between those same two people.

After a divorce in the United States, the former husband and wife separate and then live in different domiciles. If children are involved, they are routinely placed with the mother/wife and, as a consequence, their contact with the father is reduced as is his contact with them.

As seen in Table 24, over three-quarters of the children not living with both parents live with the mother only. Less than 8% of the children not living with both parents are living with their father only (or 1.5% of the total number of children). It is of some interest that the number of children living with neither parent is almost twice that of the children living with father only (2.7% versus 1.5%, U.S. Bureau of the Census, 1975).

The earlier chapters have suggested that the separation of children from adult men, in this instance the father figure, is not a trivial event. Despite wide variability in other attributes across cultures, a strong consistency is the presence and aid of men in the care and provision of children. Although the position of the man may vary, the availability of men to children is invariant. Such a strong consistency

TABLE 24
Living Arrangements of Children under 18 Years of Age, 1975

Living arrangement		Percentage	Percentage not living with both parents
Living with both parents		80.3	
Living with mother only		15.5	78.7
Mother separated	4.9		
Mother married, husband absent	0.9		
Mother widowed	2.4		
Mother divorced	5.5		
Mother single	1.8		
Living with father only		1.5	7.6
Living with neither parent		2.7	13.7

$N = 66,087,000$ children; U.S. Bureau of the Census, 1975.
[a]Adapted from Mackey, 1980.

in the face of markedly different social and ecological situations is used here to sustain the usefulness and functional importance of the adult male–child dyad. See Kleiman and Malcolm (1981), Kleiman (1977), and Katz and Konner (1981) for related discussions. If the father is the predominant male figure for his own children, then a high divorce rate would seemingly act directly against a very important cornerstone in any society and would threaten the credibility of the theory of genetic influence on the man–child bond.

Moreover, if the divorced woman/mother remarries, the new husband then invests his time, energy, and resources to raise another man's children, that is, another man's genes, with the consequence that the divorced man loses effective, if not de jure control of his children. Were the divorced man to remarry, he then quite appropriately directs his efforts toward raising any subsequent children resulting from this new union. This appropriateness arises from both a genetic as well as a cultural analysis: genetic, because they are his children (his genes), and cultural, because social rules mandate that the social father provides for his children.

Should the man remarry a divorced woman who has children living with her from her previous marriage, however, he would be devoting his time, energy, and resources to nurturing another man's children, that is, another man's genes. See Figure 3. Unlike a trend among the hanuman langurs (Hrdy, 1974, 1976), infanticide by new husbands toward stepchildren is heavily culturally proscribed in the United States. This taboo seems to be reasonably effective; yet children do appear to be at increased risk from abuse from stepparents (Lenington, 1981).

In the United States, the divorce rate (number of divorces per 1,000 population) from 1900 to 1979 increased over 700% from 0.7 to 5.4 (National Center for Health Statistics, 1950–1981). Such a rapid increase seems to argue rather forcefully and convincingly against the fundamental concepts of personal fitness and inclusive fitness and parental investment. Instead, the dynamics of divorce initiate forces which in turn pressure men to lose control of the actions of their children, as well as to lose the opportunity to nurture and to influence their "genes" in the form of their children. It thus appears that increasing numbers and increasing proportions of men are placing themselves in the position of nurturing other men's children, that is, other men's genes.

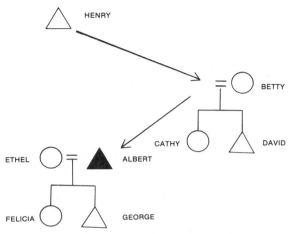

FIGURE 3. The incongruity of paternal investment and high divorce rates. If Albert divorces Betty and lives in a distant domicile, he minimizes his influence upon his children, Cathy and David, who are his genetic investment in the future, and thus jeopardizes his own inclusive fitness. To make matters worse, Albert then marries Ethel, who has children from a previous marriage—Felicia and George. Albert is expected to provide time, energy, and resources in nurturing another man's genes in the form of Felicia and George. Meanwhile, Betty has married Henry, and it is Henry who becomes the proximate male influence upon Albert's genetic investment.

Because each of his children shares one-half of his unique genetic endowment, the man has very important investments at stake in these individuals. On the average, only an identical twin or a child born to an incestuous relationship between him and a nuclear family relative would share a higher proportion of his genetic constellation. If the man, by leaving, decreases his children's viability, their social competence needed to attract mates, or their ability to rear their own offspring, then he is simultaneously decreasing his own fitness. The relative degree or amount of the man's awareness that may be involved in the unfolding of the behavioral pattern is, of course, irrelevant to the results. The consequences of the behaviors can occur as they do without regard to the intent behind those behaviors being highly focused or broadly diffused.

Recent marriage and divorce statistics illustrate that remarriage after divorce has been and still is the norm for both men and women. For men who have probably completed their marital histories, a rate of 89% remarriage has occurred (U.S. Bureau of the Census, 1975; see Table 25). Increasing numbers of men thus are placing themselves in

TABLE 25
Percentage of People, by Age and Gender, Who Did and Did Not Remarry after First Divorce (U.S. Bureau of the Census, 1976b)[a]

Age in years	Percentage remarried		Percentage not remarried	
	Male	Female	Male	Female
31 to 35	75.1	64.4	24.9	35.6
41 to 45	78.1	69.7	21.9	30.3
51 to 55	83.0	73.5	17.0	26.5
61 to 65	85.6	81.2	14.4	18.8
71 to 75	89.3	78.0	10.7	22.0

[a]Adapted from Mackey, 1980.

the position of losing their nurturing potential toward their own children to whom they have been proximate since infancy and thereby could have established unique social habits and attachments, that is, bonded to their children.

Concurrently, the men are also being given (and are accepting) responsibility for nurturing the children of other men. As a strategy to maximize one's own genetic characteristics in subsequent generations, this seems inadequate. These dynamics threaten once again to dampen, to the point of saturation, a rather nice theory.

DIVORCE AND DARWIN—A RECONCILIATION

Despite increasing divorce rates, a majority of marriages are not dissolved by divorce. The available figures vary from age cohort to age cohort, and the tentative projections similarly vary from bold to conservative (U.S. Bureau of Census, 1976a).[3] As Table 26 indicates, however, 60% to 80% of current marriages will not end in divorce; in these marriages, men have the opportunity to exercise various degrees of influence over their (they assume) immediate genetic investment.

Of those recent marriages which have already ended in divorce,

[3]Divorce statistics as used by the United States Bureau of the Census include divorces and annulments.

TABLE 26

Percentage of Ever-Married Persons Whose First and Second Marriages Have and Have Not Ended in Divorce, by Age and Gender, 1975 (U.S. Bureau of the Census, 1976b)

| Age of individual in 1975 | Percentage of ever-married persons whose first marriage, by 1975 | | | | Percentage of ever-married persons whose second marriage, by 1975 | | | |
| | Ended in divorce | | Did not end in divorce | | Ended in divorce | | Did not end in divorce | |
	Men	Women	Men	Women	Men	Women	Men	Women
26 to 30	13	17	87	83	5	8	95	92
31 to 35	17	20	83	80	6	12	94	88
36 to 40	20	21	80	79	5	10	95	90
41 to 45	18	21	82	79	8	11	92	89
46 to 50	18	21	82	79	7	14	93	86
51 to 55	18	18	82	82	9	8	91	92
56 to 60	17	16	83	84	9	11	91	89
61 to 65	17	16	83	84	7	10	93	90
66 to 70	15	15	85	85	7	9	93	91
71 to 75	13	13	87	87	6	5	94	95

approximately 40% involved no children under eighteen years of age (National Center for Health Statistics, 1960–1981).[4] This figure contrasts sharply with the 4.4% of married women 35–39 years of age who actually were childless. In addition, only 4.6% of married women 18–39 years of age expected to remain childless (U.S. Bureau of the Census, 1975, 1978). It is clear that 40% of the married women will not remain childless, nor, in the monogamous society of the United States, will 40% of the married men remain childless. The populations of men and women involved in divorces are accordingly neither physiologically sterile nor are they unwilling to have children; although a large proportion of the women will have children with men

---

[4]Of course there will be a number of women who will divorce after their youngest child reaches his or her eighteenth birthday. Consequently, as a baseline of comparison the 40% figure is necessarily a little inflated. Many of the mothers of these children would be at least forty years of age; this age bracket and those above it are well above the median age of first divorce (27.0 years), and represent very low fertility potentials. A man divorcing a woman in these age cohorts therefore risks only a small chance of losing additional genetic investment with that woman.

TABLE 27
Percentage Distribution of Divorces and Annulments by Number of Children (National Center for Health Statistics 1960–1982)[a]

Year	Number of children reported					
	0	1	2	3	4	5 or more
1978	44.3	25.4	19.5	7.4	2.3	1.0
1975	42.9	25.5	18.9	8.0	3.0	1.6
1972	39.9	25.6	18.9	9.0	4.0	2.6
1969	39.4	23.5	18.6	10.1	4.9	3.6
1966	39.7	22.8	18.2	10.4	5.3	3.6
1963	38.4	23.9	18.7	10.7	5.0	3.4
1960	43.3	23.0	17.4	9.7	4.0	2.6

[a]Adapted from Mackey (1980).

other than the ones that they have just divorced. The proportion of childless divorces has remained stable since at least 1960 with fluctuations between years averaging less than 2%. See Table 27.

Using the 1978 data as an example, childless divorces represent 44.3% of all divorces. This number (0) is also the modal figure, and although the *mean* number of children per divorce is greater than one, the *median* number of children per divorce is less than one—approximately 0.25. Over two-thirds of the divorces involved either no children or one child under 18 years of age. The 0.25 figure is obviously far below the 2.0 figure representing replacement value, and even farther below the 2.2 figure which, at the societal level, currently represents zero population growth. United States men are thereby typically leaving behind one family situation to develop another with potentially more children; few of their genes are left behind with the older families.[5] In the new families they can again father offspring, and thereby increase the number of their own genes in the next

[5]Some comment should be made on parental desertion theories, for example, those of Grafen and Sibly (1978) and Trivers (1972). Three factors preclude an easy assimilation of the data base, as presented here on divorce, with parental desertion theories: (1) the percentage of deserting fathers is low, and the disentanglement of exceptions-to-rules from examples-of-rules becomes difficult; (2) many of the theoretical models assume an imbalanced sex-ratio, and such is not the case in the United States; and (3) the sex-ratio models depend on "other things being equal," but, quite understandably, the models do not specify the character or magnitude of the important variables to be held constant in a human sociocultural environment.

generation. In other words, the cost is typically low in leaving (or being left), while the benefit is potentially high.

Of some relevance is age distribution in marital histories: the current median age of first marriage for women is 21.6 years; for the men the figure is 23.4 years—a difference of 1.8 years. The median age of the second marriage for women is 31.5 years; for men the figure is 35.3 years—a difference of 3.4 years, nearly twice the differential of first marriage (Department of Commerce, 1983).

As marital histories of men and women unfold, the United States men in second marriages marry women of increasingly greater youth than themselves. Because the age of highest actual childbearing for females in recent decades has been in the 20–29 year range (see Table 28), the closer to her early twenties that the bride is, the greater the opportunity the groom has to father more children.

Of some importance is the relationship between the women's age at divorce and their relative chances of remarrying. The younger a divorcee is, the higher the probability of her remarriage. This relationship is only marginally influenced by the number of children she has had by a previous marriage; by far the more important variable is her age. Of women 14 to 29 years of age at the time of their divorce, 76.3% eventually remarried; approximately 75% of these women with children remarried. Of the women 30 to 39 years of age at the time of divorce, 56.2% remarried; nearly 55% of these women with children remarried. At 40 to 49 years of age at time of divorce, 32.4% of the women remarried; almost 34% of these women with children remarried. At 50 to 75 years of age at the time of divorce, only 11.5% of the women remarried; remarriage rates by number of children is unavailable for this age bracket (U.S. Bureau of Census, 1977; see Table 29).

It is clear that some men are marrying women who have borne the children of other men. Although these new grooms are in the awkward Darwinian or genetic position of helping to nurture another man's genes, it is important to repeat that the percentage of these men is relatively small. It is also important to note that any theory, experiment, or strategy is going to have exceptions or error variance. In the genetic roulette of natural selection some maladapted combinations are surely going to occur; just as in the social roulette of marriage some very bad choices can occur. As will be presented in Chapter 8, an emergence of a new social or ecological environment may occur in which previously maladapted combinations may prove to

TABLE 28

Live Births in the United States by Age of Mother, 1975 (National Center for Health Statistics 1960–1975)

| | Total live births (in 1000s) | Age of mother in years | | | | | | | |
		Less than 15	15–19	20–24	25–29	30–34	35–39	40–44	45 and over
Total	3,145	12	582	1094	937	376	116	27	1
Percentage	100.0	0.4	18.5	34.8	29.8	12.0	3.7	0.8	0.0
Cumulative percentage		0.4	18.8	53.7	83.5	95.5	99.2	100.0	100.0

TABLE 29
Rates of Remarriage by Women (with 0 to 5 Children) Whose First Marriage Ended in Divorce (U.S. Bureau of the Census, 1977)[a]

| Age at divorce | Women 14 to 75 years; percentage remarried | Number of children born before divorce | | | | | |
		None	1	2	3	4	5 or more
Total	66.0	72.8	69.9	63.1	55.9	53.4	51.8
14 to 29 years	76.3	79.6	75.0	74.9	71.5	77.5	*
30 to 39 years	56.2	59.7	62.1	56.1	49.9	50.7	54.3
40 to 49 years	32.4	32.8	39.0	31.8	30.8	34.4	*
50 to 75 years	11.5	*	*	*	*	*	*

*Too few cases for analysis.
[a]Adapted from Mackey, 1980.

have been preadapted and thereby quite competitive in the new circumstances.

Table 30 illustrates that divorced men have consistently had higher rates of remarriage than have divorced women; divorced women who tend to remain unmarried are the older, less fertile women. Two previous points are worth restating here: (1) the median age of remarriage is older for men than for women; and (2) the 20–29 year age bracket is the interval of highest fecundity for women. Older divorced women (with or without children from a previous marriage) have a relatively lower rate of remarriage; these older women are also those in the less fecund categories. In the unromantic terms of increased fitness, marrying these women is not a good strategy, and such a strategy is not pursued often by United States men.

Following the lead of first marriages, second marriages do not

TABLE 30
Percentages of People Who Did and Did Not Remarry after First Divorce

| Age in years | Percentage remarried | | Percentage not remarried | |
	Men	Women	Men	Women
31 to 35	75.1	64.4	24.9	35.6
41 to 45	78.1	69.7	21.9	30.3
51 to 55	83.0	73.5	17.0	26.5
61 to 65	85.6	81.2	14.4	18.8
71 to 75	89.3	78.0	10.7	22.0

usually end in divorce. The remarried man thus has another opportunity to raise and to nurture his own children, who are carrying his genes. Nevertheless, some remarriages will end in divorce (see Table 26). The median age at second divorce is 37.5 years for women but less than 5% of all children born are born to women 37 years of age or older (see Table 28). Given these trends, a reasonable, if not socially applauded strategy for a married male's improved Darwinian success might include the following:

1. My wife has probably borne all the children that she will have.
2. The children of mine that my wife has already borne are of sufficient development to survive physically and to compete successfully for mates without large doses of my paternal time, energy, and resources.[6]
3. Hence, a divorce from my functionally sterile wife and a remarriage to a younger, more fertile female would be a genetically beneficial venture. Little is lost in an inclusive fitness sense, and much perhaps is to be gained.

That social sanction and pressures exist which temper the overt verbalization and actualization of such strategies in massive numbers would hardly seem surprising. One's curiosity would be pricked by the results of an investigation into the origin and maintenance of the social sanctions surrounding the lucid articulation of such ideas and motivations. Nonetheless, that such behaviors do occur is a fact; even though the stated or tacit motivations for them may be quite different from the one entertained here. September to May marriages are real events.

SUMMARY

Although rapidly increasing divorce rates in the United States and maximized paternal genetic investment seem mutually exclusive, the form and logistical modes of male marital and procreative patterns seem to be adjusting and accommodating to other institutions,

---

[6]It is of more than passing interest that high education, high income, and high socioeconomic status are all associated with low fertility (Kenkel, 1977; *Who's Who*, 1980). If a coldly calculating Machiavellian man were truly dedicated to maximizing his chances for the maximum number of grandchildren, he would not optimize for his own offspring the socially approved values of education, income, and status.

emerging philosophies, and *causes célèbres*. It appears that the current crop of United States men are not, in fact, examples of Darwinian ineptness; they are at least holding their own, and are perhaps exercising very adequate strategies.

For example, if a cadre of 100 typical married men are selected and the course of their probable marital histories is followed, the distribution of categories would occur as follows (see Figure 4): 60 to 80 men will not be divorced from their wives and can thereby nurture their own children to adulthood. This majority is exercising sound judgment in terms of genetic theories; there is no fault in that strategy. For those 20 to 40 men who will divorce, two-thirds (13 to 27) of their divorces will *not* involve two or more children, that is, genetic replacement for the males. The men are therefore not deserting a total complement of their genes which requires nurturance. Approximately 85% of the divorced men (17 to 34) can be expected to remarry, and 13 to 25 of these remarriages can be expected to avoid divorce. It is difficult to find genetic fault with this strategy.

Four to nine divorced men will remarry and redivorce. Some of these men will remarry again, probably to a younger, hence more fertile woman. No fault can be found there. Some of these twice divorced men will stay unmarried. If their children are viable and socially competent, the men sacrifice nothing in the way of their genetic investment. If the desertion by a man and the loss of paternal aid and comfort lessens the viability or competence of the man's children, the strategy is a poor one. This potentially poor strategy, however, affects only a small percentage of men.

Three to six divorced men will not remarry. Because the median age of first divorce for men is 29.1 years, whereas for women it is 27.0 years, the abdication of paternal nurturance toward any young children may be of some import in light of the probability that the men will not sire any more children. The young father leaves his children to the wiles of fortune, but is not expected to have any more children; when this happens, the strategy is a poor one. The percentage of men to which the above scenario applies, however, is also very small.

Because detailed statistics on individual men are unavailable, a direct quantified test of their adequacy, as defined here, is also unavailable; nevertheless, an inferred analysis is available: the United States crude birth rate has been and still is higher than the crude death rate. As of 1976, the latest figures available to me, women were expecting in excess of 2 births per female. Hence, replacement has

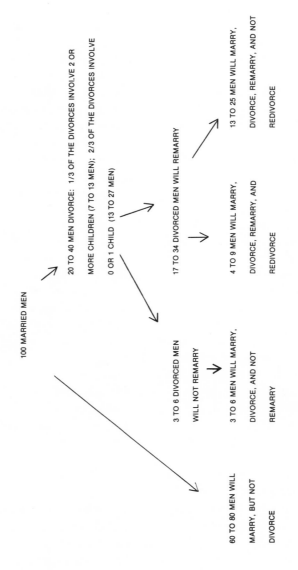

100 MARRIED MEN

20 TO 40 MEN DIVORCE: 1/3 OF THE DIVORCES INVOLVE 2 OR

MORE CHILDREN (7 TO 13 MEN); 2/3 OF THE DIVORCES INVOLVE

0 OR 1 CHILD (13 TO 27 MEN)

17 TO 34 DIVORCED MEN WILL REMARRY

13 TO 25 MEN WILL MARRY,

DIVORCE, REMARRY, AND NOT

REDIVORCE

4 TO 9 MEN WILL MARRY,

DIVORCE, REMARRY, AND

REDIVORCE

3 TO 6 DIVORCED MEN

WILL NOT REMARRY

3 TO 6 MEN WILL MARRY,

DIVORCE, AND NOT

REMARRY

60 TO 80 MEN WILL

MARRY, BUT NOT

DIVORCE

FIGURE 4. Probable marital histories for 100 married men

been and is occurring and is expected to continue (U.S. Bureau of the Census, 1978). Furthermore, as described above, only 7 to 13% of the married men divorce and leave behind their replacement value (two or more children). The odds are strong that many of these men will remarry and avoid a second divorce. Consequently, the overall corporate strategy enacted, though most assuredly not premeditated, *at a minimum*, is competent:

1. Most men remain with their wives and children.
2. Most men who do divorce from their wives do not leave behind genetic replacement to be nurtured without their influence.
3. Most men who divorce will remarry and then remain with the new spouse and any subsequent children.
4. Most remarriages for men are to younger, hence more fertile, females.
5. Most redivorces by men occur with women who are at an age at which very few children are born.

That there is not a perfect, mathematically exact congruence between genetic theory and empirical reality is not a cause for undue vexation. Human behavior patterns obviously are affected by great numbers and various kinds of influences, at a number of different conceptual levels. No one explanatory mechanism could realistically be expected to account for massive portions of the variance for any behavior pattern, especially a complex social pattern which is subject to many short-term influences. In addition, measuring instruments still lack perfect sensitivity, and countermaneuvers by subjects arise for a multitude of reasons, people forget, for instance, and they will occasionally confound surveys and surveyors, even those from the census department.

With the certainty of the changing seasons, other interpretations of the same data base are always available from other social scientists both within and across disciplines. These alternate perspectives are of course necessary to give depth, texture, and perspective to the very human phenomenon of divorce. Sociologists, anthropologists, psychologists, and family therapists each can lend insights through the different microscopes. These added dimensions will be complementary to the view presented here which allows an evolutionary theory to be supported by empirically derived data.

CHAPTER 5

The Plowman–Protector Complex

This chapter reviews the data from the project through the filter of a conventional view of culture: that is, the values and attitudes and habits passed from one generation to another via the socialization process. The data in question are the proxemic indexes that reflected variations in the size and gender composition of adult–child groups across the 18 culture sample. These indexes include:

1. The preferential association of men toward boys (rather than girls)
2. The proportion of children (associating with adults) who were with groups of men and women
3. The tendency of man–child dyads to associate with other men rather than with women
4. The tendency of woman–child dyads to associate with other women rather than with men
5. The preferential association of women toward girls (rather than with boys)

The same data from Table 16 (Chapter 2) are repeated in Table 31.

There are three points that are of immediate interest and spring from the data in the table.

1. Systematic and mutual variation did occur.
2. The systematic variations did not include the woman–girl dyad that was relatively insensitive to changes in the other indices.

TABLE 31

Correlations (Pearson's Product Moment Correlation) among the Five Proxemic Indices:
18 Cultures, (MNP Time Intervals Only), from Table 16, Chapter 2

| Index | Percentage of children who are | | | | |
	Girls associating with women-only groups	Associating with groups of men and women	Women's Plural Group Score (WPGS)	Men's Plural Group Score (MPGS)
Percentage of children who are boys associating with men-only groups	−.334	−.722***	−.562*	−.690**
Percentage of children who are girls associating with women-only groups	—	+.224	−.135	+.141
Percentage of children associating with groups of men and women	—	—	+.774***	+.665**
Women's Plural Group Score	—	—	—	+.518*

*p < .05; **p < .01; ***p < .001; two-tailed.

3. Just as in the chapters in which a genetic or Darwinian theory was necessary to hold together otherwise diffuse data, there is also a need for a cultural theory to give coherence to these figures.

Because the goal of this project is to look for some generalized processes stemming from both cultural and genetic sources, it seems a reasonable tactic to begin once again with a search for likely universals found cross-culturally and then to see if they could aid in lending unity to the data. Three universals come to mind which seem germane to this discussion and they include:

1. If a society engages in plow agriculture or the herding of large domesticates (oxen, cattle, camels), it is the male, as a class, who is invariably given charge of that task. The control of large domesticates, especially draft animals, is a male prerogative (Burton & Reitz, 1981; White, Burton, & Brudner, 1977; White, Burton, & Dow, 1981).
2. The status and role of armed combatant is a male prerogative. Men, rather than women, are the policeman and soldiers of the community of cultures. Isolate exceptions occur, of course, especially in the defense of a community (female Vietcong) or in exceptional individuals (Joan of Arc). Females also serve in logistic support of a campaign; however, when groups of soldiers leave the perimeter of a community to do battle, either in an offensive foray or as a physical deterrent, those soldiers are predictably male (Divale & Harris, 1976; Ember & Ember, 1971; Whyte, 1978).
3. The task of primary caretaker of young children, especially infants, is a female activity. Although the usual caretaker is the mother, if there are alternate or surrogate caretakers, they too are female. In an occasional culture, a young boy is under the supervision of men; but this is (a) relatively rare, (b) after infancy has passed, and (c) restricted to boys only (Barry, Josephson, Lauer, & Marshall, 1977; Barry & Paxson, 1971; Rohner & Rohner, 1982).

Earlier, in Chapters 2 and 3, it was suggested that the parenting template in men and women is relatively more sensitive to age than for gender. The data indicate that, in a basic sense, parents react more to the developmental status or the level of dependency of their children than to the children's gender. Said in another way, the starting point of parenting is egalitarianism. If all other variables are equal, then parents, both mothers and fathers, would respond very much alike to their sons and to their daughters.

Over three-quarters of a century of ethnographic research has incontrovertibly illustrated to the Western world that things across cultures are rarely equal. There are different ways to manage family networks, to organize social structures and politics, and to maintain an economic system and so on. The inventiveness of cultural types is remarkable and exploits a wide array of these options.

In the face of this variability, there are occasions when these groups of traits will cluster together in a predictable way. For example, Whiting (1964) offers evidence indicating that the ecology of a tropical climate generally is associated with a low level of protein available for consumption. The low level of protein is significantly correlated with a long post partum sex taboo. The long postpartum sex taboo in turn is significantly associated with a high level of polygyny, and, in one last linkage, high levels of polygyny are related with high incidences of patrilocality. In short, where one tends to find tropical environments is also the same sort of place where one expects to find patrilocality.

A second example: although men, across cultures, usually are in charge of housebuilding, women are occasionally the traditional housebuilders in a society. When females do construct houses, the women are usually collectors of small land fauna and wild vegetals. In addition, the women are also given the duties of preparing the vegetal foods (White, Burton, & Brudner, 1977).

A final example (from Burton & Reitz, 1981) finds that an increasing societal reliance on plow agriculture is associated with increased male participation in crop tending and a decreased participation in female crop tending, which is linked with increased tendencies toward monogamy and lessened tendencies toward polygyny.

On other occasions, cultures can resemble Brownian movements in their lack of predictability, for example, in syntax, kinship terminology, or relationships with the supernatural.

Because of the continuing awkwardness in attempting to explain a constant with a variable, the tactic used in this instance is also to take the less forboding task of trying to explain one constant with another constant, or to be more precise, to make some sense of one consistent with some knowledge of another consistent.

On one side of the ledger, we have cultural universals (constants or consistents) in the form of male prerogatives of being "soldiers" and in being "plowmen" plus the female prerogative of being primary child caretaker. On the other side of the ledger are the proxemic relationships from Table 31. The question then becomes: Can the two sets of phenomena be meaningfully integrated? This chapter attempts to make one such integration.

A number of authors have shown how the parts of any society are interrelated and tend to be mutually supportive. In their classic study, Barry, Bacon, and Child (1957) demonstrated an interdependence between socialization pressures and subsistence techniques. They showed that those societies which depended upon the males' superior strength to control large domesticates as part of their subsistence pattern also exerted differential socialization pressures on boys and girls. Their data indicated that girls, compared to boys, were expected to be more obedient, more responsible, and more nurturant. Boys were expected to be more achieving and more self-reliant. Barry, Child, and Bacon (1959) then showed the relationship between personality characteristics and the degree to which food accumulation was important in societies' economies. The more that the economy was based on accumulating and keeping food (e.g., herding), the more that the society stressed responsibility and obedience in socializing children (both girls and boys). Working from the other pole, the less that the economy depended on accumulating food (e.g., hunting), the more that the society stressed individual achievement and self-reliance or independence for children (again for boys and for girls). The kind of subsistence economy can therefore be linked to a gestalt of personality characteristics which, in turn, can be linked to socialization pressures immersing the developing children to forge the culturally appropriate gestalt.

The project presented here attempts to add one additional link to that concatenation. It will be suggested that not only do ecological parameters make some values and socialization pressures more useful than others within that ecology, but that these values and socialization pressures, reflecting the ecological conditions, also result in predictable proxemic patterns. More specifically, it is argued that selected societal variables are correlated with culturally defined gender roles and that these roles eventuate in systematic modes of proxemic behavior.

SOCIETAL VARIABLES: THE PLOWMAN–PROTECTOR COMPLEX

Given that there is a moderate or substantial societal dependence on the male's brute strength in controlling large animals, through plowing or herding, this dependence would translate into differential socialization patterns for boys and girls (Barry, Bacon, & Child, 1957; Cone, 1979). In other words, the relative dependence of a society on plowmen or herders for subsistence would affect different expectations for appropriate or model behaviors for girls and for boys.

The other status that is gender specific and must be socialized appropriately is that of active combatant or soldier/policeman. As a consequence of this male prerogative, growing boys have to be presented with the status of protector, and they then have to internalize successfully that status–role complex into their own psychoemotional identity. If the status–role complex of protector is effectively taught and is adequately learned, then, in the event that the family or community should need a physical deterrence from any potential aggression, it will be males who would be culturally prescribed to provide that deterrence. The more effectively that learning process has occurred, the more dependable will be the male's response to offer life and limb.

The actual or impending needs of a society to protect itself from internal mayhem and from external threat varies considerably (Kania & Mackey, 1977). That is, the threat of violence or social conflict, either from within a society via feuding families, lineages, or clans, or from aggression by another society is not distributed evenly across cultures. Some areas of the globe are relatively benign; others are dangerous indeed. As the felt need for active physical deterrence increases, the need to socialize males into soldiers or policemen would also increase. If domestic tranquility prevails and the borders are relatively immune from outside aggression, then a society would have minimal need to mold and infuse growing boys into the mindset of a warrior.

Therefore, two dimensions become relevant here: (1) the variable needs of a society to socialize its boys into plowmen or herdsmen; and (2) the variable needs of a society to socialize its boys into protectors. When both statuses are discussed together, they will be referred to as the *Plowman–Protector Complex*. An alternate label entitled the *Dumb Ox Factor* was suggested by a close affinal relative of the author. This suggestion was taken into advisement but eventually not accepted.

When these two continua intersect each other, four polar categories become available for analysis. Some societies may have high need of plowmen and protectors. Other societies may have low need for plowmen and protectors. Additional societies may have high need for one dimension, but a low need for the other dimension: pugnacious horticulturalists or pacifistic camel drivers. The presentation below argues that the various combinations of the two variables, working through the socialization process, will reflect predictable sets of proxemic patterns.

It might be noted that these two dimensions are not trivial attributes of a society. There are few events that are more fundamental or vital to a society than feeding itself and protecting itself from aggression within its own boundaries as well as outside them. Thus, the development and maintenance of competent plowmen–protectors for any society can be of pivotal importance to its long term survival. To help optimize the systematic development of continuing generations of plowmen–protectors, the institutionalized socialization of children would be incorporated into the other components of the social structure. A derivative of this integration is the asymmetrical division of labor by gender. As a class, males are plowman–protectors, and females, as a class, are not. For an appropriate achievement and integration of these gender specific traits within a society, attitudinal adjustments and readjustments, followed by behavioral modifications, will arise and ripple throughout the other components of the society.

For those societies with minimal reliance upon large animals and with minimal social friction or continuing conflict, either from within or without, differential responses by adults to boys and girls would be less intrusive or pervasive. The more the social structure of a culture reflects both (1) friction or violence among groups and (2) a substantial reliance upon large domesticates for subsistence (e.g., agriculture with the plow), the less egalitarian would be the behavior of adults to boys and to girls. For a more detailed account of relationships among social structure, subsistence technique, and ecology, see Ember and Ember (1971), Divale and Harris (1976), Harris (1979), Katz and Konner (1981), D'Andrade (1966), and Murdock and Provost (1973).

In contrast, the less a society relies on the plow or large domesticates, and on an imminent deterrence, the more that adults would treat boys and girls in an egalitarian manner. In this way an increased emphasis on the statuses of plowman–protector would be associated with decreased egalitarianism of adult to children. Framed in another way, the potential or actual societal conflict and the opportunities to handle large animals tend to result in different responses from men/women to boys/girls by separating men from girls and women from boys. Conversely, the removal of an emphasis on plowmen–protectors simultaneously allows adults to associate with and to respond to children in a manner regardless of gender.

Sample

An additional word is in order at this point about the 18 cultures in the sample. The 18 cultures are not independent entities, and they cannot be conceptualized as naturally occurring units. Rather, they are meant to be viewed as diagnostic units. From this perspective, they do not fulfill the rigorous standards which are utilized in cross-cultural research based on data in the *World Ethnographic Sample*, the *Ethnographic Atlas*, or the the *Human Relations Area File*. The sample of 18 cultures is derived in part from political boundaries, and, of course, other criteria are available to develop samples, for example, language and kinship (Naroll, 1973, 1971, 1970; Naroll, Michik, & Naroll, 1980). A consensus among cross-culturalists in regard to the appropriate configuration of a natural unit of culture has not yet been reached. The work by Moore (1961) gives a good historical view on the dialogue concerning cross-cultural analyses.

The data for this project were gathered in the latter quarter of the twentieth century. The people who were surveyed had lost cultural isolation decades, if not centuries, ago. Cultural diffusion, accelerated by electronic communication and the airplane, makes any attempt to separate, in contemporary societies, the independent invention of a process from the borrowing of a process, a hopelessly confounded quagmire. Galton's Problem, the term given to the dilemma of divining independent invention (functional relationships) from cultural diffusion (historical relationships), becomes not problematic, but a guarantee. Solutions to Galton's problem have been offered by a series of authors (Naroll, 1964, 1973; Rohner *et al.*, 1978; Witkowski, 1974). However, these solutions are primarily predicated upon data which are from compilations of ethnographies (e.g., *World Ethnographic Sample, Ethnographic Atlas,* and the *Human Relations Area File*). From these data banks, researchers can select samples of cultures which, at the time of analysis, were operating independently from contact with each other.

By the last quarter of the twentieth century, Western technology had altered or obliterated nearly all of the preliterate cultures. Whether this success has been a "good" or a "bad" happenstance may be a matter of discussion. That the character of Western technology has become pervasive is now simply a matter of description.

Definitions and Ranking Procedures

The procedure for ranking the 18 cultures in relationship to the plowman–protector complex was as follows. Each culture's referent population was placed into one of the cells of a 3 × 3 array. The placing was determined by the percentage of the labor force—divided into thirds—engaged in plow agriculture in the presence of large animals and by the relative social homogeneity of the immediate milieu. See Table 32. The 18 cultures were then ranked from 1–18 along the two separate dimensions: (1) percentage of labor force engaged in plow agriculture in the presence of large animals and (2) relative social homogeneity of the immediate social environment. The percentage of the labor force engaged in agriculture for each nation and reliance on large animals was obtained from the *Worldmark Encyclopedia of Nations,* the Department of State *Background Notes,* and were supplemented by the *World Ethnographic Sample* and the *Ethnographic Atlas.* The data from the Brazilian samples and on the Karaja Indians were supplied from George Donahue's fieldnotes.

To determine the reliance on men as protector, the relative de-

TABLE 32

Rankings of 18 Cultures by Homogeneity of Referent Population and by Percentage of the Labor Force of the Referent Population Engaged in Agriculture in the Presence of Large Animals; the Numbers Refer to the Ranks (1–18)

Plowman/Herder Index	Protector/Soldier Index[a]		
	Homogeneous referent population	Moderately homogeneous/ heterogeneous referent population	Heterogeneous referent population
Percentage of the labor force engaged in agriculture with large domesticates present			
67%–100%	7 Brazil (rural) 8 Taiwan (rural)	3 Sri Lanka (rural) 4 India 5 Morocco	1 Israel (kibbutzim)[b] 2 Ivory Coast
34%–66%	11 Brazil (urbanizing)	6 Mexico	9 Senufo
0–33%	13 Spain 14 Ireland 15 Hong Kong 16 Reykjavik, Iceland 17 Japan 18 Karaja	10 Lima, Peru 12 United States	

[a]A population from the referent culture is considered homogeneous if 90% or more of the population has the same group affiliation. A population is considered moderately homogeneous/heterogeneous if there are two or more groups with different affiliations and the largest group includes between 35% and 89% of the total population. A population is considered heterogeneous if there are three or more groups with different affiliations and the largest group has no more than 34% of the population.
[b]Because Israel, at the time of the survey, was involved in chronic episodes of active armed conflict, Israel's protector index was elevated accordingly.

gree of ethnic homogeneity of the group was analyzed. The rationale for this procedure was that, as tensions arise in a community, one of the earliest fractures is along ethnic group membership. When the fractures occur, the men of the community insert themselves symbolically and physically and are inserted by cultural pressures, at the interface of the various ethnic groups. Their presence serves primarily as a deterrent response; yet active defense and revenge is available for counterresponses.

The more ethnic heterogeneity within the population, the greater is the emphasis on the men of each group to assume the posture of protector. Although in a more homogeneous society different ethnic affiliation is not available, less emphasis will be needed to be placed on the role of protector. To be sure, such other fractures as religious and economic splits can occur in any society. However, ethnic affiliations are considered here to be more sensitive to social tensions than other divisions with a society. During times of stress, ethnic divisions are envisioned to be among the first to cleave societies.

For example, in the United States the relative ethnic homogeneity of states varies considerably. Some states are extremely homogeneous by ethnic affiliation, for example, New Hampshire. Other states are highly hetereogeneous, for example, Hawaii. The states can be ranked by degree of homogeneity/heterogeneity. The States can also be ranked by number of crimes reported (from data in the FBI's Uniform Crime Reports, 1980).

Using 1980 population figures, states were ranked by homogeneity/heterogeneity of their ethnic composition, and by crime rates for rape, property crime, and violent crime (minus rape). To be included in this analysis, states had to have 90% or more of their adminstrative units reporting to the FBI. Both Standard Metropolitan Areas (SMSAs) and rural areas were compared across states. Hence, six categories were available for analysis (3 categories of crime × types of loci). All six indexes showed a significant negative correlation between degree of homogeneity and rate of crime. That is, as ethnic homogeneity increased, crime rates decreased. Table 33.

Two points are needed here, The first is that in the United States, violent crime is a male, especially young male, phenomenon. For the 1980 figures, which are fairly typical, 87% of those arrested for violent crimes were male; 99% of the arrests for rape were arrests of males;

TABLE 33
Correlations between the Ethnic Homogeneity[a] across the United States[b] and
Crime Rates (per 100,000 Population): by Rural and SMSA Loci
(FBI: UCR, 1980)

Type of crime					
Violent crime (minus rape)		Property crime		Rape	
SMSA[c] $n = 47$	Rural[c] $n = 40$	SMSA $n = 47$	Rural $n = 40$	SMSA $n = 47$	Rural $n = 40$
−.382*	−.340*	−.315*	−.572***	−.378**	−.373*

$*p < .05;\ **p < .01;\ ***p < .001;$ (two-tailed).
[a]Homogeneity was determined by taking the percentage of the largest ethnic group in the state and then ranking the percentages. With the exception of the District of Columbia in which the largest ethnic group is black, the referent ethnic group for the other cases was white.
[b]Including the District of Columbia. Note that for a state to be included in the sample, the state had to have 90% or better of the administrative units reporting. For Alaska, not having any SMSA's, other cities were used.
[c]SMSA data and rural data are compiled separately in the Uniform Crime Reports, and not all states have a sufficient number of rural residents to be included. Consequently different ns are available for the two variables.

and 79% of the arrests for property crime were also male (FBI, UCR, 1980). The second point is that most crime occurs within ethnic groups (LaFree, 1982; Radelet, 1981). For 1980, over 92% of the murders where the ethnic affiliation of the assailant was known involved instances in which the ethnic affiliation of the assailant and the victim was the same (Kleck, 1981). Because the preponderance of crime is within ethnic groups, the increasing heterogeneity of a community is not necessarily increasing cross-ethnic mayhem. What may be more likely is that males are sensitized to increased social friction and tension and react to that increase within their own immediate social environment.

Even though the measuring instrument of crime rates did detect trends, it is still rather coarse and lacking in subtlety. The sensitivities of the referent ethnic communities, however, are probably not coarse but are keenly alert to dangers and problems in their own day-to-day lives. Men, often young, are thereby relied on for deterrence against the actions of other males. The young men are not only to meet what threatens but also what may be feared to arise and to threaten. The

community's men can take the form of officially sanctioned policemen or of the kinsmen—fathers, brothers, sons, uncles or the
more general: "our menfolk."

The ethnic group descriptions from the *Worldmark Encyclopedia of
Nations* (1976) were presented to seven independent raters. The countries were rated as either homogeneous, moderately homoge-
neous/heterogeneous, or heterogeneous. There was 97% agreement
between raters with $r = .99$. For ten of the cultures, ethnic affiliation
was the basis for the determination of homogeneity. For an additional
culture, India, religious affiliation is more salient than either language
or ethnic affiliation, and was the criterion used for ranking. Subsequent societies were selected for their particularistic ethnic composition.

Definitions

Homogeneous Culture.   A population from the referent culture is
considered homogeneous if 90% or more of the population was the
same group affiliation.

Moderately Homogeneous/Heterogeneous Culture.   A population is
considered moderately homogeneity/heterogeneous if there were
two or more groups with different affiliations and the largest group
includes between 35% and 89% of the total population.

Heterogeneous Culture.   A population is considered heterogeneous if there were three or more groups with different affiliations
and the largest group had no more than 34% of the population.

For each culture, the scores from the two rankings were added.
In the summing of the two rankings, the problem of weighting arises.
That is, when the final combined index was constructed, should a
culture's ranking on the plowman dimension have more or less or the
same impact as a culture's ranking on the protector dimension? Preliminary data and a conservative theoretical approach both indicated
that giving equal weight to the plowman rank and to the protector
rank was the more proper course to assume. Subsequent to the collection and analysis of the data, the results suggested that the variables,
as defined in this study, did not have equal weight in impacting on
each of the dependent variables. Whereas the plowman and protector
variables were of approximately equal influence on two of the dependent variables, the variable plowman contributed more influence on

TABLE 34
*Procedure for Ranking the 18 Cultures in Relation to the
Plowman–Protector Complex*

Culture	Plowman rank	Protector rank	Summed rank	Final rank
Israel	2.5	1	3.5	1
Ivory Coast	5	2.5	7.5	2
Sri Lanka	2.5	7	9.5	3
India	6	6	12	4
Morocco	7	8	15	5
Mexico	8	5	13	6
Brazil—rural	2.5	11.5	14	7
Taiwan	2.5	13.5	16	8
Senufo	17	2.5	19.5	9
Lima, Peru	10	4	14	10
Brazil—urbanizing	9	11.5	20.5	11
Virginia, U.S.A.	14	9	23	12
Spain	12	10	22	13
Ireland	11	15	26	14
Hong Kong	16	13.5	29.5	15
Reykjavik, Iceland	13	17	30	16
Japan	15	16	31	17
Karaja	18	18	36	18

the remaining two variables. See Appendix Table 1. A recalibration of the correlations based on the weighted figures did not substantially change the level of relationships (e.g., from $-.647$ to $-.660$, both $p <$ .001, and from $+.438$ to $+.386$, both $p < .05$).

The combined scores from the Plowman–Protector index provided the basis for ranking cultures within cells and for ranking cultures in cells equidistant from the polar categories, for example, a cell which is high in plowman but low in protector (Taiwan) is conceptually the same distance from High-Plowman and High-Protector or from Low-Plowman and Low-Protector as would be a cell which is moderate in plowman and moderate in protector (Mexico). See Table 34 for the rankings of the 18 cultures.

RESULTS

The rankings of the 18 cultures on the Plowman–Protector dimensions were compared to the other five ranked variables (Table 35)

TABLE 35

Rankings of the 18 Cultures by the Plowman–Protector Complex Index and the Four Proxemic Indexes
(from MNP Time Intervals only)

Culture	Ranking of Plowman–Protector index	Ranked percentages of children who were											
		Boys associating with men-only groups		Girls associating with women-only groups		Associating with groups of men and women		Ranking of Women's Plural Group Score (WPGS)		Ranking of Men's Plural Group Score (MPGS)	
		Rank	Percentage	Rank	Percentage	Rank	Percentage	Rank	Percentage	Rank	Percentage
Israel	1	12	60.0	7	56.2	18	14.6	12	65.2	15	84.0
Ivory Coast	2	1	77.4	2	61.0	15	15.2	18	47.7	16	83.7
Sri Lanka	3	5	70.0	16	51.9	16	14.8	16	52.6	14	85.6
India	4	11	60.6	11	53.8	12	28.5	8	73.6	11	87.7
Morocco	5	4	71.8	12	53.7	17	14.7	17	49.8	18	81.1
Mexico	6	6	69.7	5	59.4	8	35.6	10.5	67.8	8.5	92.6
Brazil—rural	7	3	73.1	4	59.6	13	22.9	14	56.8	12	87.5
Taiwan	8	10	61.5	17	49.6	14	19.2	13	62.2	6	94.5
Senufo	9	7	66.7	8.5	54.8	7	37.5	9	70.2	17	81.8
Lima, Peru	10	9	62.7	6	56.3	10	30.4	15	54.8	3	98.0
Brazil—urbanizing	11	2	77.3	10	54.5	11	29.2	10.5	67.8	13	86.3
United States	12	14	58.9	8.5	54.8	5	39.0	5	76.3	8.5	92.6
Spain	13	16	50.6	15	52.4	1	51.7	2	83.3	10	92.1
Ireland	14	15	56.8	3	60.6	4	40.6	3	82.3	4	95.6
Hong Kong	15	17	45.2	13	53.5	3	47.0	6	74.6	1	100.0
Reykjavik	16	8	65.1	14	52.7	9	31.4	4	80.9	7	93.4
Japan	17	13	59.6	18	46.7	6	38.8	1	88.8	5	95.2
Karaja	18	18	32.1	1	73.0	2	50.9	7	74.5	2	98.8

TABLE 36
Correlations (Kendall's Tau) among the Plowman–Protector Complex Index and
the Five Proxemic Indexes: 18 Cultures

| | Percentage of children who are | | | Plural Group Scores | |
| | Boys associating with men-only groups | Girls associating with women-only groups | Associating with groups of men and women | Women's (WPGS) | Men's (MPGS) |
Index					
Plowman–Protector	+.438*	+.090	−.647***	−.601***	−.555*
Plowman only	+.406*	−.013	−.667***	−.447**	−.375*
Protector only	+.264	+.183	−.330	−.410*	−.437*

*$p < .05$; **$p < .01$; ***$p < .001$; two-tailed.

and the following relationships resulted from the correlations between the Plowman–Protector Complex and the other five proxemic indices. See Table 36.

1. The Plowman–Protector Complex and the percentage of children who were boys associating with men-only groups.

   As the Plowman–Protector Index increased, there was an increased percentage of boys (rather than girls) associating with men-only groups ($r = +.438$; $p < .05$).

2. The Plowman–Protector Complex and the Percentage of children who were girls associating with women-only groups.

   As the Plowman–Protector Index increased, there was no discernable tendency for women to increase or decrease their proportions of association with girls or with boys ($r = +.090$; $p > .05$).

3. The Plowman–Protector Complex and the Percentage of children (associating with adults) who were with groups of men and women.

   As the Plowman–Protector Index increased, the proportion of children associating with adults who were with groups of men and women decreased ($r = −.647$; $p < .001$).

4. The Plowman–Protector Complex and the Women's Plural Group Score (WPGS).

   As the Plowman–Protector index increased, the more that woman–child dyads tended to associate with other women rather than with men ($r = −.601$; $p < .001$).

On the other side of the coin, as a society manifested little or minimal reliance on the male's brute strength advantage, the more women and children gravitated toward men and less toward other women.

5. The Plowman–Protector Complex and the Men's Plural Group Score (MPGS).

As the Plowman–Protector index increased, the more that man–child dyads tended to associate with other men rather than with women ($r = -.555$; $p < .05$). Analogous to the dynamics of the WPGS, it is predictable that if men are not overtly called on to perform traditional male roles, the more men and children will be with women rather than with other men.

It is of interest that the mean MPGS for the entire 18 culture sample was 90.6% ($sd = 6.0\%$). This figure was substantially and significantly larger than the corresponding WPGS mean which was 68.3% ($sd = 12.2$) ($t = 6.76$; $p < .01$; $df = 17$). This differential between MPGS and WPGS is translated to indicate that man–child groups are much more likely to associate with women (rather than other men) when compared to woman–child dyads and their likelihood to associate with men (rather than with other women). Men who are operating in a parenting manner rarely do so in contiguity with other men— but are more willing to do so when with a woman. When women are exercising their parenting role, they seem to prefer to do so with men, but are amenable to be with other women.

Theory: The Man–Child Bond as a Social Barometer

The proffered theory which is suggested to lend coherence to the data is thus: even though mens' basic parenting template is relatively more sensitive to the age of their children than to the gender of their children, cultural adaptations and adjustments to ecological parameters may necessitate emphases on brute strength, quick expenditure of energy, and uninterrupted concentration—fighting and plowing are two such tasks. Men are more available for such tasks than are women. See Maclachlan (1983) for a complementary perspective on gender role allocation.

To help socialize boys into these men-only tasks, the genders are treated differently. Part of the socialization process is to separate physically the genders in public places, especially keeping men apart from their little girls.

Accordingly, in public places, men associate preferentially with their sons rather than with their daughters and men reduce their associations with women–child dyads. Remember that in man, woman, and child triads, boys and girls tend to be equally represented (See Table 9; Chapter 2). Consequently, the reduction of man, woman, and child triads effectively reduces man–girl associations. The simultaneous reduction of man, woman, and boy triads is countered by the increase of the men's preferential association with boys rather than girls ($r = -.722$; $p < .001$).

The woman–child dyads, pulled by cultural "rules" from men, do not remain isolate, but fill the social gap with another woman. To a lesser extent, the man–child dyad, which is pulled from women, will tend to associate with other men.

The female as the universal primary child caretaker is culturally charged with the early care of children—boys and girls. Hence, she will be with both genders of children irrespective of and insulated from other processes occurring within her society.

It is the man–child bond which is more the litmus paper for societal dynamics.

So, as service economies in the world begin to become more popular and machines take the place of muscles and draft animals, it is suggested that the more the male's egalitarian parenting template will also increasingly emerge and assert itself. The cultural superstructure and dynamics which had pushed it from its original point of equilibrium would have removed themselves. New cultural norms would then be expected to track after the changing male behavior patterns. These new norms would declare the appropriateness and expectations of a more egalitarian treatment of his little boys and his little girls. The new norms would become evident after the behavior shifts have occurred, not before.

If the need for policemen and soldiers would become reduced, an additional pressure militating against egalitarian parenting would also be removed thereby more allowing men and girls the opportunity to enjoy the pleasure of each other's company.

The American Adult Male–Child Dyad

In contemporary American society, there can exist a triangulation of three sets of phenomena that describe any observable behavior pattern: (1) a symbolic or myth system referenced by the behavior, (2) a scientific paradigm, with variable levels of consensus, and (3) the actual behaviors themselves. The purpose of this chapter is to examine the correspondence among the symbolic image of the American male (as a father), the generalized paradigm of the United States father figure, and some available field data on how males actually interact with children. First a shift in paradigms will be examined which occurred in the mid-1970s and resulted in a change in the perspective of how fathers are viewed in our society. The initial perspective included an image of bumbling, irrelevance, and ineffectiveness when men were functioning in a paternal nurturing role and changed to an image of a mother substitute in which men were potentially effective and important in the social and emotional development of their children, but were not currently fulfilling that potential.

Currently, there is a lack of normative, empirical data on both the amounts and kinds of adult male–child behavioral interactions in the United States (see Peters & Stewart, 1981; and Robinson, Lockard, & Adams, 1979 for exceptions). As a result of this lack of data, the literature on the man–child relationship primarily reflects *perceptions* of the dyad and not the actual behaviors themselves. The literature on the father figure thereby becomes more amenable to analysis in the symbolic domain rather than to an analysis through descriptive statistics.

The results from this project, however, are empirically oriented and allow a comparison of levels of interaction between man–child dyads and woman–child dyads within each culture and also comparisons among the adult–child dyads across the 18 culture sample. Consequently, the American man–child dyad can be evaluated in relation both to the American women–child dyad and to the man–child dyads (compared to the respective woman–child dyads) from the 17 other cultures. This set of two empirical comparisons can then be discussed in reference to the perceptions or symbols of the American father figure as discussed by the professional and popular presses.

THE PROFESSIONAL PRESS

Recent literature from the social sciences on the American father figure can be divided roughly into two phases with the transition between the phases occurring in the early 1970s. In the earlier phase, the American father figure was (usually tacitly) assumed to be peripheralized in the socioemotional and cognitive development of the growing child (Bowlby, 1969, 1973). In their review article, Rapoport, Rapoport, Strelitz, and Kew (1977, p. 73) reported the then current expectations of parenting were that mothers were the main figures involved in parenting and that fathers were peripheral. Gorer (in Nash, 1965) suggested that because the child's early life was inundated by females, the father had become vestigial. Biller (1971) encapsulated the father's role in the first half of the twentieth century as being often ineffectual. Childrearing was viewed as the mother's responsibility and the father was not important in the socialization process. Parsons and Bales (1955) described women as the individuals who bear, nurse, and nurture children, whereas the alternative left to the men was within the domains of achievement in power and mastery of the environment. LeMasters (1974) wrote that the United States men were something less than good parents. In more than a metaphorical manner, he wrote that the human primate father is incompetent enough to give primate fathers in general a bad name.

A theme which was repeated in many variations was that the man–child interaction was essentially a derivative effect (e.g., Adams, 1960; Harlow, 1971): that is, men are found around children because men like to be around women and women like to be around children. See Mead (1949) and Count (1958) for related discussions on the male and the paternal role.

Reports on father figures were often indirect, that is, mothers' reports (e.g., Pedersen & Robson, 1969), or children's reports (e.g., Biller, 1968), and father-absent studies (see Pedersen, 1976, for a review of father-absent studies). A few reports (e.g., Tasch, 1952) on fathers were usually from questionnaires or interview formats. As an exception, Rebelsky and Hanks (1971) collected actual man–child interaction.

In the early 1970s, a transition occurred. The focus began to shift from the premise that fathers were not fundamentally important in the healthy development of their children to the premise that fathers theoretically could be quite significant in the healthy psychosexual development of their children, but that American fathers were in fact not actualizing their potential, and, thereby, were not meeting appropriate standards of paternalistic behavior. In other words, fathers can be influential, but American fathers were not fulfilling that promise. Clarke-Stewart (1977) wrote of how American fathers were "underutilized." Price-Bonham and Skeen (1979) and Parke (1979a, p. 15, 1979b, p. 577) suggested that fathers need more education and practice in their roles of father. Biller (1974, p. 4) found a picture in America of general paternal deprivation in which large numbers of fathers have little or minimal contact with their children. In his review article, Fein (1978, p. 122) noted that:

> Rather than sit by the sidelines or serve as mother's helpers, men are being urged to participate in the lives of their children, from conception on. And, apparently increasing numbers of men are reaching out for more sustaining relationships with the young in their lives.

He continued:

> What I am calling the *emergent* perspective on fathering proceeds from the notion that men are psychologically able to participate in a full range of parenting behaviors and, furthermore, that it may be good both for parents and children if men take active roles in child care and child rearing. (p. 127, emphasis in the original)

The question was posed by Levine, Pleck, and Lamb (1983):

> Why is it that more men do not assume a major role in the care of their children? Are they disinterested, thanks to their biological heritage or are they inhibited by employment practices and socioeconomic constraints that they require them to choose between paternal involvement and secure employment rather than combine the two? At this stage, we really do not know.

Russell and Radin (1983) wrote: "Modal patterns of paternal participation clearly shows that in comparison to mothers, there is plenty of scope for fathers to increase their levels of participation." Sagi and Sharon (1983) suggested that an emphasis be placed on the importance of the nuclear family and the identification of the need to encourage greater paternal participation in the family. In a more colloquial approach, Schvaneveldt (1977, p. 57) asserted that "the Father in America is a dead beat." The assumption, either stated or tacit, shared by these authors is that the American father figure is not currently dispensing acceptable levels of paternalistic behaviors. See Richards (1982) for a discussion on the form and character of the paradigmatic shift.

Technical reports on the American man–child dyad are often, as is customary, descriptive only, and the wider social contexts and implications are not included in the discussion, for example, Osofsky and O'Connell (1972) and Spelke, Zelazo, Kagan, and Kotelchuck (1973). Several of these reports described high levels of man–child interaction or levels of interaction which were quite comparable to woman–child interaction, for example, Cohen and Campos (1974), Goliknoff and Ames (1979), Pakizegi (1978), Russell (1978), Clarke-Stewart (1978), Frodi and Lamb (1978), Rohner and Rohner (1981, 1982), and Bailey (1982a,b).

For reviews on the father–child dyad, see Lynn (1974), Price-Bonham (1976), Lamb (1981, 1982), Lamb and Sagi (1983), Hamilton (1977), Macoby and Jacklin (1974), McKee and O'Brien (1982), and Parke, Power, and Fisher (1980). See Rutter (1979) for a review of the literature on maternal deprivation and the interface with the man–child bond.

Even with the available data in technical reports on extensive man–child interaction, the alternate hypothesis of American fathers actualizing adequate, if not optimum, amounts and types of paternalistic behavior was rarely discussed by either researchers or theorists. It should be noted that neither quantitative nor qualitative parameters have been established which could separate acceptable, hygienic parenting from unacceptable, pathogenic parenting. This lack of both clinical and social criteria applies equally to mothers as well as to fathers. It is of interest that with the absence of both a benchmark and correlative data, the premise of deficient fathering had become imbedded in the framework of unstated assumptions of much of American professional commentary.

THE POPULAR PRESS

The literature intended for a more general public, rather than for specialized professionals, has taken a route rather parallel to the scientific press. When discussed at all, American fathers tended to be depicted as remaining aloof from, and thereby abdicating, paternalistic responsibility, or as being good naturedly amiable toward the father role, yet uncomfortable or incompetent in exercising that role, for example, Brenton, (1966), Coon (1971), Sexton (1969, 1970), Greene (1967), Bednarik (1970), McLaughlin (1978). A syndicated cartoon exemplified the theme with the caption: "You can always tell the fathers on TV shows. They're the mindless, ineffectual buffoons." Fasteau (1976) wrote:

> Being a father, in the sense of having sired and having children, is part of the masculine image; but fathering, the actual care of children, is not. Men who spend a lot of time taking care of their children—washing, dressing, feeding, teaching, comforting, and playing with them—aren't doing quite what they should be.

In the middle 1970s, the premise began to emerge that fathers, too, could and should be positive influences upon the growing child (Fein, 1978; Levine, 1976; Rossi, 1977). In an article in the *Ladies Home Journal,* Maynard (1979, p. 152) quoted a wife as lamenting: "The truth is . . . my husband really doesn't know how to be a father." Maynard continued that "an enormously large percentage of fathers in this country are simply not involved enough in caring for their own kids." Biller and Meredith (1975) speculated that paternal deprivation is widespread enough to generate large numbers of "psychologically wounded children." Yarrow (1982) noted that:

> although many mothers want and may expect their husbands to be involved parents, sharing the tasks and the fun involved in raising a child, men's attitudes toward their roles as fathers have been changing more gradually than their wives' expectations.

The argument, in many forms, was that ways ought to be found to allow fathers more access to children and to offer men more encouragement to utilize the increased access. Again, the unstated premise was that the status quo was not adequate.

The aggregate popular press obviously prints far more pages than can be reviewed by one individual or team of researchers. Examples of items presented here that have discussed the American father

figure are necessarily selective and susceptible to either bias or circumstance. In an attempt to systematize such a review, Day and
Mackey (in press) randomly selected cartoons from the *Saturday Evening Post* to be analyzed for depiction of the adult–child relationship.
The *Saturday Evening Post* was selected as the vehicle for analysis
because of its broad, family-based target audience, its longevity, and
its abundance of cartoons. Cartoons were selected for analysis because of their tendency to reflect public assumptions and attitudes
(Berger, 1973; Houts & Bahr, 1971; Schoenfeld, 1930).

Assuming that the above constructs are reasonably accurate,
then two hypotheses could be generated relating the father figure and
the cartoons.

1. Prior to the mid-1970s, father figures, when presented, would
   be more prone to be depicted as bumbling or incompetent
   (when compared to mother figures).
2. Proportions of incidences of father–child interaction would be
   reduced in the 1970s (when compared to the 1950s).

This second prediction would result from two different social
processes occurring simultaneously. If hypothesis 1 is correct, then
there has been a tradition of portraying father figures as inept or
irrelevant. However, the newer cultural philosophy projects the father figure as potentially important. Because authors, artists, and
editors of the popular press have a strong vested interest in reading
public opinion and contemporary ideas and fashion, the media presentations of the father as competent would offend current cultural
attitudes. The only remaining strategy would be for media specialists
to eliminate the father as a topic.

PROCEDURE

Weekly issues of the *Saturday Evening Post* were randomly selected beginning with 1922 (the first year in which nonpolitical cartoons appear) and continuing through 1968. In all, 604 cartoons were
reviewed. To be analyzed further, a cartoon had to contain a father
figure or mother figure in the presence of one or more children. Next,
each cartoon was coded as to who was present (man, woman, boy,

girl). Finally coders (unaware of the hypotheses being tested) rated the men and the women in the cartoons as presenting a competent role model or as presenting an incompetent role model to the children. That is, were men and women behaving as competent or as incompetent caretakers? Prior reliability of the coders in discerning competent from incompetent behaviors had been established as quite good. A similar procedure was used for the 1971–1978 issues. Fifty-four cartoons were available for that analysis.

To test the second hypothesis, 556 consecutive cartoons were sampled from 1958–1960, and 520 consecutive cartoons were sampled from 1978–1980. These cartoons were coded for the presence of adult by gender and the presence of child by gender. Percentages of the total number of cartoons which each combination represented were then compiled.

RESULTS

The first hypothesis was confirmed: in the pre-1970 cartoons, incompetent paternal figures appeared significantly more than incompetent maternal figures. Compared to mother figures, father figures were overrepresented in perceived incompetence. The higher incidence of paternal, versus maternal, incompetence occurred when cartoons with man–child dyads (no women present) were compared

TABLE 37
Incidence of Incompetent Parenting Behavior, both Parents Present, either Gender of Child Present (1922–1968)[a]

	Cartoons with				
	Mother (father also present)		Father (mother also present)		Total (n)
	n	Percentage	n	Percentage	
Incompetent	19	23.75%	58	72.5%	77
Competent	61	76.25%	22	27.5%	83
Total	80	100.0%	80	100.0%	160

$\chi^2 = 38.08$; $df = 1$; $p < .01$.
[a] Adapted from Day and Mackey (in press).

TABLE 38

Incidence of Incompetent Parenting Behavior, Only One Gender of Parent Present, either Gender of Child Present (1922–1968)[a]

| | Cartoons with | | | | |
| | Mother (father absent) | | Father (mother absent) | | |
	n	Percentage	n	Percentage	Total (n)
Incompetent	18	31.0%	50	73.5%	68
Competent	40	69.0%	18	26.5%	58
Total	58	100.0%	68	100.0%	126

$\chi^2 = 22.75$; $df = 1$; $p < .01$.
[a]Adapted from Day and Mackey (in press).

to cartoons with woman–child dyads (no men present), and when, in cartoons of man, woman, and child triads, the man–child interaction was compared to woman–child interaction. See Tables 37 and 38.

An additional test was run on the 1971–1978 data. Because of an insufficient n when analyzed separately, the adult–child dyads were combined with the man, woman, and child triads. The incidence of incompetence was not different between men and women ($\chi^2 = 2.617$; df 1, $p > .05$). See Table 39.

The second hypothesis was also confirmed: the proportion of cartoons with adult male–child dyads was reduced in the latter 1970s (compared to the latter 1950s).

TABLE 39

Incidence of Incompetent Parenting Behavior, One or both Parents Present, either Gender of Child Present (54 cartoons); 1971–1978[a]

| | Cartoons with | | | | |
| | Mother | | Father | | |
	n	Percentage	n	Percentage	Total (n)
Incompetent	3	11.1%	9	28.1%	12
Not incompetent	24	88.9%	23	71.9%	47
Total	27	100.0%	32	100.0%	59

$\chi^2 = 2.617$; $df = 1$; $p \geq .05$.
[a]Adapted from Day and Mackey (in press).

TABLE 40

*Percentages of Cartoons Portraying Adults and Children by Gender of Adult
(1958–1960 and 1978–80) for the Saturday Evening Post and the New Yorker*

Magazine	(1) Woman–child dyads	(2) Man–child dyads	(3) Man and woman and child triads	(2) + (3)
Saturday Evening Post				
1958–60 (N = 556)	4.5%	5.2%	9.2%	14.4%
1978–80 (N = 520)	4.2%	2.5%	2.3%	4.8%
Difference				9.6%**
New Yorker				
1958–60 (N = 311)	0.6%	2.3%	4.5%	6.8%
1978–80 (N = 294)	0.3%	1.4%	1.7%	3.1%
Difference				3.7%*

*$p < .05$; **$p < .01$.

In the issues of the *Saturday Evening Post* from 1958–1960, 5.2% of the cartoons contained a man–child dyad and 9.2% contained a man, woman, and child triad. Thus, 14.4% (5.2% + 9.2% = 14.4%) of the *Saturday Evening Post* cartoons included at least one man and at least one child. In the issues from 1978–1980, 2.5% of the cartoons contained a man–child dyad and 2.3% of the cartoons contained a man, woman, and child triad. Accordingly, 4.8% of the cartoons had at least one man *and* at least one child. The difference in the percentages of man–child depiction between the two time periods was 9.6% (14.4% − 4.8% = 9.6%). This difference is significant ($\chi^2 = 34.139$, $df = 2$; $p < .001$). A similar test was then run for the *New Yorker* magazine and the difference in the incidence of the cartoon depiction of father figures was 3.7% (6.8%, 1958–60, − 3.1%, 1978–80, = 3.7%). This decrease was also significant ($\chi^2 = 6.579$; $df = 2$; $p < .05$).[1] See Table 40.

Why would depictions of the humorous father figure become more rare from the 1950s to the 1970s? Part of the explanation may involve three aspects of the United States social structure which have

[1]One additional survey of 165 cartoons from *Playboy* (1982) yielded 1 (0.6%) cartoon of man–child dyads, 0 (0.0%) of woman–child dyads, and 3 (1.8%) cartoons of man, woman, and child triads. These results would not be unexpected. In American society, the public inclusion of prepubescents in a sexual context is generally inappropriate.

undergone change within the last decade: (1) the rapid increase in the percentage of mothers of young children into the labor force, (2) the decline of birth rates/number of children per woman, and (3) the increased advocacy of egalitarianism vis-á-vis gender roles (Cherlin, 1981). As a derivative, in part, of these forces, it is suggested that formalization or ritualization of fathering expectations occurred that recasted the father status–role complex into a template equated with the mother status–role complex. For at least that segment of American society advocating more equity or identity in gender role expectations, a denigration or caricature of a humorously bumbling father figure would be inappropriate.

However, to accede to the imagery or symbolism of men as coequal primary child caretakers would be to break simultaneously with a traditional leitmotiv and with the cognitive categories and emotional cathexes of many contemporary adults who are artists (cartoonists), publishers, editors, and consumers, and who were born and socialized decades before the 1970s. The image of men competing with women for the status of primary child caretaker would be inappropriate for them.

Accordingly, a double avoidance conflict resulted for editors: (1) portrayals of father figures in competent roles shear against traditional inertia, (2) depictions of father figures in incompetent roles would be out of synchrony with emerging expectations of (large) sections of the contemporary society. Because father figures, in the main, portended offensive or nonhumorous cartoon themes, they were deleted as acceptable topics in the cartoons. Other, less ambivalent, topics took their place.

Summary

In sum, the images of the American father figure, as reflected in the printed media, ranged from aloof and distant to potentially important—especially if and when changes occur in the social structure or sex-role definition—to amiably fumbling. The assumption of adequate, if not optimal, levels of current and past paternalistic behavior on the part of American men was not systematically entertained by literature directed at either professionals or the general public. If the perceptions of the United States father figures by the artists, the journalists, and the professionals are accurate, then behavioral indices ought to exist to reflect the accuracy of those perceptions. The following section tests out the perceptions.

THE U.S. SAMPLE

A caveat was made in Chapter 2 that stated that the data sets from the 18 cultures were not intended to be ethnographic accounts of each of the cultures. As an exception to that caution, the sample from Virginia is offered as being broad enough and deep enough to index a generalized view of the American ethos.

The Virginia sample consisted of 14,499 children gathered from over 130 observation sites throughout the state. Two additional dimensions were coded for the Virginia sample. They were (1) ethnic groups: white, black, (Oriental was also coded but later deleted due to insufficiently large numbers for analysis), and (2) residence: urban and rural.

All combinations of data followed the same general pattern: (a) the percentage of children associating with men increased from the MP to MNP intervals; and (b) during MNP intervals, the children in women-only groups were pluralities, if not majorities, followed by those in groups of men and women, followed in turn by those in men-only groups. See Table 41.

For the MNP intervals, comparisons of urban versus rural data and of white versus black data revealed the following:

Urban versus Rural

In the rural sample, compared to the urban, men-only groups were overrepresented ($\chi^2 = 103.02$, $df = 2$; $p < .001$). In a comparison of 41 proxemic indices, 29 cases (70.7%) had similar outcomes for the urban and rural samples. For the remaining 12 cases, the outcomes were different, but in no instance did the two samples each reach significance in competing directions. That is, for each of the 12 different outcomes, one sample would reach the level of significance, but the other sample would indicate a nonsignificant relationship.

Compared to the 41 indices from the total sample (rural + ur-

TABLE 41

Analysis of the Four Subsamples of the Virginia, U.S. Sample by MP vs. MNP Intervals

Percentage distribution of children within the four subsamples

Adult groups	Black			White			Rural			Urban		
	MP (1)	MNP (2)	Difference (2) − (1)	MP (1)	MNP (2)	Difference (2) − (1)	MP (1)	MNP (2)	Difference (2) − (1)	MP (1)	MNP (2)	Difference (2) − (1)
Women-only	73.9%	58.8%	−15.1%*	65.0%	41.9%	−23.1%*	64.2%	38.8%	−25.4%*	66.7%	44.5%	−22.2%*
Men-only	7.0%	13.8%	6.8%	8.8%	17.9%	9.1%	17.4%	25.4%	8.0%	7.3%	15.9%	8.6%
Men and Women	19.1%	27.4	8.3%	26.2%	40.2%	14.0%	18.4%	35.8%	17.4%	26.0%	39.6%	13.6%
N	859	877		4,687	8,076		689	1,524		4,857	7,429	

*$p < .001$.

ban), outcomes from the rural sample were the same in 26 cases (63.4%) and different in 15 cases. Of the 15 differences, all 15 were examples of the data showing a significant relationship in one sample, but not in the other sample. In no instance did the two samples reach significance in a competing direction. Analogous figures for the urban sample (versus the total sample) were 36 agreements (87.8%) and 5 lack of agreements (all 5 occurred when one sample reached significance and the remaining sample did not).

Black vs. White

In the black sample, compared to the white, the women-only groups were overrepresented ($\chi^2 = 104.22$; $df = 2$; $p < .001$).[2] In the comparison of the 41 proxemic indexes, there were 28 agreements (68.3%) and 13 occasions when one sample reached significance and the other sample did not.

When compared to the total sample (white + black), the black sample was in agreement on 28 items (68.3%) and in disagreement on 13 items. Again, all 13 items represented occasions when one sample reached significance and the other failed to reach significance. Similarly derived figures for the white sample were 33 (80.5%) and 8.

Because the similarities to each other well outweighed the differences in the subsamples, the four subsamples were merged to form a "Virginia sample" which is used to index the United States. Accordingly the data gathered from Virginia will be extrapolated to the generalized United States father figure.

HYPOTHESES TO TEST PUTATIVE DERELICTION

If the American men were particularly deficient or inadequate or indifferent in their roles of father figure, then any combination of the following results could be expected:

1. No increase in the percentage of children with men would occur from MP to MNP intervals.

[2]Kauffman (1974) attributed the increased proportion of woman–child dyads in the black sample to the elevated proportions of women headed households in the black population at large (compared to the white population) and to the depressed economic condition of blacks (again, compared to whites).

2. The percentage of adult–child dyads in the American sample that was man–child dyads would be low(est) in the 18 culture sample.
3. Aberrant patterns of man–child association by gender of child in the American sample may point to deprivation in either the father–son or the father–daughter relationship.
4. Lowered levels of man–child interaction (in the context of woman–child interaction) in the American sample when compared to the man–child interactions (in the context of the respective woman–child interactions) in the other cultures would suggest reduced, potentially inadequate, parenting behaviors on the part of American father figures.

RESULTS

A point by point examination of the results reveals the following:
1. From the MP intervals to the MNP intervals, the American man–child dyads in the men-only groups increased by 9.0% (from 8.5% to 17.5%). Similarly, the man–child dyads in the men and women groups increased 13.9% (from 25.1% to 39.0%). The overall increase was significant ($p < .001$). This increase in the level of association between men and children (both girls and boys) in the American sample argues against the proposition of paternalistic neglect or indifference on the part of American men.
2. During the MNP intervals, the percentage of children with adults who were in men-only groups in the American sample was 17.5% and thus was ranked 13 in the sample of 18 cultures. The percentage of children with adults who were in the men and women groups in the American sample was 39.0% and ranked 5th. When men-only groups were added to men and women groups, the total participation level of American men was 56.5%. This figure ranked 9th in the sample of 18 cultures. See Table 42.
3. During the MNP intervals, in the American sample:
   a. Boys were overrepresented in men-only groups (58.9% to 41.1%; $p < .001$).
   b. Girls were overrepresented in women-only groups (54.8% to 45.2%; $p < .001$).

CHAPTER 6

TABLE 42
Ranked Percentages of Children with Adults who were with Men in either Men-only Groups or Men and Women Groups

Culture and number of children	Percentage of children in adult groups composed of					
	Men only	Rank	Men and women	Rank	Men only + men and women	Rank
Israel (2140)	31.9	1	14.6	18	46.5	13
Iceland (1694)	29.0	2	31.4	9	60.4	5
India (1104)	28.5	3	28.5	12	57.0	8
Morocco (1398)	28.5	3	14.7	17	43.2	15
Brazil (urbanized; 562)	24.4	5	29.2	11	53.6	10
Taiwan (2790)	23.8	6	19.4	14	43.2	15
Japan (1336)	22.9	7	38.8	6	61.7	4
Ireland (1852)	22.9	7	40.6	4	63.5	3
Brazil (rural; 549)	22.8	9	22.9	13	45.7	14
Senufo (1132)	21.0	10	37.5	7	59.5	6
Hong Kong (164)	20.7	11	47.0	3	67.7	2
Sri Lanka (1973)	20.5	12	14.8	16	35.3	17
U.S.A. (8953)	17.5	13	39.0	5	56.5	9
Ivory Coast (1642)	17.4	14	15.2	15	32.6	18
Peru (490)	17.4	14	30.4	10	47.8	12
Spain (1058)	16.8	16	51.7	1	68.5	1
Mexico (1355)	14.2	17	35.6	8	49.8	11
Karaja (399)	8.3	18	50.9	2	59.2	7
Mean/SD	21.6/5.9		31.2/12.4		52.8/10.6	

Note. The two adult groups are analyzed separately and then combined. All data are from MNP intervals.

    c. Boys were overrepresented in men and women groups (53.0% to 47.0%; $p < .05$).

    d. When all three adult groups were combined neither boys nor girls were overrepresented (50.8% to 49.2%; $p > .05$).

In the other 17 cultures, during the MNP intervals:

    a. In men-only groups, boys were overrepresented in 13 of 17 cultures (the exceptions were Spain, Peru, the Karaja, and Hong Kong). In no culture were girls overrepresented.

    b. In women-only groups, girls were overrepresented in 8 of the 17 cultures: Ireland, Mexico, India, Ivory Coast, Israel, the Karaja, the Senufo, and Brazil (rural). In no culture were boys overrepresented.

    c. Neither boys nor girls were overrepresented in men and

TABLE 43

The Relationship between Age of Child and the Level of Interaction from Adult to Child; by Men and Women Separately in both Single and Plural Gender Adult Groups: 17 Cultures;[a] Data from the U.S. Sample are Indicated by an Asterisk (*)

	Number of measurements in which there is												
	An inverse[b] relationship between age and level of interaction[c]				No relationship between age and interaction				A relationship (noninverse) between age and level of interaction				
	Gender group				Gender group				Gender group				
	Single		Plural		Single		Plural		Single		Plural		
Interaction	Men	Women	Men	Women	Men	Women	Men	Women	Men	Women	Men	Women	Total
Tactile contact	16*	16*	16*	14*	0	1	1	3	–	–	–	–	67
Personal distance	13*	13*	10*	13*	3	3	7	4	–	1	–	–	67
Visual orientation	10*	11*	5*	5*	5	3	12	9	1	3	–	3	67
Total	39	40	31	32	8	7	20	16	1	4	–	3	201

[a]The Hong Kong sample and the men-only groups in the Karaja had too few cases for analysis.
[b]An inverse relationship occurred when the youngest age bracket (birth–4 years) was overrepresented in the more active levels of interaction from adult to child.
[c]$p < .05$; χ^2, $df = 2$.

women groups in 14 of the cultures (boys were overrepresented in Ireland, Sri Lanka, and India);
d. When all three adult groups were combined, neither boys
nor girls were overrepresented in 13 cultures (boys were
overrepresented in Morocco, Taiwan, and Sri Lanka. Girls
were overrepresented in the Karaja).

When viewed within the context of these four indices, the United
States sample does not seem remarkable or unusual. The data do not
reveal any prima facie indication of paternal inadequacy in the United
States.

4. During the MNP intervals, the American sample illustrated
the following interaction patterns. See Tables 43–46. (Note
that in Tables 43–46, the data from the United States sample
are designated by an asterisk *).
a. Tactile contact—adult to child. Both men and women
touched (with their hands) younger children more than
they did older children. See Table 43. However, neither
men nor women had higher levels of touching toward the
children (both single and plural gender adult group comparisons). See Table 44. In addition, when boys and girls
were analyzed separately, in single gender adult groups.

TABLE 44

*Comparison between Men and Women in Relation to the Level of Interaction
toward all Children (Boys + Girls): 18 Cultures; Data from the U.S. Sample are
Indicated by an Asterisk (*)*

		Interaction category			
Adult group	Gender of adult responding more actively[a]	Tactile contact	Personal distance	Visual orientation	Total
Men only vs.	Men more active	4	2	4*	10
women only	Women more active	1	3	0	4
	Neither more active	13*	13*	14	40
	Total	18	18	18	54
Men (with	Men more active	1	0	1	2
women present)	Women more active	6	5	5	16
vs. women (with	Neither more active	11*	13*	12*	36
men present)	Total	18	18	18	54

[a]$p < .05$; χ^2, $df = 1$.

men and women, compared to each other, were again equally prone to touch children. In plural gender adult groups. men, rather than women, had a higher level of touching boys; but girls were touched by men and women at the same level. See Table 45. Neither men nor women preferentially touched boys or girls. See Table 46.

b. Personal distance—adult to child. In both single and plural gender adult groups, men and women were systematically closer to younger children than to older children (Table 43); and, men and women, compared to each other, were equally close to the children (boys and girls combined). See Table 44. When boys and girls were analyzed separately, neither men nor women in single gender adult groups, compared to each other, were closer to boys or to girls. See Table 45. Men, in men-only groups, were not closer to boys or to girls; while women in women-only groups were closer to girls. In the plural gender groups, men were closer to boys and women were closer to girls. See Table 46.

TABLE 45

Comparison between Men and Women in Relation to the Level of Interaction toward Children (Boys and Girls Separately): 18 Cultures;[a] Data from the U.S. Sample are Indicated by an Asterisk (*)

Adult group comparison	Gender of adult responding more actively[b]	Interaction category and gender of child						
		Tactile contact		Personal distance		Visual orientation		
		Boy	Girl	Boy	Girl	Boy	Girl	Total
Men only vs.	Men more active	1	4	2	5	1	4*	17
women only	Women more active	2	0	0	0	1	0	3
	Neither more active	14*	14*	15*	13*	15*	14	85
	Total	17	18	17	18	17	18	105
Men (with	Men more active	3*	0	2*	0	1	1	7
women present)	Women more active	0	2	0	5*	3	5	15
vs. women (with	Neither more active	15	16*	16	13	14*	12*	86
men present)	Total	18	18	18	18	18	18	108

[a]The Karaja had insufficient number of boys in the men-only groups for analysis.
[b]$p < .05$; χ^2, $df = 1$.

Table 46

Comparison of Level of Interaction from Adult (Man or Woman) to Child by
Gender of Child and Composition of Adult Group: 18 Cultures;[a] Data from the
U.S. Sample are Indicated by an Asterisk (*)

Gender of adult and adult group composition	Gender of child receiving more active responses[b]	Interaction category			
		Tactile contact	Personal distance	Visual orientation	Total
Men only	Girl	4	2	0	6
	Boy	0	0	0	0
	Neither	13*	15*	17*	45
	Total	17	17	17	51
Women only	Girl	0	3*	0	3
	Boy	0	0	2	2
	Neither	18*	15	16*	49
	Total	18	18	18	54
Men	Girl	0	0	1	1
(with women present)	Boy	2	4*	1	7
	Neither	16*	14	16*	46
	Total	18	18	18	54
Women	Girl	1	3*	0	4
(with men present)	Boy	0	0	0	0
	Neither	17*	15	18*	50
	Total	18	18	18	54

[a]The Karaja had an insufficient number of boys in the men-only groups to allow analysis.
[b]$p < .05$; χ^2, $df = 1$.

c. Visual orientation—adult to child. All four categories kept younger children in sight more so than they did older children. See Table 43. Men in men-only groups were more prone to keep children in their visual field than were women in women-only groups. Men and women, in men and women adult groups, were equally likely to keep children within view. See Table 44. With the children analyzed separately by gender, men and women in single gender adult groups kept boys in sight equally; whereas the men, compared to the women, more kept girls in their visual field. For plural gender adult group comparisons, men and women kept boys and girls within their sight at equal levels. See Table 45. For all four adult group categories, boys and girls were kept in sight in equal proportions. See Table 46.

There were 18 within (the U.S.) culture comparisons of levels of response from men and women toward children. In 13 instances (72.2%), the levels of response were equally active. In 4 instances, men had more active levels than women, and in only 1 instance were the women's responses more active than the men's.

In the other 17 cultures, during the MNP intervals, the following patterns occurred (see Table 43):

1. Tactile contact—adult to child. Of the 34 comparisons (2 adult groups × 17 cultures = 34), men and women's level of touching the children was similar in 22 cases (64.7%). In 5 cases, men touched children more often than did women (Karaja, Israel, Ivory Coast, Ireland in the single gender comparisons; Japan in the plural gender comparison). In 7 cases women touched the children more often than did men (Sri Lanka in single gender groups and Peru, Ivory Coast, Sri Lanka, Taiwan, Brazil (urbanizing), and the Senufo in men and women groups).

2. Personal distance—adult to child. In 24 of the 34 cases (70.6%), women maintained similar interpersonal distances from their children. In 8 cases women were systematically closer to the children than were the men (Ivory Coast, Brazil—urbanizing, and the Senufo in single gender comparisons, and the Ivory Coast, Sri Lanka, Brazil—urbanizing, the Senufo, and Spain in men and women groups). In 2 cases, men were predictably closer to children than were women (the Karaja and Taiwan in single gender comparisons).

3. Visual orientation—adult to child. In 25 of 34 cases (73.5%), men and women kept children within their visual field in similar proportions. In 5 cases, women were more prone to keep children within sight (Japan, Ireland, Mexico, Taiwan and India in men and women groups). In 4 cases, men were more likely to have the children within their view (Ivory Coast, Taiwan, the Senufo in single gender comparisons, and the Senufo in men and women groups).

In those comparisons between men and women in which the responses to the boys and girls were analyzed separately, 81.1% (163 of 201) of the cases found no differences in the level of interaction (Table

45). Moreover, in 86.9% (86 of 99) of the instances, men showed no gender preferences in interacting with children. A comparable figure for women was 93.1% (95 of 102). See Table 46.

DISCUSSION

Before the results are discussed as a unit, it is useful to repeat that all data were gathered in public places with equal access by gender during daylight hours and that these loci offer the men a good opportunity *not* to be found associating with their children. The data do not address adult–child interaction in private domains at which simultaneous presence of a man and a child could reflect similar schedules and residences rather than prioritized choices. Although it is self-evident that additional information from private places is important, the logistics of using a similar research paradigm in private domiciles or sites are formidable. In addition, the potential is quite real that the method of data gathering in private loci, where anonymity is unlikely, would affect the results in a massive manner. The method actually used, restricted to public domains in daylight, presumably was profiling man–child dyads in which the men were with children because they were choosing to do so—or were at least willing to be with them—even though other options competed for the men's presence. Given this restrictive framework, the procedures of data gathering were tapping the relevant behaviors in a manner as maximally sensitive to the query at hand as an otherwise imperfect world allows.

Taken as a unit, the data from the 18 cultures illustrate that men were with children less often than were women, but, once present with children, the men interacted with the children (at the proxemic level) consonant with the interaction from women to children. The American man–child dyads operated in much the same manner as the majority of man–child dyads in the other 17 cultures. The American men did not appear particularly solicitous nor particularly derelict. They appeared somewhat typical.

The argument can be made of course that, like the American men, the majority of the men in the selected countries surveyed were also deficient in adequate parenting. Such an interpretation is theoretically awkward in that a wholesale redefinition of normative paternalistic behaviors is required, that is, the statistically typical is the socially abnormal. Currently, there has been no rationale presented for such a redefinition, nor as was mentioned earlier, have criteria been established for the delineation of a threshold for healthy, adaptive parenting vis-à-vis unhealthy maladaptive parenting. Neither quantitative nor qualitative parameters have been forthcoming from the clinicians. Without such parameters, the same sterile argument of putative deficient parenting could be raised against the women in all 18 cultures.

Lacking accepted indexes of effective versus dysfunctional parenting, the more parsimonious interpretation is that American males are generating typical contact time with their offspring with typical consequences. If any deficiency does exist, it is not in the domain of American children's access to men in the public arena, during daylight hours, nor in comparable levels of interaction within man–child and women–child dyads in those loci.

A discrepancy then emerges between the empirical cross-cultural data on the man–child dyad and the images and symbols of the American father figure as reflected in the professional and popular presses. The data indicate normative contact between American men and their children. The literature suggests inadequate or deficient levels of contact between men and the children. Such a discrepancy would not be an insignificant happenstance. The importance of images and symbols operating within (and generating) a social structure has been discussed at great length, breadth, and volume, for example in, Dolgin, Kemnitzer, and Schneider (1977), Douglas (1978), Geertz (1974), Harris (1974), Leach (1971), Levi-Strauss (1963, 1969), Turner (1969).

Let it suffice that there is an ample reservoir of material sustaining the importance of the cathected symbols of a society in the day-to-day lives of the society's populace. A society's symboling system intrudes deeply into the integrated matrix of the society. The merging of the subjective reality of the psyche with the objective reality of the environment is tantamount to a given. Assuming that the disparity between the empirical data and the imagery is real, and not a derivative of sampling bias or selectivity, the reconciliation of the symbol and the behavior poses an interesting problem.

CHAPTER 7

The Myth of the Derelict Daddy

RECONCILIATION OF SYMBOL AND BEHAVIOR

One available avenue with which to conjoin the image of a deficient American father figure with the American behaviors of a typical father figure requires the two cultural universals that were introduced in Chapter 5 and one well established and widely applied theory.

The First Universal

Despite other variations and permutations of divisions of labor by gender, the primary caretaker of young children, especially infants, is invariably female (Barry & Paxson, 1971; Rohner & Rohner, 1982). Usually the biological mother is given the role of the caretaker, and she accepts the role. But if it is not the mother who assumes the predominant nurturing and custodial responsibilities, the surrogates are also female, for example, an aunt or female sibling (Wisner & Gallimore, 1977).

The Second Universal

Accordingly, other tasks which would systematically interfere with childcare are generally precluded from women and fall to the lot of men (Brown, 1970; Murdock & Provost, 1973; White, Burton, & Brudner, 1977), for example, smelting, hunting large animals, hunting sea mammals. Another of these tasks which is ill-suited to tending to small children is the status–role complex of warrior or active combatant in armed hostility (Divale & Harris, 1976; Whyte, 1978. The second universal is that men are the soldiers of community and family, and women are not. Individual exceptions will occur, especially in the defense of the domicile or community, but when armed groups of individuals leave the perimeter of the referent group to attack a second group, those individuals are invariably male (see Ember & Ember, 1971). The division of labor by gender for the two tasks *primary child caretaker* and *active armed combatant* is rather complete. Females, as a class, are the former; males, as a class, are the latter.

It is clear from the ethnographic literature that, despite widely diverse social structures, rituals, and belief systems, each society teaches females to be primary child caretakers and males to be primary soldier–protectors. In turn, females successfully incorporate the status of primary child-caretaker and actualize the appropriate roles, that is, behaviors, and males successfully incorporate the status of soldier–protector, and, if the need arises, actualize their appropriate role behaviors.

The question can be posed: Why cannot women assume both the status-role complexes of caretaker and soldier? One reasonable answer would refer to the superior physical strength that men, as a class, possess compared to that of women, as a class. Groups of men in premechanized combat would almost surely have had an advantage fighting any group of women only or of men and women. A second related answer, as suggested earlier, is that women do not readily assume behaviors that interfere with childrearing. Warfare or raiding with active fighting is certainly one of those behaviors. The loss of a fertile women, either permanently through death or for an extended convalescence through severe wounds, or temporarily through raiding forays, jeopardizes not only herself but also any nursing infant, and any subsequent children she might have borne. The loss of children jeopardizes the existence of the next generation, which in turn threatens the existence of the referent community. The smaller the community, the greater is the threat. It seems unlikely therefore that women, as a taxon, in either a hunting-and-gathering or an agrarian society would be encouraged or allowed to assume a status–role complex of primary protector–combatant.

Men, of course, cannot nurse the child, but any other nurturing behaviors between suckling episodes certainly seem available to and within the psychomotor range of males. If the cross-cultural data presented here are at all representative of the adult male–child dyads around the world, then men are with children, when they can be, in substantial proportions and are responding to children at high levels of activity.

The American adult male–child dyad is no exception to these trends. Why then would the imagery of the father figure be negative? A positive image would be more harmonious with the data. In terms of objectivity, the society's set of symbols tend to be profiled by the media. It is the negative set which is preponderant.

The Theory

It is suggested here that the negative images of the American father figure reflect the incompatibility of the status of soldier–protector with the status of primary child-caretaker. While the status of primary child-caretaker is incompatible with the status of soldier–combatant, the converse is, of course, also true. The individual or class of individuals assigned the status of soldier–combatant is simultaneously precluded from assuming the status of primary child-caretaker. It is important at this point to note the distinction, as is customarily used, between the fundamental concepts of status and role. *Status* is defined as a position within the social structure. *Role* is defined as the behavior incumbent to a status (from Gross, Mason, & McEachern, 1964). The classic theory that is applicable to this investigation is broadly referred to as *role–conflict theory*. In his seminal article within this domain, Goode (1960) wrote:

> The individual is likely to face a wide, distracting, and sometimes conflicting array of role obligations. If he conforms fully or adequately in one direction, fulfillment will be difficult in another . . . [leading to] . . . role strain . . . [that is] . . . difficulty in meeting given role demands. (p. 485)

A lack of clarity in role expectations, that is, the individual's status, can be a catalytic factor in inducing role strain or conflict within an individual or between the individual and the society at large (Getzel & Cuba, 1954; Secord & Backman, 1974; Turner, 1978). There is a consistent and general agreement by role theorists that extended role strain and conflict are not desirable states and are often dysfunctional for the personality and behavioral systems of the affected individual. In other words, an individual cannot simultaneously perform mutually exclusive or competing tasks, but if the individual is expected to perform in such a way, internal conflict results that is injurious to the personality and well-being of that individual.

If the conflict is chronic and systematic within a community, the dysfunction becomes not merely an isolated individual abberation, but a threat to the fabric of society. It is the societal level that is the analytical focus here.

The behaviors, that is, the roles, of active combatant are quite clearly incompatible with the behaviors of caregiving to infants. The role of active combatant, however, occupies only a small percentage of any man's life. The large proportion of his life would be times of noncombat. Between combat episodes, men could certainly interact actively and consistently with their children.

As the cross-cultural data from this project indicated earlier, the men not only could interact with their children, but they actually did so, under the defined conditions of the survey, in high proportions and at levels consonant with women–child dyads. The men apparently were with the children willingly, and with a modicum of speculation, also appeared to enjoy their company. The American father figure was no exception and, as has been demonstrated, was consistently typical of the surveyed sample.

A structural problem does emerge for individual men and for men as a class when they are required to prepare for physical combat. When active combat or a physical presence to attempt deterrence is necessitated to protect the community/family or to engage in offensive forays, men could be entrapped in an obvious role conflict. The man can remain at the domicile, but, if he does so, his absence threatens a successful defense at the community's perimeter or a successful raid against a traditional foe. The threat is cumulative as the percentage of men eschewing the warrior role increases. The other option is that the man can leave the domicile; yet by doing so, he cannot have continuous contact or control over his children. He momentarily deserts them. This role conflict to which the males, both individually and corporately, are susceptible becomes systematically dysfunctional and shears against one of the bases of the social structure.

It is suggested that the conflict is resolved by removing the male from the possibility of assuming the *status* of primary child-caretaker. He becomes the soldier–protector by internalizing his society's version of the status complex of soldier–protector. To reduce ambiguity, and subsequent conflict, and to reduce any potential identity problems, the competing status–role complex of primary child-caretaker is, for him, devalued and caricatured.

The symbolic cleavage would then become clean and discrete. He is one, but not the other. If a decision has to be made, his priorities are to engage a foe some distance from the nursery and not to remain in the nursery. The mental syllogism is simple: Males are soldiers. He is male. He is a soldier. Primary child-caretakers are female. He is not a female. He is not a primary child-caretaker.

Although any individual man may experience personal emotional distress such as fear or sadness or anxiety, he has no structural conflict in his expectations. He leaves the domicile or community with his fellow combatants—all of whom are males. Once the symbolic system has been successfully internalized in the growing boy and he has accepted the societal edicts, then the actual behavior of the boy, grown to a father, will not threaten his intact self-image or identity.

After the two symbolic systems are assimilated as discrete and incompatible, then the actual behaviors can be continuous and overlapping. That is, the male can be highly nurturing and can give large amounts of time and emotional support to his children. The male, symbolically, becomes a secondary or ancillary care giver to the child. He "helps out." He, as an exception, takes sole responsibility as the child's custodian. It would be irrelevant if the nurturance and contact time between the child and the male would represent over 50% of the caretaking that the child receives. The discrete symbols are in place and operant. The male perceives himself as a support or backup system. In effect, the imagery of discrete, nonoverlapping symbols serves as a shield or penumbra allowing, if not encouraging, the behaviors emanating from the statuses to overlap considerably. The male would not have to choose which behaviors he can execute: nurturer or combatant. He can *do* both. However, he cannot officially, publicly, *be* both. Males, as a class, are perceived to be soldier–protectors, but not the primary child-caretakers.

The data and the media's version of the American father figure can be reconciled.[1] Leaving aside social desirability and what the future may bring, it is clear that the cultural heritage from the American past, both on this continent as well as from Europe and Africa, has been one of intermittent, if not chronic, violence—male violence. The form of the violence varied from intracommunity friction to declaration of war. Males both metaphorically and physically placed themselves, and were placed, at the interface of the conflict separating the domiciles of the competitors.

With incurred costs as well as benefits, it was the males' status of soldier—variably accepted across individuals—but their taxon's status nonetheless. Neither their own emotional attachments nor their familial circumstances could obviate the symbol. Whether used as an excuse or as an explanation, a reference by the male to being "needed at home with the children" would not be acceptable. He was not culturally prescribed to be the primary caretaker. The female was prescribed as such, and, accordingly, she was perceived to be continuously needed at home with the children. The woman becomes, at least symbolically, the primary child-caretaker and thereby frees the male to defend or to raid.

To complete the argument, it is further suggested that the symbol of the male as primary child-caretaker was denigrated and demeaned to reinforce the statuses as distinct, while simultaneously removing from the male the option and conflict of choosing one of two competing status complexes; soldier *or* nurturer. He can actualize both role complexes if he internalizes the society's symboling system.

The dynamics of the process would thereby result in a public imagery of males as inadequate parenting figures with males actually exhibiting substantial and normative parenting behaviors. Such is the pattern that is found in America. That is, journalists and researchers in America mold (ard are molded by) the negative image of the father figure; yet the empirical data on the American man–child dyad appeared quite typical when viewed within the perspective of other cultures. It should be noted that the American journalists and social scientists operate suspended in the symbolic structures of their over-

---

[1]Although this chapter specifically addresses the United States, it would not be unexpected for similar dynamics to be extant in (the) other cultural areas: the status of father as primary child-caretaker would be devalued, whereas nurturing levels by men toward children would exist at high levels.

all society and may be no more immune from the influence of the covert givens subtending the culture than any other set of individuals. Generalized unstated presumptions, shared with the community at large, direct and orient the dynamics of the perceptions, interpetations, and reactions of the journalists and social scientists. If the interdependent weavings of the social fabric include, as a core construct, the myth of the aloof, deficient father figure, then the myth would serve as a starting point in the works of these writers. American fathers would be assumed deficient unless saliently countervailing data were presented. The analysts and observers obviously do not come to the father figure with a tabula rasa. Their own socialization refracts the incoming perceptions into the expectations of low father involvement.

The psychic inertia lies in accepting the myth. The shedding of the given negative symbolic imagery—to accept a neutral or positive imagery--requires overcoming the valence of the negative set and then reconstructing a new set of symbols for the father figure. As every fieldworker has learned, such a process can be difficult indeed. The difficulty is magnified greatly if the symbols at hand are not questioned, challenged, or examined for accuracy. The task of validating preconscious assumptions is formidable. See Arens (1979) and Freeman (1983) for excellent analyses of this process.

An interesting paradox presents itself to the American society. The delicate charade of the Dagwood Bumstead or underutilized father figure may be serving as a buffer not only protecting the fathering behaviors from social tampering, but also easing their emergence. If this is the case, then projects (including this one) that point to the importance of fathers by analyzing and revealing high levels of paternalistic behavior may act to dissolve the buffer and inhibit the very phenomenon which is under pressures to be increased.

CHAPTER 8

The American Family: A Tragedy of the Commons?

Garrett Hardin, in his seminal article "The Tragedy of the Commons" (1968), pointed out that if each individual were to maximize personal gain, the result, in many cases, would be the collapse of the social structure. That is, for a society to survive and to function effectively, the corporate good must be given priority in some instances over the individual liberty and freedom.

This relationship can be exemplified by the two otherwise disparate offenses, homicide and automobile parking. Homicide: if everyone were freely allowed to vent frustration and anger by killing the source of his or her troubles, then the social fabric would rapidly unravel, and anarchy would prevail. To facilitate an adequate, if not optimal, functioning of society, our individual citizens have accepted restriction on our freedom: we cannot kill each other with impunity. The initiator of a homicide does so, not freely, but with a penalty attached. If the individual is caught, tried, and convicted, the price paid for the murder can be a long jail sentence. The personal liberty to kill freely has been denied individuals in exchange for social stability and safety. Automobile parking: to allow open highways and the ability to move quickly from place to place, citizens have, in the main, acquiesced to the denial of parking their cars wherever they so choose. The penalty enacted by the government upon the miscreant who has parked in an area that the community has had labeled "no parking" can include loss of money, loss of car, or the loss of license to drive. Again, personal liberty is reduced to allow society to function at a more effective level. These two are fairly obvious examples. There are additional examples that are more subtle. One such unobvious candidate involving the nuclear family has been emerging and deserves increased attention by social scientists. The argument for the nuclear family in America as a bona fide candidate for an example of a tragedy of the commons begins with two decidedly uncontroversial assumptions.

There is probably a consensus among Americans that America, as a society, accepts two conditions as good. First, the maximizing of individual freedom and personal liberty is considered a good end for which to strive. Second, that America as a political entity should survive not just for one generation, but in perpetuity, is also thought a proper and good goal.

Although both of these values, taken one at a time, are without serious critics, in tandem they can mutually exclude one another. There exists for the American populace an inherent conflict within these two highly prized entities which may preclude both of them from occurring at the same time. For contemporary American society, the logic of the "tragedy of the commons" is poised to exert itself. Phrased in its bleakest form, it is argued here that American women cannot maximize their personal freedom, while—at the same time— our society is maximizing its chances for survival. It should be noted that while the exposition given below involves the analysis of the American social structure, the greater an alternate social structure compares with that of the United States, the more the arguments outlined here will apply.

INDIVIDUAL LIBERTY AND SOCIETAL VIABILITY

For personal liberty to be maximized, two necessary, but not sufficient, preconditions that must be met include (1) a maximum amount of unclaimed, discretionary time available per citizen and (2) a maximum amount of resources per citizen to use discretionary time in discretionary behaviors. The closer to 24 hours per day that a person is free to choose how, where, and with whom his or her 24 hour day is spent and his or her resources are utilized, the more freedom that person has. At the 24 hour per day mark with infinite resources, absolute freedom is reached.

On the one hand, these two conditions seem faultless goals for which to strive, and with the individual as the focus, over the short-term, there is little to dispel the aura. On the other hand, at the societal level, over the long-term, a complex problem arises.

Society is an abstraction referring to an aggregation of individuals who live out each life one at a time and who are anything but abstract. Each individual is a flesh and blood mortal. For a society to survive, there must be a continuous supply of these flesh and blood mortals who replace those individuals who have followed the "dust to dust" axiom. Currently and in the foreseeable future, the only means of replenishing a society's population is by women having babies. There is, without qualification, no substitute mechanism. Perhaps because the statement is so very obvious and without analogue, the causal nature of such a phenomenon is prone to be overlooked. Just as the Chinese aphorism tells us that the fish would be the last to discover the ocean, the pervasive presence of motherhood—everyone has a mother—may help to mask its influence on *sequelae* of perceptions attitudes, and behaviors. Nonetheless, despite its usually low analytic profile, the consequences in any qualitative or quantitative variations on the theme of women having children affect quickly and deeply the entire social structure.

If a society is to survive intact at even a steady population level, the women of that society must average two and a fraction births. The two babies replace one mother and one father. The fraction replaces those children who died before reaching a reproductive age. Because the average figure is being used, for every woman who has less than two children, another woman must have three or more children. If more than two and a fraction births per woman occur, then the population grows. If two or less children per woman are born, then the population will decline and over time can reach oblivion. For example, a one child per family average is socially maladaptive. While the familial trio may bring joy, satisfaction and contentment to each individual of the family, a society based on one child per woman cannot survive intact. In only ten generations, a society averaging one child per family would only be one-tenth of one percent of its original size $(100 \times (.5)^{10} = 0.098\%)$. From the societal perspective, at least two children per female (per family if monogamy predominates) is the minimum requirement.

It is useful to point out that there are no guarantees, nor have there ever been guarantees, on the longevity of any society. From Sodom to Carthage to Rome to Tasmania, societies can easily come and just as easily go. There is no evidence of a demographic "thermostat" which automatically responds to dysfunctional population levels.

At this juncture, the always legitimate question may be asked: So what? Assuming that all of the above is true, where is the problem of women having their freedom curtailed? The nexus comes from the fact that humans are born extremely dependent and remain so for long periods of time, that is, we are very altricial creatures. For some behaviors, such as language, humans may take years and years to assume independence and competence. Until competence in these slowly developing traits is reached, young boys and girls need continuous monitoring and nurturance.[1] As a corollary, children without guidance and nurturance suffer—in extreme cases they die. The Ik represent such an extreme case (Turnbull, 1972).

If they are to prosper and flourish, young children will consume inordinate amounts of time and resources. They put their caretakers on call for the 24 hour day, seven days a week. Each day, every day, children need not only social interaction, but also material resources in abundance, for example, food, clothing, shelter, recreation. As a norm in our nucleated society, full-time parental caretakers are essential for the children from infancy to (approximately) three years of age. From three to 10 years of age, the caretaking can be divided between school and home. As his or her maturation level develops, the child achieves more and more independence until self-sufficiency occurs. Therefore, for a base minimum of three to six years, a parent figure must be available to support and to nurture these two and a fraction young children. The closer the spacing of the children, the fewer aggregate years are mandated. The wider the spacing, the more years will be required.

If a citizen of the United States were to follow a rational strategy and demonstrate economic wisdom, the citizen should follow the scenario described below:

1. I wish to maximize my discretionary time and money.

---

[1]For further information on the nature of the caretaker role and on childrearing and child development, see Barry and Paxson (1971), Weisner and Gallimore (1977), Brown (1970), Murdock and Provost (1973), Bowlby (1969), Clarke-Stewart (1977), Rajecki, Lamb, and Obmascher (1979), Rohner and Rohner (1981), Ainsworth, Bell, and Stayton (1978). For excellent reviews of the literature, see Rapoport, Rapoport, Strelitz, and Kew (1977), Rutter (1979), Pedersen (1980), and Lamb (1981).

2. I also wish to retire and to receive social security support and to have an efficient society extant within which I can shop, be leisurely, enjoy recreational facilities, and be confident that effective medical treatment is available if needed.
3. If I eschew raising any children of my own, then I need not expend time and money rearing them; yet I can be supported by the children (grown to adulthood) of other individuals. These soon-to-be adults can guarantee social security pension payments plus operate the institutions of the society.

Again there arises an individually effective strategy which, if executed in large numbers, would be detrimental to the society as a unit.

In what can be loosely labeled "traditional" American society, females, as a class, have been socialized in preparation for the traditional role as primary child caretaker; whereas men, as a class, are socialized in preparation for their traditional role as primary economic provider and protector of hearth and kin. Over the eons, men and women have voluntarily, with various levels of enthusiasm, allocated the necessary time and resources required in caring for the needs of their children. That they were at least minimally successful is attested by America's current population level of 230 million plus citizens. One advantage to this option is the increased probability for the continuation of a stable, effective society. Other advantages would be in the proportion to (1) the number of women (and men) who are competent and satisfied in their parenting roles and (2) the number of children with a satisfactory childhood.

However, the point of interest here is that the assumption of the parental role has always been quite voluntary with no formal, legal, or official rewards or incentives. Any benefits derived from the parental roles were informal, emotional, and personal.

The United States, like other cultures, has continued to rely on what amounts to the goodwill and altruism of individuals both to procreate and to rear children with very little or no reciprocity from society as a unit, that is, the state. Such have been the dynamics for the millenium, and theoretically they can extend into the future indefinitely. Nevertheless, relatively recent social developments make such extrapolations somewhat tenuous.

The well-publicized increase in the number and proportion of women in the labor force, plus effective and available means of controlling fecundity along with increased emphasis in the media on women's automony and individuality, potentially change the milieu in which the adult–child dyad functions.

With the individual as the focus, this option of limiting fecundity and gaining a higher level entry into the labor market has a real advantage. Married women are able to compete with men and single women on an equal footing in the labor market for scarce resources in the form of high prestige, high income jobs. The larger significance of the social change becomes more apparent when these marketable women are seen in the context of the increasing numbers of women who are deciding to reduce their fecundity to low levels (which subsequently reduces the fecundity of their husbands). These women have chosen to avoid the disadvantages of being full-time child-caretakers in favour of competing for career vocations which require continuity and cumulative expertise.

It is here that we approach the conflict at its most fundamental and irreducible point: if the level of fecundity falls below replacement level for any sustained time, society is presented with the problems of populating itself for subsequent generations or of skirmishing with radically reordering its social structure, or, taken to the logical extreme, of extinction. Women are leaving the nursery quickly, and many women have decided to forego childrearing altogether. If this trend is linear and not cyclical, the logic of the "tragedy of the commons" would begin to assert itself. A society without children is decidedly short-term; yet a society with children necessitates the (voluntary) restriction of time and resources of the child-caretakers. Therefore, what is gained in freedom for the individual is seen in the context of a threat to society of not replenishing subsequent generations. The greater the number of individuals choosing to maximize freedom of discretionary time and resources by foregoing the traditional parental roles, the greater is the threat to societal viability.

When viewed from the perspective of a logical conclusion, the terminus funnels down to one of two thematic options:

1. Americans as individuals forego childbearing and childrearing and maximize discretionary freedom and resources, that is, maximize their individual liberty and freedom.
2. Sufficient numbers of Americans continue to devote substantial amounts of discretionary time and resources to bear and

to rear children who will repopulate society in subsequent generations.

There is *no* third option. It is useful to point out again that the two options are mutually exclusive. One option, if exercised to an extreme, necessarily excludes the other.

If option one were to be the destiny of the American society, there would be an unparalleled explosion of human freedom quite unmatched by any society in any other epoch. America is a very rich nation with sophisticated technology in great abundance. Millions of its citizens could enjoy extraordinary freedom and latitude of time, goods, and services. The enjoyment, of course, is finite in time if not in experience. Individuals, otherwise unfettered by the requirements of young children, are still coerced by the maturational process of aging. Thus, the unrestrained revelry would last but that one generation.

If the second option of widespread parenthood is the route taken by the American society, the population would remain stable or grow. However, people, large numbers of them, must agree to devote substantial amounts of discretionary time and resources in childrearing obligations. A second order problem then presents itself: how to allocate the inevitable sacrifices which are necessary for the successful rearing of children who will perpetuate the society. Although only women can give birth to children, there are two additional (and realistic) options over and beyond the traditional nuclear or extended family that can satisfy the requirement of systematically insuring that a populace will be nurtured in future generations: (1) mothers and fathers become coequal caretakers, and (2) a massive implementation of (all day) childcare facilities.

Fathers as Coequal Caretakers

Any vacuum of primary child-caretaker (though most certainly not genetrix) could theoretically be filled by men. As obvious a solution as it may appear, such an alternative seems less than probable. It can be, and most assuredly has been, argued that formula and bottle nursing removes suckling as a requirement of survival for infants and thereby allows anyone to be a child-caretaker if he or she is able to hold a baby and a bottle without dropping either. Gender, therefore, would be an irrelevant category in terms of who is the primary nurturant figure to children. It would follow that men could be coequal caretakers. Such a paradigm would be immediately more equitable and would satisfy more individuals of an egalitarian sociopolitical persuasion that the current rubric of the "motherhood imperative." The question may then be posed: Can a society survive in a very competitive world if it systematically relegates at least half of the child-caring responsibilities to men? A survey of other societies and cultures around the world does not offer much promise of an affirmative answer.

Of the hundreds and hundreds of societies surveyed by social scientists around the world, there is virtually no extant society in which men are even coequal partners in the caretaking of small children.[2] Despite other exotic practices on a wide range of behaviors, there is a constancy in the mother and child dyad. The world's women, as a class, are primary child caretakers; men, as a class, are not. As either cultural analogues or homologues, there are zero cases with which to compare an American prospectus of men and women as (even) equal caretakers.

The society wide experiment of men as equal or primary caretakers of infants has either never been tried or for each time it has been tried, it has been found wanting and has failed. Any society that may have attempted to equilibrate the parental roles did not compete effectively against societies stressing the mother role and has quietly disappeared with no trace.

While the theoretical category still exists that in a highly technological society such as the United States, this trend could possibly be altered through intensive socialization and resocialization, the prognosis of this society becoming the very first successful reverse-role culture seems problematic. It does not seem feasible to rely on the

---

[2]It is useful to address M. Mead's often cited discussion of the Tchambuli (*Sex and Temperment in Three Primitive Societies*, 1963). Mead suggests that the Tchambuli have developed a culture in which the roles of men and women are reversed when compared to gender roles in American society. Mead's interpretation of her own research leaves much room for debate. But that point aside, there is no evidence or mention of Tchambuli men assuming the role of either equal or primary child-caretaker. Accordingly, the Tchambuli are not available as either an exception to the rule or as an exception which disproves the rule. There is no evidence that the Tchambuli are an exception.

altruism or goodwill of men, large numbers of whom have been socialized into a traditional male role, to stay at home when increasing numbers of women, who have been actively socialized to fulfill the maternal role, are choosing to leave the nursery. It is difficult to imagine that the same forces pulling women *from* the nursery could push men *into* the nursery.

The Swedish experiment of granting, on the birth of a baby, paid paternity leave to men has produced some interesting results. The payment of the paternity leave which is parallel to payments of maternity leave, is based on a philosophical position of equilibriating gender roles. The father role is interpreted as being congruent with the mother role—both of which become parent roles. The merging of the two parenting roles is predicated on changing the traditional father role to reflect the traditional mother role. The results have indicated that Swedish men have not, as yet, responded in a manner consonant with the mother role. In 1977, only 9.7% of the eligible men availed themselves of the program at all (Lamb & Levine, 1983). Of those men who did take one or more days of paternity leave, only half (52.9%) used 30 or more days of paid paternity leave. Of additional interest is Sweden's demographic characteristics. Sweden has a very low birth rate (11.7 births per 1000 population, 1980), and a low death rate (11.0 deaths per 1000 population, 1980, *World Almanac*, 1983). With approximately two children per family (roughly per nuclear family), the men would not be in the position of tending large broods of children. A large number of fathers would be tending a first-born, hence only one, child.

There is a clear lack of correspondence between the image of men acting in a mother role and the men's behavior. If the mother role is used to evaluate the parenting quotient of Swedish men, then, by their use of paid paternity leave, the Swedish men score rather low. Again, there is a conceptual advantage of having two benchmarks against which to adjudge paternal behavior: fathers versus fathers in addition to fathers versus mothers.

A reasonable interpretation of the data suggests that Swedish fathers are not appropriate Swedish mothers. Whether Swedish fathers are appropriate Swedish fathers is an entirely different question. The Swedish data by themselves do not address that question. Other countries' fathers need be surveyed to begin to answer that question.

Feasibility and the Swedish experiment aside, the argument is still available that qualitative and quantitative changes in technology and values have prepared the first viable cultural matrix conducive to shared, egalitarian parenthood. In such an event, mothers are no more placed at a competitive disadvantage than are fathers. The "tragedy" is thereby diluted from a concentration upon female parents to one on the more inclusive parents. Parents, men and women, who have elected to raise children are placed at economic and temporal disadvantages when compared to single individuals and to married couples who have chosen to remain childless. The tragedy can be shifted, diffused, concentrated, but it cannot be eliminated. The tragedy can be focused on one gender or two. It can be nested in nuclear families or extended families. What cannot be circumvented is the societal necessity for children and the children's necessity for immense reservoirs of resources and time.

Part of the ambivalent response to entitlement programs involving unwed mothers and their children may emanate from the men's (un)conscious perception of an anomaly in the United States social structure. In past and current American society, a married father is expected to provide time and resources toward his children. This transfer of valuable commodities, time and money, occurs with surprising ease and regularity. Men seem, on the whole, remarkably agreeable to the arrangement and to the duties of the father figure. These same men may be less enthusiastic about underwriting the rearing of other men's children. The starkness of one man paying the cost of another man's children is tempered somewhat by the intermediary of the state. That is, the state collects taxes and then returns the money in the form of welfare benefits. In addition, if the number or proportion of mother–child families on welfare is low, then the economic penalty toward family men is correspondingly low. However, if a large and increasing number of woman–child dyads were to be supported by the state (through taxation), then the declining percentage of men forming a nuclear family is in a vulnerable economic position. The children of these men absorb large proportions of the income, and the men's taxes are under pressure to be elevated by demands of families with no men, that is, mother–child families. Consequently, in the face of such economic realities, young men would be expected to be more reluctant to marry, and married men would be less reluctant to desert woman–child dyads. A society can have a stable social structure if (1) the predominate family structure consists of at least one man and at least one woman plus resulting children, or (2) the woman–child dyad predominates, and men are systematically unattached to those dyads. Any intermediate form is unstable and will drift in the direction of one or the other polarity.

In a digression more apparent than real, taking a couple steps back from the American familial system reveals an interesting dynamic. After—and due to—the Great Depression and World War II, the United States embarked on a social and political course that envisioned that the government would hold itself responsible for the minimum of food, clothing, and shelter for all of its citizens. While political pundits and idealogues may well argue long and eruditely over the wisdom or folly of such an adventure, the end result is that a new environment or ecological niche was created. Part of this new environment included the latent usurpation of the traditional male role as provider. Heretofore, men were responsible for guaranteeing resources and provisions for their wives and children. The enthusiasm and realization of such responsibility may have been widely variable across the diffuse category of men; nevertheless, the responsibility was theirs to fulfill or to abdicate. For the next three decades, the government/state increasingly focused its profile as a guarantor for basic necessities.

With every new ecological niche comes (going back to Darwin), the potential for new forms of adaptation. Subsequently two competing forms of family are now available to fit with more or less success into the new niche. Again, success is measured *only* by reproductive success over generations. The Chairman of the Board with two children and three grandchildren is less of a Darwinian success than the most menial line-worker with four children and nine grandchildren. "Quality of life" is not how evolution works; the only scoreboard is quantity. Quality is only important if it serves quantity.

One form, in essence, is the woman and child(ren) family. The second form, in essence, is the man, woman, and child(ren) family.

The addition of various grandmothers or aunts or siblings might give flavor to either of the polar forms; yet the two competing taxa are woman parents with (latent or manifest) governmental support or man-and-woman parents without governmental support.

In the 1980s, women now have the option, given the availability of abortion, of having a family including a man or of having a family

without a man. Freed from the logistical imperative of a man to provide for her and her children, the United States woman behaved in a
totally expected manner. She had a baby.

From 1950 to 1979, the overall birth rate dropped from 24.1 births
per 1000 population to 15.9 births per 1,000 population. The birth rate
for unmarried women rose from 14.1 births (per 1,000 unmarried
women) to 27.8 births (per 1,000 unmarried women, *National Center
for Health Statistics*, 1982). Looked at from a different angle, in 1950,
4.0% of all births were to unmarried women. In 1979, 17.1% of all
births were to unmarried women, and over half (56%) of these births
were to women 20 years or older.

Whether other single men or married men, enjoying sexual polygyny, are mostly fathering these children is anyone's guess. What is
not problematic is the existence of two variants of the family, woman
and child versus man, woman, and child, testing themselves against
the new environment and against each other. The dynamics of the
biocultural triangle ought to keep social scientists entertained and
busy for quite some time.

Child-Care Facilities

With the advent of formula and bottle nursing, child-care facilities also become a potential source of child rearing from birth onward.
The more time that an infant or child is at the facility and the more
that the facility's resources are used in the caring for the child, the less
become the demands that are made on the parent's time and resources. Hence, the more the facilities are used, the greater the personal liberty for each participating parent.

The economics of the commercial child-care person or the child-
care center are of interest. To make a profit from her wages working
outside of the home (vs. working inside the domicile without wages),
the mother must earn the cost paid to the child-caretaker plus any
increase in taxes, transportation, clothing, and miscellaneous costs
which accrue from the job. In other words, to make economic sense,
the mother must earn more net income than are the costs of taking
care of her child (net income increase minus the cost of the child care
must be greater than zero). The dynamics of this situation imply that,
in general, the individuals receiving the payments are less marketa-

ble, competent, or skilled than the individuals giving the payments. That is, if the United States economy is based upon increased pay for increased skills or productivity, then certainly the converse would be true also: the less skillful receive less pay. By being placed in the position of buying child care, the mother is funneled into funding people less marketable or competent than herself to care for her children. If the leased caretaker were equally competent when compared to the mother, the mother would not be able to afford the cost of the caretaker. The transfer of caretaking from parent to nonparent thereby infers a lessening in the skills to which the child is exposed.

In lieu of the commercial or private sector, child-care facilities could be public or governmentally run units. To facilitate an equitable sharing of expenses, these child-care facilities would necessarily have to be supported by taxes from the spectrum of the society's classes of people: that is, the married, single, the fecund, the childless, all of whom would pay for the facilities. Individual men and women are obviously still indispensable for procreation; yet they need not be responsible for taking even the minimum hiatus involved in full-time child rearing from birth to two years. Acts of procreation can be clearly separated from acts of socialization.

Disadvantages to this option may occur at the societal level. Disregarding the child warehouses, which have few defenders, even the most progressive child-care facilities have inherent problems for a society if they are utilized on a massive scale.

Child-care workers would be working for rational reasons. That is, they have chosen to work for salaries or wages plus fringe benefits with which their own lifestyles is either maintained or upgraded. As these employees change jobs, are promoted, or move, the accelerated turnover rate would leave the child with reduced continuity of a primary nurturant figure. A traditional mother figure, however, is constant over time and her relationship to the child is perceived by the folklore and symbolic system in the United States to be irrational. The relationship is normatively and ideally viewed within the imagery of the United States as reflecting a deep emotional commitment. To paraphrase the Russian proverb: "Mothers do things for free that one cannot pay others to do."

In addition, the economics of the public child-care facilities dictate a pressure to increase the number of children per staff member. This increased ratio works in the direction of minimizing the amount of time any given staff member spends with any given child. An added disadvantage in this situation is the difficulty in the measurement and assessment of the quality of the product. In the child-care facility, one would assume that the product would be the healthy psychological and emotional development of the child. This condition is obviously very difficult to evaluate or to quantify. Any possible advantage one child-care facility would have over another would be difficult to demonstrate.[3] Without a measuring device on quality control, the inertia on labor–management conflicts would move in the direction of improving the lot of employees. The employees' needs are increased pay, shorter contact time with the children, plus fringe benefits (e.g., dental insurance). The children's needs are sustained supportive adult–child interaction. The children, however, are not in a strong bargaining position. In an analogous situation, the public school system, another arena without quality control, witnesses numbers of strikes by teachers over wages, but very rarely strikes over apathy or ineffectiveness on the part of their fellow teachers.

Accordingly, if the option of the professional parent or child-care center is put into operation on a wide scale, such a selection places a system of child rearing based primarily on rational commitments in direct competition with systems of emotional, irrational commitments. Past generations of Americans and all other societies recorded have used the irrational system, that is, emotional ties to children. Consequently, if the American society gravitates toward a rational basis of raising children, it will be without successful precedent as evidenced from the extant societies that are the current survivors in the ongoing endeavor for societal survival.[4]

Any future system of universal, subsidized day-care centers, as primary child-socialization agents, faces the problem of interculture competition. The mammoth shift in the locus of child care not only

[3]It may be important to note that there is also no quality control, per se, in the traditional American nuclear family. This is evidenced by the phenomenon of child abuse in American society (Lenington, 1981). It may be more possible to institute quality control in public child-care facilities where none can conceivably be arranged in the private home. Still, the criteria by which adequacy would be measured would be difficult to determine and would be subject to much political, ideological debate.

[4]Although the Israeli kibbutzim system could be argued to represent an idealogical commitment to child-care facilities, the behavioral referents and the longevity of such a commitment are currently equivocal (Spiro, 1979; Tiger & Shepher, 1975).

would expose the American society to the stresses and problems of restructuring the major social institutions, it also proffers the new formula of social engineering as competing candidates in the market place of cultural options. The relative viability of the new formula for child rearing as well as the viability of the society subtending that formula would be evaluated by the filter of time. If the new system is robust enough and resilient enough to secure resources, protect its members, and produce competent citizens, it will be a success and enjoy an extended longevity. If not, the society either reverts to other social formulas or is absorbed into better adapted systems.

SOCIETAL RESPONSES TO THE TRAGEDY

It is useful to reiterate that new generations are necessary, if not sufficient, for a society to persevere over time. Disregarding re-population by immigration,[5] the most realistic thematic choices on how to insure effectively future generations are either: (1) to depend on the continuance of the traditional division of labor and the al-truism of the traditional family, thus assuming that the much her-alded, newly found freedom of American women, as a class, is a short-lived epicycle in the longer rhythms of the society's lifespan; or (2) dilute the tragedy to encompass fathers as well as mothers, or (3) to promote child-care facilities financed by the public coffers, thereby distributing the tragedy more equitably across a wider swathe of soci-ety's peoples; or (4) reciprocity on the part of the society toward the American females.[6] An example of the fourth avenue for developing a more equitable exchange between mothers and society could follow the pattern of the G.I. bill. In fulfilling the traditional mother role, women remove themselves from equal competition with most men

---

[5]Several of the northern European countries, for example, Great Britain, Germany, Sweden, currently entertain lowered birth rates (numbers of deaths are approximately the same as the number of births). Consequences of this trend include an aging population and the importation of foreign workers. The derivatives of this repopula-tion by immigration are beginning to be felt in these countries and the resultant fractures and dislocations indicate the process is not welcomed by the indigenous citizenry.

[6]For related discussions upon alternate options, see Mackey (1979b), Huber (1980), Lorber (1980), and Reiss and Hoffman (1979).

and single women in the market place of employment. A societal response to the loss of equity could be a reimbursement through a major conduit to preferred job choices—higher education. That is, society can make the decision to exchange free education (room, board, tuition, and a stipend) for the next generation: women who have finished childrearing can enroll, at public expense, at a school of their choice. The extent of the scholarship awarded to the mother would be related to the number of children and the numbers of years spent nurturing them. The scholarship can be for professional, vocational, or liberal arts training. The choice would belong to the mother. The free education would act to help generate a more egalitarian competition between mothers, men, and single/childless women.

This linkage of fecundity and education would not initiate a totally new relationship. An interaction between education and fecundity has long existed and been recognized. With the focus, not on the individual, but on the society, a current pattern in the United States may have long term consequences upon the character, direction, and qualities of the culture. With an increase in the educational level of women there is a clear and substantial decrease in the number of children those women will have. Framed differently, female fecundity is negatively correlated with female education. With the attainment of a high school diploma, replacement value is still occurring. Added years of formal training progressively results in fewer children until the mean number of children per woman is 1.5 for college graduates and postgraduates. This figure is well below replacement levels. For women in *Who's Who* (1980), the figure is 1.07 children per woman.[7] See Table 47.

It certainly may be argued that not all traits or personality characteristics of highly educated individuals who succeed in the quest for high grades and advanced degrees are appropriate to be uniquely promulgated or increased within a population; yet in the context of a society which places high value on the concept of education and in

---

[7]The *Who's Who* compilation may be viewed, in a generalized manner, as reflecting achieved status by the individuals involved. On the other hand, the *Social Register* may be viewed, in an equally generalized manner, as illustrating ascribed status of the participants. A sample number of listed children in the *Social Register* from 1,246 families revealed an average of 1.97 children—a level of reproduction below replacement value. Accordingly, the high-born and the highly motivated within the U.S. are both underrepresented in subsequent generations.

TABLE 47
Educational Level and Mean Number of Children Born per Married Woman (15–44 Years of Age)[a]

Education level	Children born per woman			
	1950	1960	1969	1974
College, 4 years or more	1.3	1.7	1.8	1.5
College, 1–3 years	1.4	2.0	2.1	1.7
High school, 4 years	1.5	2.1	2.3	2.1
High school, 1–3	1.9	2.5	2.9	2.6
Elementary school, 8 years	2.1	2.6	3.2	3.1
Elementary school, less than 8 years	2.6	3.1	3.4	3.5

[a]W. F. Kenkel, *The Family in Perspective.* Santa Monica, California: Goodyear, p. 225 (1977).

the context of individuals who accept and thrive on that value, the consistent draining of these people and their attributes from the population over generations must surely have an effect, probably not beneficial, on that society. Viewed from the other side of the coin, the idea that the eventuation of the society's values, a highly educated citizenry, is detrimental to that society would seem peculiar. It is more likely that there may be some penalty to be paid by a society when the brightest members of a gender are increasingly underrepresented in subsequent generations. Hardin's logic is relevant once more. An individual's excitement and curiousity and ambition are certainly laudable when viewed from the perspective of the American socioeconomic ethos. The individuals, taken as a unit, who possess these traits are systematically deleting themselves from influencing subsequent generations and affecting the character of that society accordingly.

Any of the options could be the response to the tragedy of the commons or some combination could be the direction taken by aggregate America. Our society can (1) stay with the traditional emotional commitment from parent (man or woman) to child with no formal compensation or (2) institutionalize a large scale child-care system based on rational committment on the part of the worker toward the child or blend the rational with the irrational by having 24 hour "drop-in" child-care centers, thereby blending the irrational commitment of the parent with the rational commitment provided by the professional, or (3) develop a G.I. bill analogue to compensate the woman for her service to society by providing the mother with educational advantages in exchange for the next generation.

Whatever the response, the logic of the tragedy of the commons is neither averted nor removed. For a society to exist, an average of two and a fraction children per woman must be constantly nurtured and monitored by adults for at least 2–4 years each at high costs to those adults in the form of time and resources: no children, no society. However, the divesting of large amounts of time and resources—with no rational incentives—by adults toward children diminishes personal freedom for those adults and places the caretaking adults at a marked disadvantage in the quest for highly pursued, high paying occupations.

Although the sacrifice of time and resources by child-caretakers can be distributed in various ratios, formats, and formulas, the sacrifice cannot be reduced to zero. Similarly, part of the cost to a nation—any nation—for its survival depends upon the willingness of its individual citizenry, taken one at a time, to surrender part of his or her freedom and treasure for the corporate good. The continuity of a society and the total freedom within that society cannot coexist at the same time—such is the nature of tragedies.

CHAPTER 9

Conclusion

SUMMARY

The argument presented so far has traveled a circuitous route and has touched a wide array of conceptual and empirical bases. To help crystalize and profile the structure of the argument that has been presented, it may be useful to summarize the key points of the argument. The two basic questions this exploration addressed were (1) what were the behavior patterns that existed between men and children and (2) what were the forces which generated and reflected these patterns of behavior.

The one condition that was fundamental at the inception of the project was the requirement of letting the men and children who were to be surveyed to act on their own priorities, preferences, and agendas. Ad lib or feral behavior on the part of the respondents was essential. So, methods of surveying the interaction between men and children were designed which would be unintrusive and would leave the man–child relatively unfettered by the form and texture of my speculations and intuitions. At that juncture, thousands of men, women, and children around the globe were consigned to the honor of being stared at by various cuts of social scientists when they, scientists and subjects alike, were in public places during daylight hours. Once the decision was made to use naturalistic observation upon feral humans in their play and recreation, the next problem was the selection of which spots on the globe were to be surveyed. Ruing for the moment the problems that geopolitics tend to serve for the social scientist, vast areas of interesting places and people were unavailable for scrutiny. Although I was tempted to accept a volunteer who thought a combination of urban guerilla-anthropologist-lay missionary was attractive as a summer adventure, I ended by restricting observation sites to those places that were safe, politically insensitive, and with relatively unrestricted access. Eventually 18 samples were collected in 15 countries on 5 continents with over 49,000 adult–child dyads recorded. The samples were selected in part on their reliance on men to perform traditional tasks which called on their superior brute strength. A second criterion was based on urban-rural distinctions. The idea underpinning the first of these two variables was that gender and age were important variables in any society and that the structuring of any culture would include ordered allocations of the presence or absence of males versus females and younger versus older. In addition, it was accepted that a populace with a rural, agrarian lifestyle may well develop different values and habits toward their children when compared to the lifestyle in an urban service-oriented lifestyle.

If the cultures were changed systematically, then the question becomes: Would the allocations of people by age and gender also change, and change systematically? On the other side of the coin, it was also of interest whether there would be cross-cultural consistencies or constants in the behavioral patterns that would complement any putative variations. The answer, happily enough, to both questions turned out to be *yes*. Predictable variations occurred and so did predictable constants.

In essence, the constants included the following tendencies (from Chapter 2; Tables 2–14):

1. During discretionary times and in discretionary places, men were with their children in fairly appreciable proportions (compared to the woman–child dyad).
2. Men responded to children in a basically similar way when the responses were compared to the way woman responded to children. Said in a different way, men were not with children as often as were women, but once they were present, they behaved with their children not unlike the way the women did.
3. Compared to gender, the age of the children seemed much more important in influencing the level or intensity of interaction received from the adults—men and women. Younger children, not surprisingly, received more active levels of re-

sponse from adults than did older children. What was somewhat surprising was that men, as well as women, responded
toward children in a manner that was gender neutral. That is,
boys and girls were treated rather similarly. While it is true
that the measuring instruments were necessarily coarse
grained to allow cross-cultural comparability, the tenacious
manner in which man–boy interactions paralleled man–girl
interaction and in which man–child interaction paralleled
woman–child interaction was still a surprise.

My intuition would have been that woman–child interaction
would have been substantially higher than man–child interaction and
that men would have behaved preferentially toward boys, and wom-
en preferentially toward girls. My intuitions are occasionally offered
large doses of humility.

Given that higher levels of paternalistic behavior occurred than
were anticipated, the question presented itself: why? Why were men
behaving paternalistically at all—and why were they doing so in such
large numbers and so intensely? The easy facile answer would be that
they "wanted" to behave that way, they were enjoying what they
were doing, and that they had learned the appropriate father role
from their relevant socialization agents.

A more rigorous answer initially involves the (consensual) construction of an evolutionary history of our genus *Homo* as a hunter-
scavenger-gatherer. It is generally agreed that early *Homo* emerged
with a lifestyle in which men-only groups hunted and scavenged and
then returned to the women and children to share food with them.
The argument is then presented that sharing food is not a light and
trivial matter; but that such sharing is continguent upon the men
wanting and willing to do so. In turn, with a couple of ratchet-turns
in speculation, the wanting and willingness to share is predicted on
affectional bonds mediated by the motivational system (the central
nervous system and the endocrine system). Said much more briefly:
men *like* children. Although the sentence "men like children" is brief
and, I think, rather accurate, the processes and dynamics which have
led to that affection are fundamental and complex—not facile and
simple.

Men have been forged and tempered by the pressures of natural
selection acting over enormous spans of time to be triggered and

motivated by the actions, shenanigans, and hurts of children who have grown up with those men since birth in close proximity and in intimacy. That fathers will walk colicky children at wee hours, lose consistently at Uncle Wiggley and Chutes and Ladders, invariably be the Old Maid, buy braces and Barbi's and 10-speed bikes, provide tuitions and supply the "but I *must* have. . . " items, are all of no mere accident or examples of serendipity for a few lucky children. Men, as a class, are built to protect and provision bonded children.

The building is probably found in some form of neurohormonal circuitry which would allow for a quick, efficient, well-integrated learning of how to be fond of children. When given the chance to be fond of their children, I suspect most men would succeed swimmingly. It would surprise me, however, if all men are loving or that all children are lovable. Because there are so many factors that allow such huge variability and diversity, for 100% of any human category to act identically seems most unlikely. It would not surprise me at all, if, allowed a normal environment, most men would love most of their children most of the time.

The phrase which encapsulates this genetic template for paternalistic behavior is that parenting behavior is not gender dimorphic in humans, but that the threshold for initiation and maintenance of the parenting behaviors is lower for men than for women. Removing the jargon for the minute, it is suggested that it is harder to motivate men, compared to women, to act in a nurturing way toward children, but, once motivated, men are as nurturing to their children as would be the woman.

Sentences such as "men like children" and "there is a fathering instinct" are very much easier to write than to substantiate. The idea of a genetic basis to the father–child bond, that is, a fathering instinct, is not an idea everyone will embrace enthusiastically in the 1980s. To some, the idea will reek of a Rudyard Kipling Just so Story: "How the Father Became the Child of Man." To others, the idea will be viewed as another fiber in the halyard depicting the innate depravity and immutability of the human condition. To still others, the idea will be dismissed as a senseless and inefficient exercise in an attempt to reduce humanity to an automaton governed by a black box of drives, needs, and appetites. Separate from these individuals, there will be others with a healthy skepticism, but equally healthy ability to suspend judgment and remark: "Put your evidence in the market place of ideas and let us scrutinize that evidence and then make a decision from our apperceptive masses." These individuals will be comfortable with the notion that a Newtonian proof is currently and truly unavailable in regards to finding causal factors in the development of human behavior, but that evidential shreds can be mustered to bolster a case. The fewer and increasingly amorphous the shreds, the weaker the case. The more and increasingly clear the shreds, the stronger the case. That point at which high quality shreds of evidence can present themselves to make an argument or case strong enough to be a good case then becomes matter of individual taste, judgment, and opinion.

For those people who are interested in weighing the evidence, two bits of evidence can be marshalled to lend support to a biological basis for paternalistic behavior.

1. The descriptive data are there to illustrate high levels of fathering behaviors. The high levels are consistent across otherwise divergent and unique cultures. Behavioral consistency was found in the face of cultural variability. This consistency is awkward to explain using a variable as the explanatory device. Another consistency in the project is the genotype of *Homo sapiens*. One consistency can be considered a reasonable candidate with which to help explain the existence of a second consistency. Unless a third force is conjured that can be seen to influence human behavior, cultural traditions and genetic heritage are the only two candidates competing for the opportunity to effect human actions. The removal of one, cultural traditions, would leave the field open to the other, genetic heritage. The project was designed to move in the direction of neutralizing unique cultural traditions; yet the results still found consistent systematic patterns of man–child behavior across those same cultures. Consequently, it is suggested that the genetic explanation is the stronger case than is the cultural explanation.

2. A deductive development of an hypothesis, if sustained, is normally viewed as lending credibility to the theory or axiom generating the dynamics of the hypothesis. In the instance of this project, two hypotheses can be deduced from the premises supporting the notion of a genetic template or fathering. The premises are (a): behavioral tendencies are inherited in blueprint or recipe form and these tendencies are best viewed as biased motivational states: some responses feel better and are more impelling than other responses at

specified times and places, (b): the ecological heritage of men acted to select in those genetic recipes that favored the men to stay with and to associate with those children who had grown-up proximate to the men. Presumably those children were close kin, usually the men's (assumed) offspring or his sister's offspring; Premise (c): the ecological heritage of men also selected in those genetic recipes that favored recruitment of pubescent boys into all-male groups—hunting groups. Given these three premises, it can be deduced that:

1. Men would be unlikely to leave through divorce—read desert—their own children (See Chapter 4, Table 27).
2. Men and pubescent boys ought to be overrepresented in feral groups across societies (compared to the other five adult–child groupings) (See Chapter 2; Table 8).

Both of these proposed patterns were tested and supported. The deductive route was a success. It is not a success in terms of a mathematical proof; we are long treks away from proofs; however, we did have a success in terms of predictability. For the moment such a success in such a difficult field is not bad at all. At the least, an argument was placed in that market place of ideas and the argument was geared to help account for some of the data gathered. These data were similarities of behaviors across cultural boundaries. Now, what about the systematic differences?

The systematic differences in behavioral patterns across the 18 culture sample seemed to reflect a generalized cultural event: the relative reliance by a referent group on their men to perform tasks which depended on the men's superior brute strength (compared to women).

When these tasks, plowing and protection are good examples, were salient and important, several trends occurred (see Chapter 5: Tables 35 and 36):

1. Men increased their associations with boys (compared to girls).
2. Men decreased their associations with women (and as a derivative with infants).
3. Men increased their associations with other men (rather than with women).

4. Women increased their associations with other women (rather than with men).

When these tasks of male prerogatives were minimized or reduced in a society, then the reverse happened:

1. Men associated with boys and with girls more equally.
2. Men decreased their associations with other men and increased their associations with women (and thereby with infants).
3. Women also decreased their associations with other women and increased their associations with men.

Presented more succinctly, the reliance on male strength separates the two genders in a culture. The removal of such a reliance allows females and males to associate with each other in a more egalitarian manner.

At this point two major effects had been made available for pondering and for bracketing the man–child bond: the natural tendencies of the species, however thematic or generalized, and the cultural traditions of any society being investigated.

A third lens with which to see the man–child bond is the unique symbolic system of the culture in question. Although all of cultures in this sample certainly have symbolic systems, and it is probably a safe bet to assume that all of the cultures have had one or more social scientists who keenly scrutinized those systems, the only symbolic system analyzed in this project was that of the United States.

The United States data in the context of the 17 other cultures were then compared to the perceptions of American authors writing about American father figures. In a bit of discontinuity there was a rather bad fit between United States father data (again, the United States sample was represented only by Virginia), and the writings of individuals reporting upon the American father figure. Both the professional and popular presses inferred or boldly asserted that fathers in America were either irrelevant to the appropriate psychosocial development of their children and were somewhat inept parents (an earlier stereotype) or were potentially useful but still derelict in fulfilling that potential (a more current stereotype). Because no real evidence was given to support the allegations, these allegations must stem from images or symbols within the folklore or the myth system of the American culture.

The available data in this project lent support to the notion that American men, compared to other men in other cultures, were doing typical and unexceptional things with their children. No signs or indications of a super dad or of a derelict dad emerged. (See Chapter 6; Tables 42–46). American men were rather bland examples of the way men and children acted toward each other across the globe. Imagery and behavior were not congruent.

An explanation was then presented which suggested that men who arrogated the role of primary child caretaker would be ridiculed or mocked in that society's myth system. That is, men would not be encouraged or allowed to compete with women for the status of primary child-caretaker. Such competition is prevented or reduced so that men can avoid any role conflict which would interfere with their own gender specific tasks (e.g., plowing, protecting, raiding, hunting) which would be incompatible with child care. In spite of the caricature and denigration of the man when he acted as a mother substitute, the actual behaviors of the surveyed men did illustrate high levels of epimeletic or caretaking behaviors. The men can and do act as solicitous parents, but the cultural filters are set in place such that the caregiving by these men is seen and interpreted by the natives as exceptions or as sporadic, but not chronic.

Subsequently, the images would allow both sets of male behaviors to exist simultaneously: the traditional male role and the caregiving parental role. The symbols for the status of the traditional male would be emphasized whereas the symbols for the status of the highly nurturant male would be rebuked.

The historical dynamics of the cultural construction of the myth of the derelict daddy in America then become understandable: tasks that are incompatible with continuous child care or which require sheer bulk of muscle power were given to males. To make sure that the men were available to perform those tasks, the mutually exclusive task of continuous child caregiving was deleted from the expectations of what men would do.

Part of the process of removing men from competing with women for the status of primary child care-taker was the ridicule and mockery of the man when he was pictured as a mother substitute.

Both men and women, in the past as well as currently, have been presented with the same tapestry of the father figure as they have been socialized. They accept and incorporate the image of the male as somewhat deficient in the realm of proper parenting. The myth becomes the reality. The myth becomes the tacit and real starting point in an analysis of or inquiry into the American father figure. In a nearly metaphorical way, the mental gymnastics begin with "The American father figure is inadequate because. . . ." The reasons for the alleged inadequacy can become erudite or simplistic, convoluted or direct, microanalytical or macroanalytical. Whatever the conclusions are, they are based upon a perception of a myth which has more functional impact in the symbolic realm than descriptive accuracy in an empirical realm. Conclusions based on a faulty premise tend not to be particularly useful.

Once the tripartite analysis (biology, culture, imagery) was complete, an attempt was made to divine some of the current forces that push-and-pull, hew-and-haul at the American parent. The perspective of *Homo sapiens*, the Rational Creature, was assumed in the attempt to find incentives for men and women to become parents who will raise and nurture children from birth to independence. In a rational analysis based on the economics of time, money, and resources, children are heavily counterproductive. They are expensive and cost-ineffective. The truly rational person is far better off letting other people have children who, in turn, will serve as the labor force maintaining the good life for that person.

Because children are so essential to the perpetuation of each and every cultural group, incentives for parenting have to be extant if the culture is to continue as a discrete entity. If the benefits of rearing children are decided to be worth the costs, then the next question becomes: Who bears those costs?

The allocation of childrearing costs in terms of time, resources, and money becomes a nontrivial problem when the costs are heavy, the distribution is unequal, and the alternatives are very appealing. Currently, societies do rely on the altruistic sacrifice of people who decide to become parents. These parent-folks seem to be deciding to be parent-folks on the basis of irrational commitments—read "emotions." At what point the rational penalities begin to outweigh the joys of irrational commitments is a matter social scientists will be squinting at for years to come.

CONCLUSION

When it has all been said and done, what has been gained from analyzing over 49,000 adult–child dyads from five continents along the three maps of (1) evolutionary history, (2) cultural ecology, and (3) symbolic systems? What of value bubbles out of the cauldron of the hordes of numbers and the diversity of theories?

Let me suggest that five points are potentially useful to ponder. The pondering would not exemplify any brand new or inchoate ideas. The Greeks seem to have anticipated most of the really interesting problems that humans would face either as individuals or as members of a tribe. Having anticipated, they were rather talented in discussing and presenting our lives to us. Because these Greeks wrote down their mental meanderings, they receive a good deal of credit for the development of Western philosophy (see Russell, 1945, for a review of some of their ruminations). In addition to clever Greek scholars, there may well more have been many cerebral sheperds or prescient peasants who (only) imagined the unimaginable and who (only) fathomed the course and destination of the human condition without writing down their mental adventures cum signature (cf. Gray, 1751). Their wisdom has filtered down to us via folklore, fables, and cliches—all signed "anonymous." The literate Greeks with intimations of immortality signed their written thoughts, and we can know their ideas and their personalities individually across the millenia. So, with a respectful nod to anonymous sheperds, far-flung peasants, and literate Greeks, I proffer some ideas in the form of reminders rather than as illusions of innovation.

A key feature to the study presented in the preceding chapters is the comfortable placement of humans in Mother Nature's domain. We are a part of the natural world and not apart from it. The data insert us into a zoological niche, and the insertion did not hurt a jot— the beast within everyone of us was not so bad after all. The specific example or vehicle for this idea was the man–child bond. It was suggested that, given a reasonably stable environment with at least minimum levels of creature comforts, men in a tribe or community will gravitate toward their children and nurture, cuddle, and play with them. They will love their children. They will love their children not because of magic, not because of a lack of alternatives, and not because they are expected to do so by significant others—again the content of emotion cannot be taught, only experienced. They will love their children because they are built to love them. The substratum in the form of the motivation system (central nervous system and endocrine system) was and is passed from generation to generation in the form of the genetic recipe or blueprint on how to construct a human who will survive to construct culture. The culture, in turn, will create a subjective reality enmeshing the human in a milieu such that men and women can find each other and will create issue who will play out the cycle of life once again. It is my guess that this form of biological determinism is one with which most people can find an easy accommodation.

The conjunction or reciprocal character of the relationship between genetic information and culture introduces a second point. The genetic recipe for humans is, for specific behaviors, flexible and malleable enough to entertain complexities, subtleties, and nuances of great variability. At least from the human point of view, our human culture is rich in detail and texture. From the perspectives of termites, elephants, or Venutians, we may appear as very boring, predictable robots with no surprises at all—but that evaluation would belong in their chronicles, not in this one. Despite the assumed realities of our human cultural diversity for particular behavior complexes, it is suggested that the *themes* of our behaviors are much less arbitrary and that these themes, over ontogenic and phylogenetic time spans, maintain the core of humanity.

A useful metaphor should be introduced here, and this is the metaphor of the rubber band. Any rubber band worthy of its name can be stretched, bent, folded, and pulled in an infinite number of patterns. However, when the forces manipulating the rubber band's configuration are removed, it will return, either slowly or quickly, to its original shape. The more it is stretched, the greater the rubber band will exert a counterforce to return to its base condition. Continuous force may, of course, be applied to the rubber band and perpetually keep it from its original condition. Such force, however, can be expensive and wearisome, thereby progressively encouraging the forces to be removed and their energies to be saved for more rewarding escapades elsewhere.

Over the individual's time–space continua, as well as over the species's history, short term stretches undoubtedly have occurred and will occur again—but for slower, more fundamental rhythms and

themes of life-death-and-life-again, the core matrix of the human condition seems to have inertia firmly on its side. Any given man or any
given tribe's men can be kept from interacting with their children at
mutually satisfying levels for days, months, or perhaps generations.
Nonetheless, I would venture that individual prerogatives and social
formulas, which funnel men and children together and allow them to
find mutually satisfying equilibria of social interaction, will emerge
and solidify themselves in the proximate culture. The achievement of
equilibrium may be slow and steady or rapid and decisive. Other
cultural chips in the overall societal mosaic can catalyze or obstruct
temporarily—the occurrence of men associating and interacting with
their children however does not seem problematic.

A second metaphor presents itself. Just as we can choose either a
vanilla ice cream cone or a chocolate ice cream cone in order to eat ice
cream, we are still eating ice cream if either of the conditions occur.
Although we can choose to eat ice cream or something else, we are
still eating food. But note that the choice of eating food or not eating
at all is a self-correcting program: those that choose not to eat soon
lose the option of having choices at all. Some strategies encourage
their own perpetuation; other strategies discourage perpetuation.

Similarly, we can choose a myriad of rationales or procedures in
regards to bearing and rearing children. Fathers can be strict or per-
missive or inconsistent. Fathers can foster traditional gender roles for
boys and girls, or they can foster androgeny in their children. These
are options which, from a distance, are not of import. For fathers to
be with their children and share their social lives *is* of import, for
children and for men. Such sharing is, in part, what men are about,
and such sharing is, in part, what children are about. How to config-
ure the social milieu is quite optional. To have or not to have the
social milieu is less optional. The rubber band, when stretched, either
strives to return to its original form or, if stretched too far, will snap.
Another self-correcting program is in effect, if rubber band lineages
are to continue.

The third point of attention is more technical. In the analysis of
human social behavior, the validation of any hypothesis concerning
the behavior must occur through behavior, that is, only recorded
behavior can validate conjectures about behavior. Neither neu-
rophysiological mapping nor interpretations of folk wisdom, current
or past, can validate what people *do*. How people behave can be

ascertained only by finding out how they behave. These is no substitute. Questionnaires, surveys, and interviews tell us how people
respond to questionnaires, surveys, and interviews. They can also
suggest what to look for in the form and frequency of behavior. What
they cannot do is tell how in fact the people in question actually
behave. To quiz fathers and their spouses about father–child interaction gathers interesting information to be sure; but that information
reflects directly on the perception of a father role and may or may not
reflect the behavioral antecedents to that role. It is a bold and swash-
buckling scientist who assumes accurate, unbiased, undistorted, and
unfiltered verbal and written responses from those fathers and
spouses. The existence of such childlike innocence and faith which
presupposes truth from parents' intuitions and feelings and memo-
ries is awkward to point out—no one wants to toss soot on Snow
White. Nevertheless, the Western cultural traditions proclaiming
honesty is a good thing—for example, "An honest man is the noblest
work of God" (Pope, 1734)—may also covertly teach that any following of that dictum of honesty ought more be observed in the breach
than in the observance. At that juncture, we have an empirical question to be tested rather then a premise crystalized on which further
constructs are to be placed. The presumption of subjects' veracity is a
luxury social scientists simply do not have. Fathering, as a behavior
pattern, can be best known by profiling the behavior and not by
recording culturally tinted images or expectations of that pattern.

A fourth idea concerns the starting point for analyzing a sample
of fathers. Deleting cross-species comparisons for the moment, the
two main candidates become "mothers" and "other fathers." If one
begins with the premise that there are parents—male-types and
female-types—and that the gender of the parent is irrelevant to parenting, then it makes reasonable sense to compare fathers with mothers. To date, such comparisons have made fathers look rather bad
and mothers look rather good. If a society wishes to remedy this
asymmetry, mothering quotients could be lowered or fathering quotients could be raised.

On the other hand, one could begin with the premise that there
are male-parents and there are female-parents and that the gender of
the parents, taken over a population rather than each individual one
at a time, does make a difference. With such a beginning, fathers
from one setting would then be compared to fathers from alternate

settings, that is, fathers are compared to other fathers—not with mothers.

As presented earlier, the data from this project indicate that American fathers are typical, normative, and anything but aberrant. American fathers are doing just fine when compared to other cultures' fathers. In terms of fathering, not mothering, there is no available data base that suggests, much less demonstrates, that American fathers are not doing normal things in normal amounts for normal durations. Any attempt to raise or lower fathering quotients would have to be justified by reasons other than those found in available data.

Which of the two starting points someone would choose may serve to reflect that person's sense of aesthetics, politics, social justice, economics, ego, or vested interest. For whatever reason that one beginning premise is preferred over the alternate beginning premise, the conclusions which emanate from that initial difference in starting place will also be fundamentally different. If important decisions are to be made that might impact on men as fathers and on children as progeny, both views might be considered thoroughly before those decisions are made and implemented. Rubber bands can stretch; rubber bands can snap.

The fifth and final point concerns temporocentrism: the evaluation of events, past and future, from the attitudes and values belonging to one moment in time—usually the present. In the latter years of the 20th century, the scientific establishment has amassed an amazing and prodiguous amount of information on human behavior, any trip to any reference library's stacks and microfilm can clearly attest to the volume. What is less clear is the amount of ignorance which is still available concerning the human creature. The volume of the unknown may be infinite, or it may merely be enormous.

Looking back on other epochs, we can, after a fashion, see foolishness and folly in abundance: alchemy, flat earths, Lamarckisms, rabbits' feet, Piltdown man, astrology, thalidomide, and swine-vaccines. Such mistakes generally lend humility toward others who have gone by—and not to us (cf. Minor, 1956). Our own errors in concept in (misplaced) faith, and tribal yearnings for group or peer approval tend to be far less obvious to ourselves, but probably not to those others to come who will decide to look back at us.

Fathering behavior is, I would posit, a very complex business indeed, and fathering behavior is only a small part of the overall repertoire of human resources. Fathering involves neural tissues collecting data, organizing that data into emotions and thoughts, and then delivering those emotional-motivational states transcribed into behavior. Fathering also involves hard to plumb social processes deeply woven within those neural tissues via some, equally difficult to plumb, mechanism. I can think of no imperative on the part either of the social processes or of the neural tissues which finds accuracy or truth to be of any consistent and inherent value over and beyond illusion or camouflage. Only the scientific community is more or less aligned with the premise that truth is an unqualified good thing and that knowledge is always better than ignorance. Other taxa serve other masters' other priorities.

If it can be agreed that the adult male–child bond is a major and irreducible facet of the human biogram, there is probably something to be said for treating it carefully and with respect for what it is and what it does across generations and not necessarily what we would momentarily like it to be or not to be.

Appendix: Coding System

TACTILE CONTACT—ADULT TO CHILD

As soon as the group composition is determined, a thirty second observation interval is begun. Within the 30 seconds, the *most* active physical contiguity from the adult's hands to the child is recorded. See below for the coding system for tactile contact—adult to child.

0 carressing and holding   (*Most Active Tactile Contact*)
1 feeling or caressing
2 extended or prolonged holding (holding for the entire 30 second interval)
3 holding (holding for a portion of the 30 second interval)
4 spot touching (e.g., a hand peck)
5 accidental touching (e.g., brushing)
6 No contact whatsoever   (*Least Active Tactile Contact*)

PERSONAL DISTANCE—ADULT TO CHILD

With the adult's head and trunk as the locus, the closest in terms of (spatial) distance that the adult comes to the child, within the 30 second observation limit, is recorded. See below for the coding system of personal distance—adult to child.

 11 touching with head or trunk   (*Closest Distance*)
101 just outside body contact
 12 touching with forearms, elbows, or knees
102 within forearm distance, but not touching
 13 touching with arms fully extended

Statistical instrument: Chi-square extension of the median test.

182

103 within arm reach, but not touching
14 touching with arm extended and body leaning
104 within reach if body is leaning and arm is extended
55 outside the system; applicable only with extensions (*Farthest distance*)

VISUAL ORIENTATION—ADULT TO CHILD

The immediate visual field is considered to be directly in front of any individual's eyes plus segments to the left and right of center. The coding interval for Visual orientation is the *last* 5 seconds of the 30 second observation interval. If, during the full 5 seconds, the child is never in the visual scan of the adult, the child is recorded as being out of the adult's visual field (coded NONSEE). If during any portion of the 5 seconds, the child is within the visual scan of the adult, then the child is recorded as being in the adult's visual field (coded SEE). Figure A-1 reflects the coding system of visual orientation—adult to child.

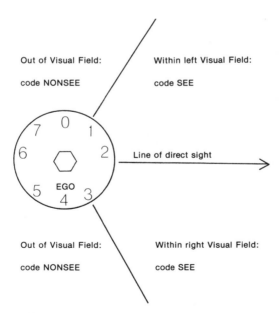

FIGURE A-1. Statistical instrument: chi-square.

APPENDIX TABLE 1

Correlations and Beta-Weights for the Four Patterned Proxemic Behaviors.
The Protector Index and the Plowman Index are Analyzed Separately.

Proxemic behavior	Protector		Plowman	
	r	Beta-weight	r	Beta-weight
Percentage of children who were boys associating with men-only groups	+.264	+.155	+.406*	+.359
Percentage of children who were associating with groups of men and women	−.330	−.141	−.667**	−.624
Women's plural group score (WPGS)	−.410*	−.302	−.447*	−.356
Men's plural group score (MPGS)	−.437*	−.356	−.375	−.268

$*p < .05; **p < .01.$

References

Adams, R. N. An inquiry into the nature of the family. In G. E. Dole & R. L. Carneiro (Eds.), *Essays in the science of culture in honor of Leslie A. White*. New York: Thomas Y. Crowell, 1960, pp. 30–49.

Ainsworth, M. D., Bell, S. M., & Stayton, D. J. *Patterns of attachment*. Hillsdale, N.J.: Erlbaum, 1978.

Alexander, R. D. *Darwinism and human affairs*. Seattle: Univ. of Washington Press, 1979.

Alexander, R. D. & Noonan, K. M. Concealment of ovulation, parental care, and human social evolution. In N. A. Chagnon & W. Irons (Eds.), *Evolutionary biology and human social behavior: An anthropological perspective*. North Scituate, Mass.: Duxbury Press, 1979, pp. 436–453.

Allen, D. L. *Wolves of Minong: Their vital role in a wild community*. Boston: Houghton Mifflin, 1979.

Andrews, P. Hominoid evolution. *Nature*, 1982, *295*, 185.

Appleton, W. S. *Fathers and daughters*. Garden City, New York: Doubleday, 1981.

Ardrey, R. *African genesis*. New York: Delta Books, 1961.

Ardrey, R. *Territorial imperative*. New York: Atheneum, 1966.

Ardrey, R. *The social contract*. New York: Atheneum, 1971.

Ardrey, R. *The hunting hypothesis*. New York: Atheneum, 1976.

Arens, W. *The man eating myth: Anthropology and anthropophagy*. New York: Oxford Univ. Press, 1979.

Bailey, W. T. Affinity: An ethological theory of the infant–father relationship. *Infant Behavior and Development* (Special ICIS Issue), 1982a, *5*, 12.

Bailey, W. T. Affinity: An ethological perspective of the infant–father relationship in humans. *International Journal of Primatology*, 1982b, *3*, 257.

Bales, K. B. Cumulative scaling of paternalistic behavior in primates. *American Naturalist*, 1980, *116*, 454–461.

Barash, D. P. *Sociobiology and behavior*. New York: Elsevier, 1977.

Barkow, J. Biological evolution of culturally patterned behavior. In J. Lockard (Ed.), *The evolution of human social behavior*. New York: Elsevier, 1980, pp. 277–290.

Barry, H., Bacon, M. K., & Child, I. L. A cross-cultural survey of some sex differences in socialization. *The Journal of Abnormal and Social Psychology*, 1957, *55*, 327–332.

Barry, J., Child, I. L., & Bacon, M. K. Relation of child training to subsistence economy. *American Anthropologist*, 1959, *61*, 51–63.

Barry, H. & Paxson, L. Infancy and early childhood: Cross-Cultural codes 2. *Ethnology*, 1971, *10*, 466–508.

Barry, H., Josephson, L., Lauer, E., & Marshall, C. Agents and techniques for child training: Cross-Cultural codes 6. *Ethnology*, 1977, *16*, 191–230.

185

Beach, F. A. The descent of instinct. *Psychological Review*, 1955, *62*, 401–410.

Bednarik, K. *The male in crisis*. New York: Knoph, 1970.

Benbow, C. P. & Stanley, J. C. Sex differences in mathematical ability: Fact or artifact? *Science*, 1980, *210*, 1262–1264.

Berger, A. A. *The comic stripped American*. New York: Walker, 1973.

Biehler, R. F. *Child development: An introduction*, (2nd ed.). Boston: Houghton Mifflin, 1981.

Biller, H. B. A Multiaspect investigation of masculine development in kindergarten age boys. *Genetic Psychology Monographs*, 1968, *78*, 89–137.

Biller, H. B. *Father, child, and sex role*. Lexington, Mass.: Heath Lexington Books, 1971.

Biller, H. B. *Paternal deprivation*. Lexington, Mass.: Heath Lexington Books, 1974.

Biller, H., & Meredith, D. *Father power*. Garden City, New York: Anchor Books, 1975, pp. 1–9.

Bowlby, J. The nature of the child's tie to his mother. *International Journal of Psycho-analysis*, 1958, *39*, 350–373.

Bowlby, J. *Attachment and loss. Vol I. Attachment*. New York: Basic Books, 1969.

Bowlby, J. *Attachment and loss. Vol. II. Separation, anxiety, and anger*. London: Hogarth, 1973.

Breland, K. & Breland, M. The Misbehavior of Organisms. In T. E. McGill (Ed.). *Readings in animal behavior* New York: Holt, Rinehart & Winston, 1965, pp. 455–460.

Brenton, M. *The American male*. Greenwich, Connecticut: Fawcett, 1966.

Brito, E. M. *La poblacion en Mexico*. Mexico: Centro de Investigacion Y Accion Social, 1969.

Broude, G. J. Extramarital sex norms in cross-cultural perspective. *Behavior Science Research*, 1980, (15), 181–218.

Broude, G. J. & S. J. Greene. Cross-Cultural codes on twenty sexual attitudes and practices. *Ethnology*, 1976, *15*, 409–429.

Brown, J. L. *The evolution of behavior*. New York: W. W. Norton, 1975.

Brown, J. K. A note on the division of labor. *American Anthropologist*, 1970, *72*, 1073–1078

Bunn, H. T. Archaeological evidence for meat-eating by Plio-Pleistocene hominids from Koobi Fora and Olduvai Gorge. *Nature*, 1981, *291*, 574–575.

Burton, M. L. & Reitz, K. The plow, female contribution to agricultural subsistence and polygyny: A log-linear analysis. *Behavior Science Research*, 1981, *16*, 275–306.

Busse, C. & Hamilton, III, W. J. Infant carrying by male chacma baboons. *Science*, 1981, *212*, 1281–1283.

Chagnon, N. *Yanomano*. New York: Holt, Rinehart, & Winston, 1977.

Chagnon, N. & Irons, W. *Evolutionary biology and human social behavior: An anthropological perspective*. North Scituate, Mass.: Duxbury Press, 1979.

Cherlin, A. J. *Marriage, divorce, remarriage*. Cambridge, Mass.: Harvard University Press, 1981.

Child Development, 1983, *54*, 253–528.

Chivers, D. J. The siamang and the gibbon in the Malay peninsula. *Gibbon and Siamang*, 1972, *1*, 103–135.

Chivers, D. J. The siamang in Malaya: A field study of a primate in a tropical rain forest. *Contributions to Primatology*, 1975, *4*, 1–335.

Clarke-Stewart, K. A. *Child care in the family*. New York: Academic Press, 1977.

Clarke-Stewart, K. A. And daddy makes three: The father's impact on mother and young child. *Child Development*, 1978, *49*, 466–478.

Cohen, L. J. & Campos, J. J. Father, mother, and stranger as elicitors of attachment behaviors in infancy. *Developmental Psychology*, 1974, *10*, 146–154.

Colman, A. & Colman, L. *Earth father/Sky father.* Englewood Cliffs, NJ.: Prentice-Hall, 1981.

Cone, C. Personality and subsistence: Is the child the parent of the person? *Ethnology,* 1979, *17,* 291–301.

Coon, C. S. *The hunting peoples.* Harmondsworth, England: Penguin Books, 1971.

Cooper, J. E., Holman, J., & Braithwhite, V. A. Self-Esteem and family cohesion: The child's perspective and adjustment. *Journal of Marriage and the Family,* 1983, *45,* 153–159.

Count, E. W. The biological basis of human sociality. *American Anthropologist,* 1958, *60,* 1049–1085.

Count, E. W. *Being and becoming human: Essays on the biogram.* New York: Van Nostrand, 1973.

Crook, J. H., Ellis, J. E., & Goss-Custard, J. D. Mammalian social systems: Structure and function. *Animal Behaviour,* 1976, *24,* 261–274.

D'Andrade, R. G. Sex differences and cultural institutions. In E. E. Maccoby (Ed.), *The development of sex differences.* Stanford, Calif. Stanford Univ. Press, 1966, 174–204.

Daniels, D. The evolution of concealed ovulation and self-deception. *Ethology and Sociobiology,* 1983, *4,* 69–88.

Darwin, C. *On the origin of species by means of natural selection.* London: J. Murray, 1859; New York: Appleton, 1960.

Dawkins, R. *The selfish gene.* Oxford: Oxford Univ. Press, 1976.

Day, R. & Mackey, W. C. The role image of the American father: An examination of media myth. *Journal of Comparative Family Studies,* in press.

Department of Commerce. *General social and economic characteristics: Virginia.* Washington, DC.: U.S. Government Printing Office, 1972.

Department of Commerce. *Statistical abstract of the United States* 1982–1983. Washington, DC.: U.S. Governmental Printing Office, 1983, 82.

Department of State. *Background notes.* Wash., DC.: Department of State, 1980.

Dewsbury, D. A. Dominance rank, copulatory behavior, and differential reproduction. *The Quarterly Review of Biology,* 1982, *57,* 135–159.

Divale, W., & Harris, M. Population, warfare, and the male supremacist complex. *American Anthropologist,* 1976, *78,* 521–538.

Dobie, J. F. *The voice of the coyote.* Boston: Little, Brown and Co., 1949.

Dolgin, J. L., Kemnitzer, D. S., & Schneider, D. M. (Eds.) *Symbolic anthropology: A reader in the study of symbols and meanings.* New York: Columbia Univ. Press, 1977.

Douglas, M. *Purity and danger: An analysis of concepts of pollution and danger.* New York: Routledge & Kegan, 1978.

Durham, W. H. Toward a coevolutionary theory of human biology and culture. In N. Chagnon & W. Irons (Eds.), *Evolutionary biology and human social behavior.* North Scituate, MA.: Duxbury Press, 1979, pp. 39–58.

Eimerl, S., & DeVore, I. *The primates.* New York: Time-Life Books, 1965.

Ekman, P. Darwin and cross-cultural studies of facial expression. In P. Ekman (Ed.), *Darwin and facial expression: A century of research in review.* New York: Academic Press, 1973, pp. 1–83.

Ekman, Paul. *The face of man.* New York: Garland Press, 1980.

Ember, C. R. Myths about hunter-gatherers. *Ethnology,* 1983, *22,* 439–448.

Ember, M. & Ember, C. R. The conditions favoring matrilocal versus patrilocal residence. *American Anthropologist,* 1971, *73,* 571–594. Ethnographic atlas (see G. P. Murdock, 1967).

Fasteau, M. F. Men as parents. In D. S. David & R. Brannon (Eds.), *The forty-nine percent majority: The male sex role.* Reading, Mass.: Addison-Wesley, 1976, pp. 5–49.

Fein, R. Research on Fathering: Social Policy and an Emergent Perspective. *Journal of Social Issues*, 1978, *34*, 122–135.

Fisher, R. A. *The genetical theory of natural selection.* Oxford: Clarendon Press, 1930.

Foss, E. M. *Determinants of infant behavior Vol. I-IV*, London: Metheun, 1961–1969.

Fox R. *Kinship and marriage.* London: Penguin Books, 1967.

Fox, R. *The Tory islanders: A people of the Celtic fringe.* New York: Cambridge Univ. Press, 1978.

Fox, Robin. *The red lamp of incest.* New York: E. P. Dutton, 1980.

Freedman, D. G. *Human infancy: An evolutionary perspective.* Hillsdale, NJ.: Erlbaum, 1974.

Freedman, D. G. *Human sociobiology: A holistic approach.* New York: The Free Press, 1979.

Freeman, D. *Margaret Mead and Samoa.* Cambridge, Mass.: Harvard Univ. Press, 1983.

Frodi, A. M. & Lamb, M. E. Sex differences in responsiveness to infants: A developmental study of psychophysiological and behavioral responses. *Child Development*, 1978, *49*, 1182–1188.

Gardner, H. *Developmental psychology* (2nd ed.). Boston: Little, Brown and Co., 1982.

Gaulin, S. J. C. & Schlegel, A. Paternal confidence and paternal investment: A cross-cultural test of a sociobiological hypothesis. *Ethology and Sociobiology*, 1980, *1*, 301–309.

Geertz, C. (Ed.), *Myth, symbol, and culture.* New York: Norton, 1974.

Getzel, J. W. & E. C. Cuba. Role, role conflict, and effectiveness. *American Sociological Review*, 1954, *19*, 164–175.

Goliknoff, R. M. & Ames, G. H. A comparison of father's and mother's speech with their young children. *Child Development*, 1979, *50*, 28–52.

Goodall, J. Warfare and cannibalism among Gombe's chimpanzees. *National Geographic*, 1979, *155*, 592–621.

Goode, W. J. A theory of role strain. *American Sociological Review*, 1960, *25*, 483–496.

Goss-Custard, J. D., Dunbar, R. I., & Aldrich-Blake, F. P. G. Survival, mating and rearing strategies in the evolution of primate social structure. *Folia Primatologica*, 1972, *17*, 1–19.

Grafen, A., & Sibly, R. A model of mate desertion. *Animal Behavior*, 1978, *26*, 645–652.

Grants register. Chicago: St. James Press, 1983.

Gray, T. "Elegy Written in a Country Churchyard." In *The literature of England.* Chicago: Scott, Foreman and Co. 1958, pp. 50–52.

Greene, T. A. *Modern man in search of manhood.* New York: Association Press, 1967, pp. 9–23.

Gross, N., Mason, W. S., & McEachern, A. W. *Explorations in role analysis.* New York: Wiley, 1964.

Guggisberg, C. A. W. *Simba: The life of the lion.* Philadelphia: Chilton Books, 1963.

Haldane, J. B. S. *The causes of evolution.* London: Longmans, 1932. (Reprinted as a paperback, Ithaca, New York: Cornell Univ. Press, 1966).

Hall, E. T. *The silent language.* Garden City, New York: Doubleday, 1959.

Hall, E. T. A system for the notation of proxemic behavior. *American Anthropologist*, 1963, *65*, 1003–1026.

Hall, E. T. *The hidden dimension.* Garden City, New York: Anchor Books, 1966.

Hamburg, D. Emotions in perspective of human evolution. In P. Knapp (Ed.), *Expression of emotions in man.* New York: International Univ. Press, 1963, pp. 300–317.

Hamilton, M. L. *Father's influence on children.* Chicago: Nelson Hall, 1977.

Hamilton, W. D. The genetical theory of social behaviour. *Journal of Theoretical Biology,* 1964, *7,* 1–52.

Hardin, G. The tragedy of the commons. *Science,* 1968, *162,* 1243–1248.

Harlow, H. F. *Learning to love.* San Francisco: Albion, 1971, pp. 63–64.

Harris, M. *The rise of anthropological theory.* New York: Thomas Y. Crowell, 1968.

Harris, M. Why a perfect knowledge of all the rules one must know to act like a native cannot lead to the knowledge of how natives act. *Journal of Anthropological Research,* 1974a, *30,* 242–251.

Harris, M. *Cows, pigs, wars, and witches.* New York: Random House, 1974b.

Harris, M. *Cultural materialism.* New York: Random House, 1979.

Hinde, R. A. *Ethology: Its nature and relations with other sciences.* New York: Oxford Univ. Press, 1982.

Hinde, R. A. & J. Stevenson-Hinde. *Constraints on learning.* New York: Academic Press, 1973.

Hofferth, S. L. Childbearing decision making and family well-being: A dynamic sequential model. *American Sociological Review,* 1983, *48,* 533–545.

Houts, T. C., & Bahr, R. M. *Native Americans: A sociological perspective.* New York: Harper & Row, 1971, pp. 110–114.

Hrdy, S. Male–Male competition and infanticide among the langurs (Presbytis entellus) of Abu Rajasthan. *Folia Primatologica,* 1974, *22,* 19–58.

Hrdy, S. Care and exploitation of nonhuman primate infants by conspecifics other than the mother. In D. S. Lehrman et al. (Eds.), *Advances in the study of behavior VI.* New York: Academic Press, 1976, 101–158.

Hrdy, S. *The woman that never evolved.* Cambridge, Mass.: Harvard Univ. Press, 1981.

Huber, J. Will U.S. fertility decline toward zero? *The Sociological Quarterly,* 1980, *21,* 481–492.

Human Relations Area File. New Haven, Connecticut: HRAF Press, 1949.

Hunter, D. E. & Whitten, P. (Eds.), *Encyclopedia of anthropology.* New York: Harper & Row, 1976, 134.

Hurlock, E. B. *Developmental psychology: A life-span approach* (5th ed.). New York: McGraw-Hill, 1983.

Immelmann, K., Barlow, G. W., Petrinovich, L., & Main, M. (Eds.) *Behavioral development.* New York: Cambridge Univ. Press, 1981.

Inglis, R. *Sins of the fathers: A study of the physical and emotional abuse of children.* New York: St. Martin's Press, 1978.

Isaac, Glynn. Food sharing and human evolution: Archaeological evidence from the Plio-Pleistocene of East Africa. *Journal of Anthropological Research,* 1978, *34,* 311–325.

Itani, I. Paternal care in the wild Japanese monkey *Macaca Fuscata.* In C. H. Southwick (Ed.), *Primate social behavior* NY: D. Van Nostrand, 1963, pp. 91–97.

Jensen, A. R. *Genetics and education.* New York: Harpers & Row, 1972. pp. 104–114.

Johanson, D. C., & White, T. D. On the status of Australopithecus afarensis. *Science,* 1980, *207,* 1104–1105.

Jolly, A. *The evolution of primate behavior.* New York: MacMillan, 1972,

Kania, R. E., & Mackey, W. C. Police violence as a function of community characteristics. *Criminology,* 1977, *15,* 27–48.

Katz, M. M., & Konner, M. J. The role of the father: An anthropological perspective. In M. E. Lamb (Ed.) *The role of the father in child development* (2nd ed.). New York: Wiley, 1981, pp. 155–186.

Kauffman, D. *Father–Child interaction as related to family structure among blacks and whites in Virginia.* Unpublished MA thesis, University of Virginia, 1974.

Kempe, R. S., & Kempe, C. C. *Child abuse*. Cambridge, Mass.: Harvard Univ. Press, 1978.

Kenkel, W. F. *The family in perspective*. Santa Monica, California: Goodyear, 1977, p. 225.

King, G. Socioterritorial units among carnivores and early Hominids. *Journal of Anthropological Research*, 1975, *31*, 69–87.

King, G. Alternative uses of Primates and carnivores in the reconstruction of early Hominid behavior. *Ethology and Sociobiology*, 1980, *1*, 99–110.

Kleck, G. Racial discrimination in criminal sentencing: A critical evaluation of the evidence with additional evidence on the death penalty. *American Sociological Review*, 1981, *46*, 783–805.

Kleiman, D. Monogamy in mammals. *Quarterly Review of Biology*, 1977, *52*, 39–69.

Kleiman, D., & Malcolm, J. R. The evolution of male parental investment in mammals. In D. J. Gubernick & P. H. Klopfer (Eds.), *Parental care in mammals*. New York: Plenum Press, 1981, pp. 347–387.

Kruuk, H. *The spotted hyena: A study of predation and social behavior*. Chicago: Univ. of Chicago Press, 1972.

Kühme, W. Communal food distribution and division of labour in African hunting dogs. *Nature*, 1965, *205*, 443–444.

Kuhn, T. S. *The structure of scientific revolutions*. Chicago: Univ. of Chicago Press, 1962.

Kummer, H. *Social organization of Hamadryas baboons*. Chicago: Univ. of Chicago Press, 1968.

LaFree, G. D. Male power and female victimization: Toward a theory of interracial rape. *American Journal of Sociology*, 1982, *88*, 311–328.

Lamb, M. E. *The role of the father in child development* (2nd ed.). New York: Wiley, 1981.

Lamb, M. E. (Ed.) *Nontraditional families: Parenting and child development*. Hillsdale, NJ.: Erlbaum, 1982.

Lamb, M. E., & Levine, J. A. The Swedish parental insurance policy: An experiment in social engineering. In M. E. Lamb & A. Sagi (Eds.), *Fatherhood and family policy*. Hillsdale, NJ.: Erlbaum, 1982, pp. 39–45.

Lamb, M. E., & Sagi, A. *Fatherhood and family policy*. Hillsdale, NJ.: Erlbaum, 1983.

Lancaster, Jane B., & Lancaster, Chet S. *Parental investment: The hominid adaptation*. In D. Ortner (Ed.), The 7th International Smithsonian Symposium. Washington, D.C.: Smithsonian Institution, Government Priting Office, 1982, pp. 1–49.

Laughlin, W. S. Hunting: An integrating biobehavior system and its evolutionary importance. In R. B. Lee & I. DeVore (Eds.), *Man the hunter*. Chicago: Aldine, 1968, pp. 304–320.

Lawick-Goodall, J. van. *In the shadow of man*. Boston: Houghton Mifflin Co., 1971, p. 34.

Lawick, H. van, & Lawick-Goodall, J. van *Innocent killers*. Boston: Houghton Mifflin, 1971.

Lawton, J. T. *Child development*. New York: Wm. C. Brown, 1982.

Leach, E. *Rethinking anthropology*. Atlantic Highlands, NJ.: Athlone, 1971.

Leakey, R. E. F., & Walker, A. On the status of Australopithecus afarensis. *Science*, 1980, *207*, 1103.

Lee, R. B., & DeVore, I. (Eds.) *Man the hunter*. Chicago: Aldine, 1968.

LeMasters, E. E. *Parents in modern America*. Homewood, Ill.: The Dorsey Press, 1974.

Lenington, S. Child abuse: The limits of sociobiology. *Ethology and Sociobiology*, 1981, *2*, 17–29.

Levine, J. *Who will raise the children? New options for fathers (and mothers)*. Philadelphia: Lippincott, 1976.

Levine, J. A., Pleck, J. H., & Lamb, M. E. The Fatherhood Project. In M. E. Lamb & A. Sagi (Eds.) *Fatherhood and family policy.* Hillsdale, NJ.: Erlbaum, 1983, pp. 101–103.

Levinson, D., & M. J. Malone. *Toward explaining human culture: A critical review of the findings of worldwide cross-cultural research.* New Haven, Conn.: HRAF Press, 1980.

Levi-Strauss, C. *Structural anthropology* (C. Jacobsen, trans). New York: Basic Books, 1963.

Levi-Strauss, C. *The raw and the cooked: Introduction to a science of mythology* (Johan & Doreen Weightman, Trans.). (Vol. I). New York: Harper & Row, 1969.

Lewis, M., & Rosenblum, L. *The effects of the infant on its caregiver.* New York: Wiley, 1973.

Lorber, J. Beyond equality of the sexes: The question of children. In J. M. Henslin (Ed.), *Marriage and Family in a Changing Society.* New York: The Free Press, 1980, pp. 522–533.

Lorenz, K. The evolution of behavior. *Scientific American,* 1958, *199,* 68–78.

Lorenz, K. *On aggression.* New York: Harcourt, Brace & World, 1963.

Lorenz, K. *Evolution and modification of behavior.* Chicago: Univ. of Chicago Press, 1965.

Lovejoy, C. O. The origin of man. *Science,* 1981, *211,* 341–359.

Lynn, D. B. *The father: His role in child development.* Monterey, Calif.: Brooks/Cole, 1974.

Maccoby, E. E., & Jacklin, C. N. *The psychology of sex differences.* Stanford, Calif.: Stanford Univ. Press, 1974.

Mackey, W. C. The adult male–child bond: An example of convergent evolution. *Journal of Anthropological Research,* 1976, *32,* 58–73.

Mackey, W. C. Parameters of the adult male–child bond. *Ethology and Sociobiology,* 1979a, *1,* 59–76.

Mackey, W. C. The American woman: A tragedy of the commons? *South Dakota Social Science Association Journal,* 1979b, *9,* 15–19.

Mackey, W. C. A sociobiological perspective on divorce patterns of men in the United States. *Journal of Anthropological Research,* 1980, *36,* 419–430.

Mackey, W. C. A cross-cultural analysis of recruitment into all male groups: An ethological perspective. *Journal of Human Evolution,* 1981, *10,* 281–292.

Mackey, W. C. A preliminary test for the validation of the adult male-child bond as a species-characteristic trait. *American Anthropologist,* 1983, *85,* 391–402.

Mackey, W. C., & Day, R. Some indicators of fathering behaviors in the United States: A cross-cultural examination of adult male–child interaction. *Journal of Marriage and the Family,* 1979, *41,* 287–299.

Mackinnon, J. The behavior and ecology of wild Orang-utans (*Pongo pygmaeus*). *Animal Behaviour,* 1974, *22,* 3–74.

Maclachlan, M. D. *Why they did not starve.* Philadephia: Ishi, 1983.

MacRoberts, M. The social organization of Barbary Apes (*M. sylvana*) on Gibraltar. *American journal of physical anthropology,* 1970, *33,* 83–95.

Maynard, J. Do fathers make good mothers? *Ladies Home Journal,* 1979, *96,* 152–154.

Maynard-Smith, J. Group selection and kin selection. *Nature,* 1964, *20,* 1145–1147.

McKee, L., & O'Brien, M. *The father figure.* New York: Tavistock, 1982.

McLaughlin, B. Second look: The mother tongue. *Human Nature,* 1978, *1,* 89.

McMahan, P. The victorious coyote. *Natural History,* 1976, *84,* 42–51.

Mead, M. *Sex and temperment in three primitive societies.* New York: Morrow, 1935.

Mead, M. *Male and female.* New York: Morrow, 1949, 185–190.

Mead, M. *Sex and temperment in three primitive societies.* New York: Dell, 1963 (from Morrow, 1935).

Mech, L. D. *The wolves of Isle Royale.* Washington, DC.: Government Printing Office, 1966.

Mech, L. D. *The wolf.* Garden City, New York: The Natural History Press, 1970.

Miner, H. Body ritual among the nacirema. *American Anthropologist,* 1956, *58,* 503–507.

Mitchell, G. *Behavioral sex differences in non-human primates.* New York: Van Nostrand Reinhold, 1979.

Moehlman, P. D. Jackals of the Serengeti. *National Geographic,* 1980, *153,* 840–843.

Money, J., & Ehrhardt, A. A. *Man & woman, boy & girl.* Baltimore: The Johns Hopkins Press, p. 258.

Montagu, A. *Man and aggression.* New York: Oxford Univ. Press, 1973.

Moore, F. (Ed.), *Readings in cross-cultural methodology.* New Haven, Conn.: HRAF Press, 1961.

Morris, D. *The naked ape.* New York: McGraw-Hill, 1967.

Morris, D. *The human zoo.* New York: McGraw-Hill, 1969.

Mowat, F. *Never cry wolf.* Boston: Little, Brown and Co., 1963, pp. 96–108.

Murdock, G. P. Comparative data on the division of labor by sex. *Social Forces,* 1937, *15,* 552.

Murdock, G. P. World ethnographic sample. *American Anthropologist,* 1957, *59,* 664–687.

Murdock, G. P. Ethnographic atlas. *Ethnology,* 1967, *6,* 109–236.

Murdock, G. P., & Provost, C. Factors in the division of labor by sex: A cross-cultural analysis. *Ethnology,* 1973, *12,* 203–225.

Murie, A. *The wolves of Mount McKinley.* Washington, DC.: U.S. Government Printing Office, 1944.

Naroll, R. On ethnic unit clasification. *Current Anthropology,* 1964, *5,* 283–312.

Naroll, R. The culture-bearing unit in cross-cultural surveys. In R. Naroll & R. Cohen (Eds.), *A handbook of method in cultural anthropology.* Garden City, New York: Natural History Press, 1970, pp. 721–765.

Naroll, R. The double language boundary in cross-cultural surveys. *Behavior Science Notes,* 1971, *6,* 95–102.

Naroll, R. Holocultural theory tests. In R. Naroll & F. Naroll (Eds.), Cultural Anthropology. New York: Appleton-Century Crofts, 1973, pp. 309–384.

Naroll, R., Michik, G. L., & Naroll, F. Holocultural research methods. In H. C. Triandis & J. W. Berry (Eds.), *Handbook of cross-cultural psychology* (Vol. 2). Boston: Allyn & Bacon, 1980, pp. 479–521.

Nash, J. The father in contemporary culture and current psychological literature. *Child Development,* 1965, *36,* 260–297.

National Center for Health Statistics. *Vital Statistics of the United States.* Washington, DC.: U.S. Government Printing Office, 1950–1982.

Nelson, H., & Jurmain, R. *Introduction to physical anthropology* (2nd ed.). New York: West Publishing, 1982.

Osofsky, J. D., & O'Connell, E. J. Parent–child interaction: Daughters' effects upon mothers' and fathers' behaviors. *Developmental Psychology,* 1972, *7,* 157–168.

Pakizegi, B. The interaction of mothers and fathers with their sons. *Child Development,* 1978, *49,* 479–482.

Parke, R. D. The father of the child. *The Sciences,* 1979a, (April) *19,* 12–15.

Parke, R. D. Perspectives on father–infant interaction. In J. D. Osofsky (Ed.), *The handbook of infant development.* New York: Wiley, 1979b, pp. 549–590.

Parke, R. D., Power, T. G., & Fisher, T. The adolescent father's impact on the mother and child. *Journal of Social Issues,* 1980, *36,* 88–106.

Parsons, T & Bales, R. F. *Family, socialization and interaction process*. New York: The Free Press, 1955.

Pedersen, F. A. Does research on children reared in father-absent families yield information on father influences. *The Family Coordinator*, 1976, *25*, 459–464.

Pedersen, F. A. (Ed.) *The father–infant relationship*. New York: Praeger, 1980.

Pedersen, F. A., & Robson, K. S. Father participation in infancy. *American Journal of Orthopsychiatry*, 1969, *39*, 466–472.

Peters, D. L., & Stewart, R. B. Father–child interactions in a shopping mall: A naturalistic study of father role behavior. *The Journal of Genetic Psychology*, 1981, *138*, 269–278.

Piaget, J. *Behavior and evolution*. New York: Pantheon, 1978.

Pilbeam, D. New Hominoid skull material from the Miocene of Pakistan. *Nature*, 1982, *295*, 232.

Potts, R., & Shipman, P. Cutmarks made by stone tools on bones from Olduvai Gorge, Tanzania. *Nature*, 1981, *291*, 577–580.

Price-Bonham, S. Bibliography of literature related to roles of fathers. *Family Coordinator*, 1976, *25*, 489–512.

Price-Bonham, S., & Skeen, P. A comparison of black and white fathers with implications for parent education. *Family Coordinator*, 1979, *28*, 53–59.

Rabb, G. B., Woolpy, H. H., & Ginsberg, B. E. Social relationships in a group of captive wolves. *American Zoologist*, 1967, *7*, 305–311.

Radelet, M. L. Racial characteristics and the imposition of the death penalty. *American Sociological Review*, 1981, *46*, 918–927.

Rajecki, D. W., Lamb, M. E., & Obmascher, P. Toward a general theory of infantile attachment: A comparative review of aspects of the social bond. *The Behavioral and Brain Sciences*, 1978, *3*, 417–464.

Rapoport, R., Rapoport, R. N., Strelitz, Z., & Kew, S. *Fathers, mothers, and society*. New York: Basic Books, 1977.

Rebelsky, F., & Hanks, C. Father's verbal interaction with infants in the first three months of life. *Child Development*, 1971, *42*, 63–68.

Redican, W. K., & Taub, D. M. Male parental care in monkeys and apes. In M. E. Lamb (Ed.), *The role of the father in child development* (2nd ed). New York: Wiley, 1981.

Reiss, D. & H. Hoffman (Eds.), *The American family: Dying or developing?* New York: Plenum Press, 1979.

Richards, M. P. How should we approach the study of fathers? In L. McKee & M. O'Brien (Eds.), *The father figure*. New York: Tavistock, 1982, pp. 57–71.

Robinson, C. L., Lockard, J. S., & Adams, R. M. Who looks at a baby in public. *Ethology and Sociobiology*, 1979, *1*, 1979.

Roe, A., & Simpson, G. G. *Behavior and evolution*. New Haven, Conn.: Yale Univ. Press, 1958.

Rohner, R. P. *They love me, they love me not*. New Haven, Conn.: HRAF Press, 1975.

Rohner, R. P., & Rohner, E. C. Parental acceptance–rejection and parental control: Cross-cultural codes. *Ethnology*, 1981, *20*, 245–260.

Rohner, R. P., & Rohner, E. C. Enculturative continuity and the importance of caretakers: Cross-cultural codes. *Behavior Science Research*, 1982, *17*, 91–114.

Rohner, R. P., Naroll, R., Barry, H., Divale, W. T., Erickson, E. E., Schaefer, J. M., & Sipes, R. G. Guidelines to holocultural research. *Current Anthropology*, 1978, *19*, 128–129.

Rosenblatt, P. C., & Hillebrant, W. J. Divorce for childlessness and the regulation of adultery. *Journal of Sex Research*, 1972, *8*, 117–127.

Rosnow, R. L. When he lends a helping hand, bite it. In J. B. Maas (Ed.), *Readings in psychology* (3rd ed.). Del Mar, Calif.: CRM Books, 1974, pp. 22–24.

Rossi, A. S. A biosocial perspective on parenting. *Daedalus*, 1977, *106*, 1–31.

Rubin, Z. Jokers wild in the lab. In J. B. Maas (Ed.), *Readings in psychology* (3rd ed.). Del Mar, Calif.: CRM Books, 1974, pp. 25–27.

Ruddle, K., & Barrows, K. *Statistical abstract of Latin America*. Los Angeles: Univ. of California Press, 1974.

Rudnai, J. A. *The social life of the lion*. Wallingford, Pennsylvania: Washington Square East, 1973.

Russell, B. *A history of Western philosophy*. New York: Simon & Schuster, 1945.

Russell, G. The father role and its relation to masculinity, femininity, and androgyny. *Child Development*, 1978, *48*, 1174–1181.

Russell, G., & Radin, N. Increased paternal participation: The fathers' perspective. In M. E. Lamb & A. Sagi (Eds.), *Fatherhood and family policy*. Hillsdale, NJ.: Erlbaum, 1983, pp. 139–145.

Rutter, M. Maternal deprivation 1972–1978: New findings, new concepts, new approaches. *Child Development*, 1979, *50*, 283–305.

Ryden, H. The "lone" coyote likes family life. *National Geographic*, 1974, *146*, 279–294.

Sagi, A., & Sharon, N. Costs and benefits of increased paternal involvement in child-rearing: The societal perspective. In M. E. Lamb & A. Sagi (Eds.), *Fatherhood and family policy*. Hillsdale, NJ.: Erlbaum, 1983, p. 39.

Schaller, G. B. *The Serengeti lion*. Chicago: Univ. of Chicago Press, 1972a.

Schaller, G. B. Are you running with me, Hominid? *Natural History*, 1972b, *81*, 60–69.

Schaller, G. B., & Lowther, G. R. The relevance of carnivore behavior to the study of early Hominids. *Southwestern Journal of Anthropology*, 1969, *25*, 307–336.

Schlegel, A. *Male dominance and female autonomy*. New Haven, Conn.: HRAF Press, 1972.

Schoenfeld, A. The laugh industry. *The Saturday Evening Post*, (1930, February) *20*, 12.

Schvaneveldt, J. D. Proceedings of the third annual conference up-date in quality parenting. *Fatherhood*. Univ. of Utah, 1977, 57.

Secord, P. F., & Backman, C. W. *Social psychology* (2nd ed.). New York: McGraw-Hill, 1974.

Seligman, M. E. P., & J. L. Hager. *Biological boundaries of learning*. New York: Appleton-Century Crofts, 1972, 1–6.

Sexton, P. *The feminized male*. New York: Random House, 1969.

Sexton, P. How the American boy is feminized. *Psychology Today*, 1970, *3*, 23–29.

Simons, E. L. *Primate evolution*. New York: MacMillan, 1972, 288–289.

Spelke, E., Zelazo, P., Kagan, J., & Kotelchuck, M. Father interaction and separation protest. *Developmental Psychology*, 1973, *9*, 83–90.

Spiro, M. E. *Gender and culture: Kibbutz women revisited*. Durham, North Carolina: Duke Univ. Press, 1979.

Spuhler, J. N. Continuities and discontinuities in anthropoid-Hominid behavioral evolution: Bipedal locomotion and sexual receptivity. In N. Chagnon & W. Irons (Ed.), *Evolutionary biology and human social behavior*. North Scituate, Mass.: Duxbury Press, 1979, pp. 454–461.

Starr, R. Child abuse. *American Psychologist*, 1979, *34*, 872–878.

Stephens, W. N. *The family in cross-cultural perspective*. New York: Holt, Rinehart & Winston, 1963.

Starin, E. D. Food transfer by wild Titi Monkeys (Callicebus torquatus torquatus). *Folia Primatologica*, 1978, *30*, 145–151.

Stewart, F. H. *Fundamentals of age-group systems*, New York: Academic Press, 1977.

Sturm, S. C. Primate predation: Interim report on the development of a hunting tradition in a troop of Olive baboons. *Science*, 1975, *187*, 755–757.

Szasz, T. *The myth of mental illness*. New York: Dell, 1967.

Szasz, T. *The manufacture of madness*. New York: Harper & Row, 1970.

Tasch, R. J. The role of the father in the family. *Journal of Experimental Education*, 1952, *20*, 319–361.

Teleki, G. The omnivorous chimpanzee. *Scientific American*, 1973, *228*, 33–42.

Teleki, G. Primate subsistence patterns: Collector-predators and gatherer-hunters. *Journal of Human Evolution*, 1975, *4*, 125–184.

Tiger, L. *Men in groups*. New York: Random House, 1969.

Tiger, L. *Optimism: The biology of hope*. New York: Simon & Schuster, 1979.

Tiger, L., & Fowler, H. T. (Eds.) *Female hierarchies*. Chicago: Beresford Book Service, 1978.

Tiger, L., & Fox, R. *The imperial animal*. New York: Delta Books, 1971.

Tiger, L., & Shepher, J. *Women in the kibbutz*. New York: Harcourt Brace Jovanovich, 1975.

Tinbergen, N. *The study of instinct*. Oxford: Clarendon Press, 1951.

Trivers, R. L. Parental investment and sexual selection. In B. H. Campbell (Ed.), *Sexual selection and the descent of man, 1871–1971*. Chicago: Aldine, pp. 136–179.

Trivers, R. L. Parent-offspring conflict. *American Zoologist*, 1974, *14*, 249–264.

Turnbull, C. *The mountain people*. New York: Simon & Schuster, 1972.

Turner, R. H. The role and the person. *American Journal of Sociology*, 1978, *84*, 1–23.

Turner, V. *The ritual process*. Chicago: Aldine, 1969.

Uniform crime reports. Washington, DC.: U.S. Government Printing Office, 1980.

United Nations. *Demographic yearbook*. New York: United Nations, 1974–1976.

U.S. Bureau of the Census. *Marital status and living arrangements: March 1975*. Current population reports series P-20, 287. Washington, DC.: U.S. Government Printing Office, 1975.

U.S. Bureau of the Census. *Number, timing, and duration of marriages and divorces in the United States: June 1975*. Current population reports series P-20, 297. Washington DC.: U.S. Government Printing Office, 1976a.

U.S. Bureau of the Census. *Fertility of American women: June 1975*. Current population reports series P-20, 301. Washington, DC.: U.S. Government Printing Office, 1976b.

U.S. Bureau of the Census. *Marriage, divorce, widowhood, and remarriage by family characteristics: June 1975*. Current population reports series P-20, 312. Washington, DC.: U.S. Government Printing Office, 1977.

U.S. Bureau of the Census. *Perspectives on American fertility; Special studies series*. Current population reports P-23, 70. Washington, DC.: U.S. Government Printing Office, 1978.

van den Berghe, P. L. *Human family systems*. New York: Elsevier, 1979.

van den Berghe, P. L. Incest and exogamy: A sociobiological reconsideration. *Ethology and Sociobiology*, 1980, *1*, 151–162.

Waddington, C. H. *The evolution of an evolutionist*. New York: Cornell Univ. Press, 1975.

Weisner, T. S., & Gallimore, R. My brother's keeper: Child and sibling caretaking. *Current Anthropology*, 1977, *18*, 169–190.

White, D., Burton, M. L., & Brudner, L. A. Entailment theory and method: A cross-cultural analysis of the sexual division of labor. *Behavior Science Research*, 1977, *12*, 1–24.

White, D. R., Burton, M. L., & Dow, M. M. Sexual division of labor in African agriculture: A network autocorrelation analysis. *American Anthropologist*, 1981, *83*, 824–847.

White, L. K. Determinants of spousal interaction: Marital structure of marital happiness. *Journal of Marriage and the Family*, 1983, *45*, 511–519.

Whiting, B. B., & Whiting, J. W. M. *Children of six cultures: A psycho-cultural analysis.* Cambridge, Mass.: Harvard Univ. Press, 1975.

Whiting, J. W. M. Effects of climate on certain cultural practices. In W. H. Goodenough (Ed.), *Explorations in cultural anthropology.* New York: McGraw-Hill, 1964, pp. 511–544.

Who's who. Chicago: A. N. Marquis, 1980.

Whyte, M. K. Cross-Cultural codes dealing with the relative status of women. *Ethnology*, 1978, *12*, 211–237.

Wilson, E. O. *Sociobiology.* Cambridge, Mass.: Harvard Univ. Press, 1975.

Wilson, E. O. *On human nature.* Cambridge, Mass.: Harvard Univ. Press, 1978.

Witkowski, S. Galton's Opportunity: The hologeistic study of historical processes. In J. M. Schaefer (Ed.), *Studies in cultural diffusion: Galton's problem.* New Haven, Conn.: HRAF Press, 1974, pp. 84–112.

World almanac. New York: Newspaper Enterprise Association, 1983.

World ethnographic sample (see G. P. Murdock, 1957).

Worldmark encyclopedia of nations. Volumes 2–6. New York: Wiley, 1976.

Yablonsky, L. *Fathers and sons.* New York: Simon & Schuster, 1982.

Yarrow, L. How to get your husband to help. *Parents*, 1982, May: 55–59.

Young, S. P., & Jackson, H. T. *The clever coyote.* Washington, DC.: Wildlife Management Institute, 1951, 82–88.

Yunis, J. J., & O. Prakash. The origin of man: A chromosomal pictorial legacy. *Science*, 1982, *215*, 1525–1529.

Zihlman, A., & Tanner, N. Gathering and the Hominid adaptation. In L. Tiger & H. Fowler (Eds.), *Female Hierarchies.* Chicago: Beresford Book Service, 1978, pp. 163–194.

Author Index

197

Subject Index